PRESBYTERIANS AND PENSIONS

The Roots and Growth
of Pensions in the
Presbyterian Church (U.S.A.)

R. Douglas Brackenridge
and
Lois A. Boyd

John Knox Press
ATLANTA

Library of Congress Cataloging-in-Publication Data

Brackenridge, R. Douglas.
   Presbyterians and pensions : the roots and growth of pensions in the Presbyterian Church (U.S.A.) / R. Douglas Brackenridge and Lois A. Boyd.
     p. cm.
   Bibliography: p. 176
   Includes index.
   ISBN 0-8042-1050-0
   1. Presbyterian Church (U.S.A.). Board of Pensions—History.
   2. Presbyterian Church (U.S.A.)—Clergy—Pensions—History.
   3. Presbyterian Church—United States—Clergy—Pensions—History.
I. Boyd, Lois A. II. Title.
BX9195.B67 1988
262'.05137'0683—dc19   88-23060
                                                                                                     CIP

© Copyright John Knox Press 1988
10 9 8 7 6 5 4 3 2 1
Printed in the United States of America
John Knox Press
Atlanta, Georgia 30365

Presbyterian Historical Society Publications

1. *The Presbyterian Enterprise* by M. W. Armstrong, L. A. Loetscher and C. A. Anderson (Westminster Press, 1956; paperback reprinted for P.H.S., 1963 & 1976)
2. *Presbyterian Ministry in American Culture* by E. A. Smith (Westminster Press, 1962)
3. *Journals of Charles Beatty, 1762-1769,* edited by Guy S. Klett (Pennsylvania State University Press, 1962)
4. *Hoosier Zion, The Presbyterian in Early Indiana* by L. C. Rudolph (Yale University Press, 1963)
5. *Presbyterianism in New York State* by Robert Hastings Nichols, edited and completed by James Hastings Nichols (Westminster Press, 1963)
6. *Scots Breed and Susquehanna* by Hubertis M. Cummings (University of Pittsburgh Press, 1964)
7. *Presbyterians and the Negro—A History* by Andrew E. Murray (Presbyterian Historical Society, 1966)
8. *A Bibliography of American Presbyterianism During the Colonial Period* by Leonard J. Trinterud (Presbyterian Historical Society, 1968)
9. *George Bourne and "The Book and Slavery Irreconcilable"* by John W. Christie and Dwight L. Dumond (Historical Society of Delaware and Presbyterian Historical Society, 1969)
10. *The Skyline Synod: Presbyterianism in Colorado and Utah* by Andrew E. Murray (Synod of Colorado/Utah, 1977)
11. *The Life and Writings of Francis Makemie,* edited by Boyd S. Schlenther (Presbyterian Historical Society, 1971)
12. *A Younger Church in Search of Maturity: Presbyterianism in Brazil from 1910 to 1959* by Paul Pierson (Trinity University Press, 1974)
13. *Presbyterians in the South,* Vols. II and III, by Ernest Trice Thompson (John Knox Press, 1973)
14. *Ecumenical Testimony* by John McNeill and James H. Nichols (Westminster Press, 1974)
15. *Iglesia Presbiteriana: A History of Presbyterians and Mexican Americans in the Southwest* by R. Douglas Brackenridge and Francisco O. García-Treto (Trinity University Press, 1974; 2nd edition, 1987)
16. *The Rise and Decline of Education for Black Presbyterians* by Inez M. Parker (Trinity University Press, 1977)
17. *Minutes of the Presbyterian Church in America, 1706-1788* edited by Guy S. Klett (Presbyterian Historical Society, 1977)
18. *°Eugene Carson Blake, Prophet with Portfolio* by R. Douglas Brackenridge (Seabury Press, 1978)

19. *Prisoners of Hope: A Search for Mission 1815–1822* by Marjorie Barnhart (Presbyterian Historical Society, 1980)
20. *From Colonialism to World Community: The Church's Pilgrimage* by John Coventry Smith (Geneva Press, 1982)
21. *Facing the Enlightenment and Pietism: Archibald Alexander and the Founding of Princeton Theological Seminary* by Lefferts A. Loetscher (Greenwood Press, 1983)
22. *Presbyterian Women in America: Two Centuries of A Quest for Status* by Lois A. Boyd and R. Douglas Brackenridge (Greenwood Press, 1983)
23. *Kentucky Presbyterians* by Louis B. Weeks (John Knox Press, 1983)
24. *Merging Mission and Unity* by Donald Black (Geneva Press, 1986)
25. *Gilbert Tennent, Son of Thunder* by Milton J. Coalter, Jr. (Greenwood Press, 1986)
26. *A Guide to Foreign Missionary Manuscripts in the Presbyterian Historical Society* by Frederick J. Heuser, Jr. (Greenwood Press, 1988)
27. *The United Synod of the South: The Southern New School Presbyterian Church* by Harold M. Parker, Jr. (Greenwood Press, 1988)

°Out of print

Chronology of Important Events

1706 First presbytery (Philadelphia) organized
1717 The Fund For Pious Uses begun
1754 The Widows' Fund created
1759 The Widows' Fund chartered
1761 First insurance policies issued
1789 General Assembly (PCUSA) organized in Philadelphia
1849 The Fund for Disabled Ministers (Old School) begun
1856 Widows' Fund name changed to the Presbyterian Annuity Company
1861 Civil War and division of Presbyterians north and south
      The Aged and Infirm Ministers' Fund (UPNA) created
1868 The Invalid Fund (PCUS) instituted
1870 The Relief Fund for Disabled Ministers (PCUSA) begun
      The Relief Fund for Widows and Orphans (PCUS) begun
1875 Presbyterian Annuity Company name changed to the Presbyterian Annuity and Life Insurance Company
      The Board of Ministerial Relief (UPNA) chartered
1876 The Board of Ministerial Relief (PCUSA) chartered
1881 Cumberland Presbyterian Board of Ministerial Relief chartered
1883 First ministerial retirement home opened at Perth Amboy (PCUSA)
1888 Presbyterian Annuity and Life Insurance Company name changed to The Presbyterian Ministers' Fund
1901 Executive Committee of Ministerial Relief chartered (PCUS)
1904 Executive Committee of Ministerial Education and Relief (PCUS) instituted
1906 Cumberland and PCUSA denominations united
1909 Sustentation Fund (PCUSA) chartered
1910 Executive Committee of Christian Education and Ministerial Relief (PCUS) begun
1912 Board of Ministerial Relief and Sustentation Fund (PCUSA) federated
1915 Interdenominational Secretaries Conference formed
1917 Ministerial Annuity Fund (UPNA) established
1918 Board of Ministerial Relief and Sustentation (PCUSA) chartered

1927	Board of Pensions (PCUSA) chartered and Service Pension Plan put into operation
1928	UPNA General Assembly approves new pension plan and a new Board of Ministerial Pensions and Relief is chartered
1931	Interdenominational Secretaries Conference name changed to Church Pensions Conference
1933	First Joy Gift (PCUS) received
1934	Employees Pension Plan (PCUSA) begun
1940	Ministers' Annuity Fund (PCUS) put into operation
1942	Employees' Annuity Fund (PCUS) begun
1949	Board of Annuities and Relief (PCUS) chartered
1951	Employees Pension Plan (PCUSA) closed; lay employees eligible for Service Pension Plan
1955	Ministers become eligible for participation in Social Security
1958	Union of UPNA and PCUSA to form the United Presbyterian Church in the United States of America (UPCUSA)
1983	Union of UPCUSA and PCUS to form the Presbyterian Church (U.S.A.)
1986	Board of Annuities and Relief and Board of Pensions united into one organization, the Board of Pensions (U.S.A.)
1987	New Benefits Program put into operation

Acknowledgments

The authors acknowledge with gratitude William B. Miller, director of the Presbyterian Historical Society, and Arthur M. Ryan, copresident of the Board of Pensions of the Presbyterian Church (U.S.A.) and former president of the Board of Pensions of the United Presbyterian Church in the U.S.A., for implementing the research project that has led to this study of the history of pensions in the Presbyterian Church. With the expansion of the initial project to include the Board of Annuities and Relief of the former Presbyterian Church in the U.S., we have been warmly supported by J. Phillips Noble, copresident of the Board of Pensions of the Presbyterian Church (U.S.A.) and former executive general secretary of the Board of Annuities and Relief. We are pleased that it will become a title of the Presbyterian Historical Society Publications series.

The staffs of both boards have been of invaluable assistance in locating records and illustrations and providing information both in informal conversations and in structured interviews. We are particularly appreciative of the time given by the incumbent board executives and those recently retired who shared their memories with us: Arthur W. Brown, Charles C. Cowsert, Donald L. Hibbard, and George H. Vick. In addition, Robert L. Moreland, vice-president, assistance and homes secretary of the Board of Pensions, recently retired, gave us access to the results of his research on the Homes Program and explained the policies of the Assistance Program.

In our research travels to Philadelphia and Montreat the staffs of the Historical Foundation of Presbyterian and Reformed Churches, Inc., the Presbyterian Historical Society, and the Presbyterian Ministers' Fund have given cordial and efficient assistance. Other persons connected with both the former UPCUSA and PCUS denominations have given interviews and materials that made this history more complete.

During the years we researched this topic, accommodations were provided for us in Prentiss House, the Board of Pensions's former congregate retirement home in Philadelphia. In 1985, Professor Brackenridge had the privilege of spending the summer there as a guest. The residents incorporated him into their fellowship community, and he had the opportunity not only to establish friendships but to benefit from their collective experiences. Because Prentiss

House was in the process of being closed, there were only a few people in residence that summer: Louisa Eakin, Katherine Hendrickson, Agatha Little, Henry Little, Margaret Murdoch, Elizabeth McConnell, Grace Reifsnyder, Albert J. Sanders, and administrators Judy and Robert Sandercock.

We also thank the administration at Trinity University for its continuing support of our research in the area of church history. Finally, we appreciate the encouragement of our colleagues, relatives, and friends who listened to our stories and supplied information helpful to our research. This sharing enabled us to put such a case study into a broader context and to produce a work that we hope will be useful to Presbyterians and others who wish to study this subject.

Contents

Introduction	1
PART ONE: Beginnings 1707–1870	7
Chapter 1 Colonial Efforts	7
Chapter 2 The Widows' Fund	19
Chapter 3 The Presbyterian Annuity Company	30
Chapter 4 The Fund for Disabled Ministers	40
PART TWO: Denominational Boards and Agencies 1870–1930	51
Chapter 5 The Board of Ministerial Relief	51
Chapter 6 The Board of Ministerial Relief and Sustentation	63
Chapter 7 Cumberland and United Presbyterian Relief Traditions	77
Chapter 8 Executive Committee of Christian Education and Ministerial Relief	87
PART THREE: Modern Pension Programs 1930–1986	107
Chapter 9 The Board of Annuities and Relief	107
Chapter 10 The Board of Pensions: PCUSA	119
Chapter 11 A Decade of Controversy and Change 1973–1983	133
Epilogue	148
Notes	152
Bibliography	176
Index	181

Introduction

The Board of Pensions of the Presbyterian Church (U.S.A.) is a one-and-a-half-billion dollar private pension institution in the United States with a diversified program including medical and life insurance, disability coverage, retirement homes, and welfare grants. Combining the assets and traditions of the former Board of Annuities and Relief of the Presbyterian Church in the United States (PCUS) and the Board of Pensions of the United Presbyterian Church in the United States of America (UPCUSA), beginning in 1987 the board administered a Benefits Plan for more than 30,000 persons, both lay and ordained, and their families.

This book represents the first effort to understand the historical roots of a denominational organization that affects the lives of many people. In essence, it is a case study of how a fairly representative middle- to upper-middle class social institution, the Presbyterian Church (U.S.A.) and its antecedent denominations, produced its present retirement and protection program for church employees. Although it focuses on one American theological tradition, the study does not exclude parallel developments in other denominations. Nor does it ignore the social and economic contexts in which mainline Protestant churches developed their pension programs over a period of nearly three hundred years. Like its secular counterparts, the Presbyterian Church interacted with and was influenced by a variety of societal factors, all of which in one way or another shaped its structures.

Within its cultural context, the Presbyterian Church expresses a tradition that had its origins in the Reformation of the sixteenth century, especially as the theology relates to John Calvin. Imbued with a high regard for the Bible, American Presbyterians supported a variety of humanitarian ventures not simply because they seemed "right" but because they were viewed as theological responses to relevant issues in human life. The church's concern for the well-being of its ordained ministry and church employees represents one dimension of its theological application of biblical insights to a particular aspect of social responsibility.

We have divided our narrative into three major sections, each of which corresponds to a pattern of development in the pension program. The first period begins with the colonial era and continues to the end of the Civil War. During this time, Presbyterians tended to view the cause of "ministerial relief," as it was then called, as primarily a responsibility of families and/or local churches. The ideal of a loyal son or daughter or of a faithful congregation dutifully attending the physical and financial needs of the aged dependent was extolled in the denomination's inspirational and programmatic literature. One exception occurred with the creation of the Widows' Fund in 1759 by the Synod of Philadelphia and New York. Conceived by Francis Alison, the Widows' Fund was the first life insurance company to be organized in colonial America and reflected the prevalent belief that a minister should work in a pastorate until he died and the church should care for his widow and dependent children. Although the Widows' Fund exists today as a highly successful secular insurance company (The Presbyterian Ministers' Fund), it languished during most of the nineteenth century as a quasi-official denominational agency with a limited constituency.

The second section describes developments beginning in the 1870s, when denominational "relief" boards came into being, up to the 1920s when the church began to emulate the contributory pension plans of industry and corporations that had been springing up since the end of the nineteenth century. These boards did not come into existence without controversy. Adherents of the familiar system of local support strongly resisted what they considered to be impersonal bureaucratic agencies of questionable efficiency and uncontrolled authority. Limited in funds and lacking adequate staff, the boards were not able to match the growing needs of an expanding ministerial population, many of whom had no independent sources of income. The congregations of ministers who served small churches and mission stations were unable to provide much more than a small piece of land and infrequent salary payments. A survey taken in 1871 indicated that a third of the 61,000 Protestant ministers existed on a salary of less than $500 a year.

As an alternative to cash payments, several denominations, including the Presbyterian Church in the United States of America (PCUSA), opened ministerial retirement homes in which clergymen and their wives could live without charge in lieu of receiving relief pensions. Burdened by a societal image of a "poor house," these homes never attracted a large number of residents. Nevertheless, they served a small percentage of churchworkers who were unable to live with relatives or friends. Despite a high cost factor, the PCUSA managed to keep a few homes operating as part of its relief program.

In another effort to remove the stigma of relief from its ministerial retirement program, the PCUSA in 1909 implemented the Sustentation Fund, the first attempt by an American Protestant denomination to establish a contributory pension plan. Instead of relying solely on church benevolence, ministers were asked to contribute one-fifth of the amount required to produce a pension of $500 at age seventy. The balance was to be raised by canvassing the denomination for contributions. When these funds never materialized, the Sustentation Fund was forced to cease operations.

The third section discusses the development of the Ministers' Annuity Fund of the Presbyterian Church in the United States (PCUS) and the Service Pension Plan of the PCUSA. Both programs, modeled after secular plans, featured actuarial calculations, accumulation of adequate reserve funds, and the inauguration of a system of management in which congregations included as part of the ministerial salary a fixed payment to the denominational pension plan. Along with the minister's contribution, the plans anticipated awarding a minimum pension of $600 after forty years of service to the denomination. The UPCUSA program initially did not require retirement at sixty-five and visualized the "pension" partially as a salary supplement for those who continued to work as interim pastors.

Both plans experienced strong opposition from those who viewed them as a rejection of the biblical injunctions to live by faith and depend on congregational charity; this opposition diminished after the plans became operational. More devastating, however, was the economic impact of the Depression of the 1930s that slowed the anticipated growth of accumulated funds. In the aftermath, the directors of both programs became extremely conservative in their investment portfolios and thus limited adjustments to changing economic conditions in post-World War II America.

The 1950s brought a number of programmatic changes to the Board of Pensions and the Board of Annuities and Relief. During this period benefits were expanded to include such items as medical insurance, disability payments, psychological counseling, and educational assistance. These more comprehensive protection plans mirrored those of other mainline Protestant denominations who offered such features either on a self-administered basis or through external insurance organizations. The benefits were periodically upgraded in order to keep pace with rising medical costs and inflation; in most instances this necessitated an increase in payment of dues.

An important development of the 1950s was the amendment of the Social Security law, which made the coverage of ordained ministers possible as of January 1, 1955. This coverage tended to make denominations adopt noncontributory pensions, primarily because ministers paid Social Security taxes as self-employed individuals so as to maintain a clear separation of church and state. Since local churches could not assist ministers with their payments, each congregation was encouraged to pay all of the pension contributions.

With the advent of the social change in the 1960s and 1970s, the pension boards found their retirement programs being challenged by various constituents. Churchwomen, for example, noted features that discriminated against female participants. Other organizations called for a reexamination of the basic philosophy of the plans, as they were tied to income level and penalized those who served small congregations in which salary scales were low. Although the UPCUSA in 1980 inaugurated an "alternative pension" based on the average of median salaries, the boards attempted to address this criticism primarily through assistance or subsidy grants to individuals. In 1986 the new Benefits Plan introduced a minimum pension based on the average median salary of employees in comparable work categories.

In recent years the General Assemblies and the pension boards have also addressed the issue of the use of investment policies as a means of social witness and responsibility. Various General Assemblies have endorsed the use of such tactics as proxy votes, shareholder resolutions, and total or selective divestment. Advocates of these measures have argued that the church must utilize its financial power as a moral force and that such activity can be pursued within the bounds of responsible trusteeship of church funds. The boards, while acknowledging a dimension of social responsibility in developing investment portfolios, have responded that unlike other program boards and agencies, they have a binding contractual obligation to plan members who expect expert management of funds in order to insure maximum retirement benefits. From their perspective, moving investment capital in order to make a social witness carries certain risks in terms of financial viability and legal culpability. Although both boards have demonstrated a willingness to implement investment guidelines approved by the General Assembly, they have maintained that their participation is voluntary, not mandatory. Moreover, in situations in which they deemed guidelines to be in conflict with "prudent-person trusteeship," the boards have affirmed their right to take alternative measures.

This discussion of the control of investment policies reflects the presence of a wider question. Precisely how is the relationship between the Board of Pensions and the General Assembly defined? Unlike other boards and agencies of the church, it has contractual obligations to its constituents and is legally bound to fulfill those obligations according to established guidelines. At the same time, it is historically and theologically perceived as an integral part of the total life and work of the denomination. The nature and responsibility of such a relationship continues to be addressed.

We have tried in this history to be accurate, descriptive, analytical, and nonjudgmental. We have conscientiously cited sources for the information included. Although our research has been supported financially by the Board of Pensions and the Board of Annuities and Relief, we have not written an "authorized" history. Board members and staff have been generous in supplying interviews, explanations, and materials. They have had the opportunity to review the manuscript, as has the Editorial Committee of the Presbyterian Historical Society. We remain, however, solely responsible for the content of the book and take responsibility for any errors.

We regret that space makes it impossible to include extensive biographies of those who have played a part in the development of the pension program of the Presbyterian Church. Although we have included photographs and brief descriptions of some of the major figures, many other individuals—clergy, lay, volunteers—have made significant contributions. It is to them that we dedicate this volume.

PART I
Beginnings 1707–1870

Chapter 1
Colonial Efforts

> The Synod of Philadelphia have often Seriously considered the many distresses of this infant Church, & how thro the smiles of Providence they might best releive [sic] them; and were deeply Sensible that among other things, the small and uncertain Stipends of ministers, and the Poverty & Distress of their widows & children, were great discouragements to many Pious & able men in the ministry, & great hinderances to Parents, from educating their children for this Necessary & honourable, but laborious, Employment, So that ye Gospel ministry was like to fall into weak hands, & many People were like to be without the benefit of Ministers & ordinances.
> —*Charter Petition for the Widows' Fund, 1756*

Colonial Presbyterians belonged to a theological tradition that placed high priority on an educated ministry and thus on candidates who showed intellectual promise as well as spiritual commitment. Congregations believed that the clergy should be set apart to "a high and holy calling" and pledged financial support so that ministers could devote all their energy to ecclesiastical duties. Recognizing how essential forceful leadership was to the struggling church, Presbyterians asked a great deal of the ministers, and furthermore, expected them to perform their duties until they died. Retirement in the modern sense was unknown in America in the seventeenth and eighteenth centuries. "Let the aged endeavor to be as useful as they can, even to the last," wrote John Brock, who lived only two weeks after preaching his last sermon.[1] Consequently, the first organized effort to help ministers financially, The Fund for Pious Uses (1717), was designed to support frontier missionaries and to provide for their widows and children.[2]

Of diverse origins, American Presbyterianism primarily grew out of English Puritanism and Scottish Presbyterianism. Early Presbyterian settlers located throughout virtually all of the original colonies, although their presence was most visible in New Jersey, Pennsylvania, New York, Delaware, and Maryland. Only after a large emigration of Scots-Irish in the seventeenth and eighteenth centuries did Presbyterians have sufficient strength to warrant a formal organizational structure. Francis Mackemie, whose defense of religious freedom before the Governor of New York became a cause célèbre among the colonists, helped mesh disparate elements of Presbyterianism to form the Presbytery of Philadelphia in 1706.[3]

By 1716 emigration of dissenting clergy from Ireland and Scotland to America raised the membership of the Presbytery of Philadelphia to seventeen, and new congregations and mission stations in the middle colonies required closer supervision than what one presbytery could provide. In response, the Presbytery of Philadelphia in 1716 approved the creation of a general synod with four presbyteries: Long Island (New York and New Jersey), Philadelphia (Pennsylvania), New Castle (Delaware), and Snow Hill (Maryland), although the latter never came into being.[4]

New judicatories notwithstanding, colonial Presbyterianism resembled a frontier mission rather than an established denomination. With a membership of three thousand scattered throughout some forty congregations, the new church faced many obstacles. Most Presbyterians lived in unsettled areas where poverty and poor communication made it difficult to adhere to traditional Presbyterian polity. Because of a paucity of ordained ministers and of facilities for training new ones, the church lacked strong leadership and administration.[5]

Throughout the colonial period, Presbyterian ministers, especially those in frontier communities, existed on meager stipends, and most pastors had "to work for their living and preach for charity" if they hoped to sustain themselves.[6] Prior to 1760 any congregation extending a pastoral call was required to have sufficient pledges to guarantee a minister an annual income of about £60, the equivalent of the average income of a Philadelphia seaman. After that date stipends gradually increased until by the end of the century they ranged between £100 and £150 for ministers in established congregations.[7]

On the American frontier, Presbyterians were reluctant to pay a minister from their own small incomes. The Scots-Irish immigrants from Ulster had not formerly had to supply ministerial salaries since the Crown had subsidized their pastors. Not uncommonly presbyteries dissolved pastoral relationships between ministers and congregations because of chronic nonpayment of salaries.[8] In other situations, clergy received compensation in forms other than currency. The Presbytery of Donegal reported that one of its congregations paid a minister £60 in yearly support and supplemented this with linen yarn or linen cloth at market price.[9] Ministers in the New York presbyteries of Oneida and Utica traditionally received part of their salary in firewood, and then, according to presbytery records, congregations rarely delivered the full amount of wood agreed upon.[10]

These early Presbyterians placed great emphasis on charitable and benevolent responsibilities. Much of the actual assistance was given privately—to the poor, elderly, infirm, widows, orphans—thus making historical documentation difficult. There could have been those such as Catherine Steel, a Presbyterian in Derry, Pennsylvania, whose only record of Christian humanitarianism is to be found on her tombstone: "In her lifetime raised 19 orphan children."[11] On many occasions, however, when church members needed financial assistance, sessions and presbyteries aided them. The Presbytery of Donegal in 1737 considered an application from Margaret Wright whose husband had died in an accident. She was left with several children and a large debt. The presbytery decided that she was "justly an object of Christian Charity" and recommended that every congregation within its bounds raise money for her support.[12] The records of New Castle Presbytery (1716-1736) contain several similar references. In 1731 an entry noted that "the Brethren who have not collected for ye widow and her son in Nottingham . . . be mindful of it at our next meeting." On another occasion the record reported that the presbytery had made "a Collection for ye relief of Margaret McAdam, a distressed girl at Upper Elk."[13]

Cognizant that uncoordinated efforts by individual presbyteries were inadequate to deal with growing needs, the Synod of Philadelphia at its initial session in 1717 designated a "Fund for Pious Uses" that became a foundation for subsequent missionary, educational, and charitable activities. Annual offerings taken up at congregational and presbytery meetings and gifts solicited from wealthy individuals provided income. The Fund began its operations with the modest sum of £18, administered by a synodical committee with Jedidiah Andrews, pastor of First Presbyterian Church in Philadelphia, as treasurer. The Fund was intended to provide financial assistance to ministers and their families, to build new churches, and to maintain frontier missionaries.[14]

Initially disbursements from the Fund for Pious Uses were small and infrequent. The first mention of aid either to ministers or their families appeared on September 21, 1719, when the synod voted to give the widow of John Wilson "four pounds and not more than three additional pounds at the discretion of the committee."[15] Considerable funds went to support missionary activities. The synod issued a pastoral letter in 1719 appealing for money "for the carrying on of the said noble and pious design of planting and spreading the everlasting Gospel in these Provinces."[16] In 1723 grants of £3 each were awarded to the Octorara and Hanover congregations and in 1724 a similar one to "the people of Broad Creek" who apparently were having difficulty meeting basic needs.[17] In 1741 the committee gave £10 to assist Presbyterians in Wilmington who wanted to erect a meeting house. The committee also agreed to loan them an additional £30, interest free for three years and repayable at £10 year. On other occasions, the committee simply reported that it had "disposed of funds for the relief of indigent places" scattered through the synod.[18]

Because needs were great, the synod made repeated appeals to congregations for contributions to the Fund for Pious Uses. In 1738, to stimulate interest, the synod proposed that each minister assess himself £10 which he could pay personally or raise from congregational contributions. Records show that several ministers failed to contribute and were billed for these accounts.[19] Aided by substantial gifts from Scottish churches and other generous individuals, the Fund gradually increased. From 1733, when treasurer Andrews reported assets of approximately £508, to 1739, shortly before the Old Side-New Side schism, assets had reached nearly £600.[20]

Theological developments during this time overshadowed the Fund's growth. Colonists were in the midst of the so-called Great Awakening, a time of revivalistic fervor that had begun in the 1720s and reached a peak in the 1740s. Led by Jonathan Edwards, a Congregational pastor at Northampton, Massachusetts, and George Whitefield, an itinerant evangelist of exceptional ability, revivalism touched Presbyterian clergymen such as Gilbert Tennent, Jonathan Dickenson, Samuel Davies, and others. These "New Side" ministers tried to infuse their religious enthusiasm into a denomination that they believed was a victim of declining spirituality and piety.[21]

Many ministers criticized the new movement for its emotional excesses and disagreed with its theology. Their opposition caused them to be termed "Old Side" clergy. When Tennent preached a sermon in 1740 entitled "The Danger of an Unconverted Ministry," in which he denounced Old Side clergy as "blind and natural" leaders who were unworthy of congregational support, he angered and consolidated the opposition. The Synod of Philadelphia, meeting in 1741, expelled revivalist supporters who then formed a rival Synod of New York. This bitter and often hostile division continued until both parties negotiated a reunion in 1758.[22]

During the schism (1741-1758), the Old Side Synod of Philadelphia controlled the Fund for Pious Uses. When the revivalists requested a share of the Fund in 1744, the Synod of Philadelphia ruled that New Side ministers had by their conduct "forfeited their right to membership among us, and of consequence of all the privileges thereof."[23] The Synod of New York attempted to create its own fund for "ministers' widows and orphans" in 1755 but had not done so before reunion in 1758. Bitter feelings engendered by this Old Side rebuff carried over into discussions after the merger concerning how resources from the Fund should be dispensed.[24]

While New Side revivalists flourished and produced a number of outstanding leaders, the Old Side party made few lasting contributions. One exception was Francis Alison, a pastor, academician, and advocate of reunion. Alison argued that demands on the Fund for Pious Uses were so diverse that families of deceased ministers received insufficient attention. In 1754 he proposed the creation of a "Widows' Fund" based on the principle of life insurance. Approved by the Synod of Philadelphia in 1755 and chartered by the colony of Pennsylvania in 1759, the Widows' Fund was the first life insurance company established in America. Formal ties between the Widows' Fund and the church ended in 1789 when the Fund was not included in the new General Assembly structure. The Widows' Fund continued to insure Presbyterian ministers, however, and exists today as the Presbyterian Ministers' Fund.[25]

Alison became interested in a Widows' Fund through his correspondence with Scottish clergy who introduced him to the newly emerging field of actuarial studies and individual life insurance. Although life insurance companies had existed in England since the late 1700s, they were primarily marine and fire underwriters, and their ventures into individual life insurance were handicapped by inadequate mortality statistics and unscientific actuarial computations. In the early 1740s, however, two Edinburgh clergymen who had proclivities for mathematics, Alexander Webster and Robert Wallace, drew up a proposal for a Widows' Fund featuring an annual premium based on actuarial research. Various plans for such a fund had been considered in Scotland for a number of years but rejected "because of their limited nature and from want of a common rule and proper authority to enforce it."[26] Approved by the British Crown in 1744, the Scottish plan was optional for ministers already ordained but compulsory for future clergy. Participants could select an annual rate of £2 to £7 expecting that after their death an annuity based on their annual contributions would be paid to their survivors.[27]

Following the "laudable example of the Church of Scotland," Alison sought to put the American version of the Widows' Fund on a sound legal basis by obtaining a charter so that the Fund could enforce contracts and receive money. In 1756 Alison and Robert Cross, pastor of First Presbyterian Church in Philadelphia, signed a petition directed to Thomas and Richard Penn, sons of William Penn, requesting a charter for the new corporation. The Penns approved, noting that "Presbyterian ministers... have generally endeavored to promote Religion virtue and industry among the people under their care, and have behaved as loyal and dutiful subjects to His Majesty, and as quiet and inoffensive Neighbours."[28] Alison and Cross recorded the charter in Philadelphia on May 2, 1759. The complete title was "The Corporation for Relief of Poor and Distressed Presbyterian Ministers and of the Poor and Distressed Widows and Children of Presbyterian Ministers." Abbreviated titles such as the "Widows' Fund" or simply the "Corporation" were commonly used.

The Widows' Fund provided for a whole life insurance policy with survivorship annuities. A minister could pay the £2 to £7 a year and provide his widow and/or children with an annuity about five times the amount contributed. Widows received life payments unless they remarried, at which time they received one-half of the original stipend. Children were entitled either to a lump sum or thirteen annual payments at the Corporation's discretion. Once having selected a rate, policyholders could not increase the amount of insurance at a later date, a provision designed to prevent people from raising insurance benefits when their health was more precarious. Although the Corporation did not initially require medical examinations, it retained the right to reject applicants who appeared to be in poor physical condition or had a history of bad health. The Corporation further limited its risks by excluding transfers from other synods and confined new policyholders to ordained men from twenty-five to thirty years of age.[29] Given the danger of frontier life and the impecunious status of many colonial congregations, mandatory membership in the Widows' Fund was not considered feasible. The Corporation could only "recommend to every Presbytery to engage as many ministers in their bounds, as they can to become subscribers."[30]

Alison labored to make the Widows' Fund represent both Old and New Side constituents. A committed ecumenist, Alison told synod members that "We must maintain union in essentials, forbearance in lesser matters, and charity in all things."[31] The twelve who signed the original charter reflected Alison's desire to make the Widows' Fund a visible symbol of reunion. Along with Alison, Cross, and local merchants who identified with the Old Side, the original incorporators also included New Side ministers Gilbert Tennent, Samuel Finley, Richard Treat, and layman Andrew Reed.

Although the Corporation composition was ecumenical, its initial officers were all from the Old School. The first president, Robert Cross, had been closely associated with Alison in securing the charter, but by the time of his appointment was seventy years old and in poor health. Alison served as the first secretary until his death in 1779. During his tenure he dominated the Corporation, especially in maintaining its relationship to the synod and the Church of Scotland. As its first treasurer, the Corporation elected a layman, William Allen, Chief Justice of the Province of Pennsylvania. One of the wealthiest and most influential people in the colony, Allen attended First Presbyterian Church in Philadelphia and was active in many religious, educational, and civic organizations. All of the initial officers served without remuneration. In later years the Corporation provided modest salaries for the president and the treasurer.[32]

With no guaranteed clientele and virtually no capital fund, the Corporation immediately launched a campaign to secure sufficient endowment to commence issuing policies. One of the trustees, Robert Smith, was ordered "to excite the Moderators of the Presbyteries to take Subscriptions from the

Ministers and send them in to the Secretary." They also solicited support from individuals and congregations and received a variety of contributions including cash, real estate, and personal goods. One individual gave "twelve pounds twelve shillings and sixpence and two lottery tickets in ye lottery for the Presbyterian Church in Lancaster." The ticket numbers were 565 and 571 but Corporation records do not indicate if they proved to be winners.[33] Another entry notes that Colonel Peter Boyard "generously bestowed ten pistoless" along with a small sum of money. Although these gifts were gratefully received, they did not generate enough income to underwrite the company.[34]

Because of limited resources, Corporation trustees realized that they needed to seek assistance overseas. In 1760 the Corporation dispatched Charles Beatty to Scotland and England to solicit funds. In light of its charter provision not only for life insurance but "to assist ministers of our Synod in frontier settlements, or such as by age or infirmities are not able to get a Subsistence," Beatty based his appeals on the Fund's missionary and charitable features. He described frontier scenes of nearly destitute clergy and congregations under constant threat of "Indian attack." Donors responded with gifts amounting to nearly £4,000, some of which they designated for missionary work rather than capital income. Beatty's money-raising tour angered Anglicans who viewed his mission as a clandestine campaign to create a Presbyterian Society for the Propagation of the Gospel, a charge which the Corporation vehemently denied.[35]

Since the Corporation had been successful in raising money for frontier missions and because its activities duplicated the Fund for Pious Uses, the synod agreed to turn over the assets of the Fund for Pious Uses (1717) to be administered "in trust" by the Corporation. The synod specified that the money should be used initially to provide for those who had been receiving assistance before the institution of the Widows' Fund.[36] In 1761 Alison reported that he had money from the Fund for Pious Uses and the gifts from England and Scotland specially designated for frontier missions that were not legally secured by corporate statute. This money was given to the Corporation with the proviso that the synod would help decide when and where it would be dispensed. The Corporation accepted and the synod appointed a committee to work with the Corporation to make appropriate distributions.[37]

On May 22, 1761, twenty-one Presbyterian ministers applied for insurance and received the first such policies issued in colonial America. Based on available data, the average age of the initial policyholders was 42.7 and the average age of death was 66.6, surprisingly high for that period of history. All of them were men of modest income. Of this initial group, five let their policies lapse shortly after they joined the Fund. A sixth paid premiums until 1792 at which time he withdrew his policy. The remaining fifteen paid premiums until their death, and their families received full annuities.[38]

New subscriptions trickled in following the initial policies. In 1763, although there were fifty members, some already had ceased making payments. Between 1763 and 1789 only thirty-six Presbyterian ministers became policyholders. Equally disappointing was the number who allowed their policies to lapse. The original register book of subscribers to the Fund shows that before 1789 no fewer than thirty-two entries had the word "lapsed" written in red ink beside their name. The inability or unwillingness on the part of ministers to maintain regular payments proved to be a financial burden to the Fund throughout its early history.[39]

As trustee of the Fund for Pious Uses and with the donations from Scotland for frontier missions, the Corporation in its early years functioned both as an insurance company and a missionary society. This has caused some business historians to question the Corporation's claim to be the first American life insurance company. One author deemed the Widows' Fund "a half-charitable, half-insurance" institution that served as a link between individual and corporate forms of underwriting.[40] Another excluded the Widows' Fund from a list of colonial companies because it was supposedly established "for other purposes than business."[41] Most historians, however, have argued that the missionary and charitable features of the Widows' Fund did not impinge on its primary role as an insurer of human life. Before the end of the century the Corporation had completely divested itself of these ancillary responsibilities and was concentrating on insurance-related activities.[42]

Early Corporation minutes corroborate that trustees intermingled insurance, missionary, and charitable interests, noting that it had funds for "distressed frontier inhabitants and for settling ministers and for the propagation of the gospel and paying ransom to free people taken captive by Indian tribes." Its stated policy was to help "those only that are exceeding poor of all Denominations without exception."[43] In 1763 it reported funds dispatched to free "Christian friends and their children who have long endured a most distressing captivity among Savage and Barbarous Nations." In the same year it gave £25 to Moses Tuttle, "a poor and distressed Presbyterian minister, who was driven from the Frontiers in the late Indian War," to support himself and his family.[44] In 1764 a woman who had escaped from captivity applied for assistance. Her husband had been scalped and murdered and her four children remained incarcerated. She received money to make back payments on land she was about to lose.[45]

The Corporation also supported Native American converts and dispatched missionaries to establish more churches in frontier settlements. In fact, the Corporation financed one of the first missionary expeditions in colonial America with some of the money raised in England and Scotland. In 1766 Charles Beatty and George Duffield traveled as far west as the Muskingum River in Ohio where they made contact with various tribes and distributed religious literature.[46] Another missionary, David Brainard, received £40 to assist the converts "in building them a few cabins, or in clearing some lands for the support of their families."[47] In sending out missionaries, the Corporation enjoined missionaries from preaching to colonists who had settled on lands not yet legally acquired from the tribes because "we think this practice of encroaching on these nations Unjust in its Self, and likely to prevent the Success of the Gospel among these people."[48]

During the next decade the synod and the Corporation clashed over the dispensation of money not clearly designated for insurance purposes. Repeatedly the synod asked the Corporation to clarify its financial statements, but each time the requests were met either with silence or inconclusive generalities. In 1767 a synod committee reported that it could not "Ascertain the Sum" nor come to an agreement with the Corporation about the allocation of disputed funds. The following year the synod again pressed for specific information about the "Scottish money," and the Corporation agreed to consult with the synod's committee "and mutually to propose and to agree with one another in the uses to which the Money is to be applied." Simultaneously it asserted its independence from synodical jurisdiction by claiming the power to dispense funds if the synod failed to send members to Corporation meetings when such decisions were made.[49]

The two parties did not resolve their differences until 1771 when the Corporation agreed to set aside £600 of the Scottish money which would yield about £30 interest annually, "to end all debates and for the sake of peace." The synod was empowered to use the £30 interest to assist needy ministers, to aid weak churches, to secure pulpit supply, to build places of worship, and to assist friendly Native Americans who lived on the frontier in proximity to Presbyterian congregations. The Corporation reserved the right to utilize the £600 in the event that it was unable to make annuity payments as stipulated in the thirteenth article of agreement between the contributors and the Corporation.[50] This settlement did not entirely reduce tension between the two bodies. In 1774, for example, the synod reported to the Corporation that it had given £16 in support of "a poor and distressed Congregation" in Haddiston, New Jersey, to provide them with a small meeting house.[51] The Corporation approved the expenditure but expressed irritation. "We would have been glad to have conversed with the Committee to know the necessity of giving that Money to build this New Church . . . and We think it fit to converse with the Committee thereafter, on all their Applications, that we may know their reasons for acting in cases that we are unacquainted with."[52]

As a result, the synod created a new "Fund for Pious Uses" similar to the one that had been given over in trust to the Corporation. In 1766 the synod authorized congregational collections "to raise a Fund for the Propagation and Support of the Gospel in such Parts as cannot otherwise enjoy it."[53] The following year it appointed presbyterial treasurers to collect and send contributions to a synodical treasurer. In a pastoral letter the synod specified that the Fund would give priority to assigning missionaries, distributing religious literature, and "propagating Christian knowledge among the Indians—And for such other Pious Uses as may occur from time to time."[54]

The synod and the Corporation also clashed over the treatment of widows whose husbands had permitted their coverage to lapse. The synod frequently intervened to make exceptions to policy in hardship cases, even though the Corporation had no legal obligation to provide a survivors' annuity. In 1768 the Corporation denied a request for aid from the widow of Adam Boyd who at his death was three years delinquent in premiums, noting that "to relax this point would be inconsistent with our obligation to the Public."[55] Under pressure from the synod it reconsidered and voted her £20 "in Consideration of the Services done . . . by her deceased husband in promoting this Fund."[56] After a number of similar cases the Corporation announced publicly in 1773 that "We do determine, that it is inconsistent with the design of this Charitable Institution, to encourage such failures in payment, and therefore, in justice, we can do nothing for such Families."[57]

External financial problems also affected the Fund. Economic chaos—inflation, undervaluation of property, nonpayment of taxes, and a generally weakened currency—during and after the Revolutionary War jeopardized investments and drained capital. In such an unsettled economic environment, the Corporation relied heavily on unsecured personal bonds and mortgage bonds secured on real estate for initial investments. Sometimes funds were used to finance business ventures or to purchase local real estate. Two so-called "directors' loans" resulted in losses to the Corporation, and another investment in the Continental Loan Office, authorized in 1777, proved to be equally unproductive. The Corporation did not meet between May 1777 and May 1779 because it had been "dispersed by the English Army" from Philadelphia. Only after revolutionary forces had retaken the city could the Corporation conduct business in any systematic fashion.[58]

Subsequently, economic misfortune pushed the Corporation to the brink of financial collapse. In 1780 it reported to the synod that its capital had "suffered greatly by the depreciation of the Currency" and that it was unable to make full annuity payments.[59] The synod agreed in 1782 to relinquish its claim to interest payments (£30) from the Scottish money "in consideration of the difficulties under which the Corporation labour, through the decay of their Funds."[60] The synod's gesture was insufficient to rescue the Corporation. Directors of the Widows' Fund, appealing to the agreement between the Corporation and synod in 1771, encumbered the entire £600 of the Scottish money. Although the synod appointed several committees to investigate the Corporation's financial status, none ever made a formal report of its findings.[61]

Even with cessation of interest payments to the synod, the Corporation came close to bankruptcy. Newly ordained ministers chose not to become members of the Widows' Fund, and many participants were delinquent in annual payments. In 1784 the Corporation threatened to admit lay persons as policyholders "for the preservation of the Fund" unless more ministers subscribed and present members maintained their payments.[62] Three years later it urged the synod to use its influence to recruit new members and to apply pressure on ministers who were not meeting their financial obligations.[63] Although it reaffirmed its support of the Corporation, the synod declined to take disciplinary action against delinquent members or to make membership in the Widows' Fund mandatory for married clergy.[64]

The Fund also suffered from the prolonged Old Side-New Side power struggle. The reconciliation had been a "union without love" in which personal jealousies and theological differences had not been resolved. Alison's inclusion of New Side men in the first set of incorporators proved to be more symbolic than actual. Old Side sympathizers continued to control the Fund, especially after Alison's death in 1779. Opposition to Old Side domination of the Widows' Fund surfaced in 1771 when John Witherspoon proposed a rival organization in New Jersey entitled "The New Jersey Society for the Better Support of the Widows and the Education of Destitute Orphans of Presbyterian Ministers." Although the governor of New Jersey approved Witherspoon's petition in 1775, the outbreak of war and uncertain economic conditions prevented its implementation.[65]

Collectively these ecclesiastical, theological, and economic factors placed the Widows' Fund in a precarious relationship with the synod as it was planning a major judicatorial restructuring including the creation of a General Assembly. As synod committees worked on a *Constitution and Directory of Worship* for the proposed General Assembly, confidence in the Widows' Fund was extremely low. Since the beginning of the American Revolution only a dozen ministers had taken out policies, and many in the denomination feared that the Fund would not recover its financial equilibrium in time to satisfy its constituency. Nevertheless, the initial draft of a *Plan of Government* published in 1786 gave the Widows' Fund official status in the new structure. In the procedures for ordaining and installing ministers, the *Plan* specified that neither ordination nor installation could take place "until that congregation shall have engaged to contribute to the widows' fund a certain yearly rate as he shall choose, for the benefit of his family after his decease, which shall be considered part of his salary that they shall have promised to pay him."[66] If approved, this proviso would have mandated that every ordained and installed minister in the denomination be a member of the Widows' Fund and would have given the organization constitutional authority to conduct its business.

This compulsory feature concerned clergy and laypersons who argued on the basis of their freedom of choice and their individual rights. Moreover, they reasoned, since so many congregations could not provide their ministers with living wages, how could they be expected to shoulder additional financial responsibilities? Although no detailed account of the debate regarding the Widows' Fund exists, the result does: the synod voted to omit the mandatory membership in the 1787 draft of the *Plan of Government*. In its place the synod granted the Corporation permission to publish its terms of membership in the *Constitution and Directory of Worship*. For all practical purposes, the Fund functioned solely as a secular insurance company. Its relationship to the General Assembly of the Presbyterian Church was to be informal rather than official.[67]

Despite this beginning, the Widows' Fund introduced to American society an economic example that transcended denominational policies. With personal life insurance companies not appearing until the last decade of the eighteenth century, the Widows' Fund supplied actuarial data and stimulated an interest in life insurance. Future commercial companies learned from its successes and failures. Moreover, the Widows' Fund provided a model for a similar society in the Protestant Episcopal Church. William Smith, provost of the College of Philadelphia and personal friend of Francis Alison, became interested because of it. Largely through Smith's efforts, Pennsylvania approved a charter for the "Corporation for the Relief of the Widows and Children of the Clergymen in the Communion of the Church of England in America" in 1769. The Anglican Corporation secured substantial capital funds and began to provide support.[68]

These positive factors did not lessen the reality that the Presbyterian Church in 1789 had no official provision for the care of retired or disabled ministers and their dependents. This consideration would claim the attention of a new generation of church leaders.

Chapter 2
The Widows' Fund

The Widows' Fund was originally a charitable institution but ceased to be either charitable or Christian when it incorporated the principle of "Life Insurance" in its terms.
—*The Southern Presbyterian Review*, 1869

A new era for Presbyterians began in 1789 when John Witherspoon, distinguished patriot and president of the College of New Jersey, called to order the first General Assembly of the new national church. The commissioners gathered in Philadelphia's Second Presbyterian Church represented an ecclesiastical body that had survived both internal schism and political revolution and had emerged as a respected "denomination" in the nation's pluralistic religious milieu. Although Baptists and Methodists would make great gains in the coming century, Presbyterians and their Congregational allies maintained their intellectual and social leadership. Halfway through the nineteenth century, historian Philip Schaff characterized Presbyterians as "without question one of the most numerous, respectable, worthy, intelligent, and influential denominations" which had "a particularly strong hold on the solid middle class."[1]

By coincidence the year 1789 also was a significant year for the life insurance industry, which had made little headway in pre-Revolutionary America. The French Revolution and the subsequent war between England and France, which continued intermittently until 1815, set up conditions whereby American business could expand its programs with minimal competition from Europe. As this country's shipping industry grew after 1789, fire and marine insurance companies formed. Between 1787 and 1799 at least twenty-four American insurance companies received charters, and of this number five were authorized to insure lives. Although the few policies written usually covered exceptional risks such as capture by pirates or perhaps a hazardous journey to India, they signaled the beginning of insurance coverage for the general public by companies rather than by underwriters.[2]

Mortality tables were first published in the United States in 1789. Although such tables had existed for more than a century, the most notable being the Northampton Tables devised by an English minister Richard Price, they were not widely used in America. Professor Edward Wigglesworth of Harvard University instigated development among insurance companies when he presented his version of an actuarial table in 1782 to the American Academy of Arts and Sciences in Boston. Undergirded by these actuarial studies, joint stock companies chartered to insure human life as well as marine and fire liabilities multiplied in the last decade of the eighteenth century. The Insurance Company of North America (INA) opened in 1792 and by 1830 thirty-one companies were in operation, twenty-four of which had been chartered since the Constitutional Convention of 1787. In 1812 the Pennsylvania Company for Insurance on Lives and Granting Annuities became the first commercial company organized on a sound actuarial basis and devoted solely to insuring human lives. Many early companies failed either because of poor management or economic recessions; nevertheless, their increasing presence attested to a growing confidence in life insurance as an integral part of business life.[3]

The Widows' Fund entered this new era under the leadership of John Redman, a Philadelphia physician who had been a trustee when the Fund was incorporated in 1759. A graduate of Gilbert Tennent's "Log College," Redman was a scholar and civic leader. He was nearly seventy when he became president of the Corporation in 1791 and administered an organization with forty-seven ministerial policyholders and assets of $118,885. Annuities of $10,615 were paid annually to twenty families of deceased ministers. Although these statistics attest to the Fund's solvency, they also indicate that the Corporation had experienced little growth since its inception in 1759.[4]

During Redman's presidency (1791–1796), the Widows' Fund modified its regulations in an effort to increase denominational participation and to broaden its financial base. Under "The Plan of 1792," it removed the restriction that policyholders had to reside within the bounds of the Synod of New York and Philadelphia and allowed "any minister of the gospel in communion with the General Assembly of the Presbyterian Church" to join. The plan opened membership to unordained ministerial candidates who were under presbyterial care. It also enabled clergy over the age of twenty-eight to become policyholders by paying an additional sum based on the number of years beyond that age. Robert Patterson, a noted mathematician and trustee since 1785, calculated these new insurance rates. His "annexed table" was the first such actuarially based set of premiums for various ages published in the United States and became the basis for similar tables produced by other insurance companies.[5]

The 1792 plan also liberalized procedures for payment of premiums. The old system required premiums to be paid annually throughout the participant's lifetime. Now the corporation offered the alternatives of either submitting an initial lump sum or making a large enough deposit to generate sufficient interest to cover annual premiums. The deposit was to be returned to the survivors at the death of the insured. Another innovation was an option whereby congregations or educational institutions could pay premiums for their pastors or professors by providing a "permanent deposit" similar to the program offered to individuals. These provisions were forerunners of various payment plans common in modern insurance programs.[6]

By providing reinstatement procedures, the Plan of 1792 also modified the forfeiture penalty for delinquent premiums, which jeopardized coverage even after years of prompt payment. Although not identical to modern nonforfeiture value, they moved toward instituting basic policyholder rights. Other innovations included the opportunity to increase coverage at a later date and to allocate part of the annuity to the widow and part to the children. Finally, the new plan increased the maximum annual premium from £7 to £9 and offered a higher annuity rate set at five times (instead of four) the annual contribution.[7]

Despite its new inclusiveness and liberalized conditions, and even though the Plan of 1792 was endorsed by the General Assembly during several of its meetings, it failed to attract many new members. Eleven ministers joined from 1794 to 1797. From 1798 to 1801 no minister applied for membership and for the next decade only ten new names appeared in the company's register book. Between 1800 and 1825 only forty-two new policies came into force, and of that number thirteen eventually lapsed.[8]

This poor growth can be attributed in part to competition from the secular sector. Commercial insurance companies paid field agents handsome commissions and advertised their products throughout the country. In contrast, the Widows' Fund remained essentially a Philadelphia company that relied on occasional "Addresses" to the General Assembly for publicity. Because such meetings were normally held right in Philadelphia, the Corporation used these occasions for personal contact with commissioners. Moreover, Corporation trustees and officers, volunteers who worked gratis or received only token salaries, usually met only once a year just prior to sessions of the General Assembly. Even then, officers were not always reliable; one president did not attend a meeting of the company for two years. Since actions were often deferred, the efficiency and the reputation of the Fund suffered.[9]

Concurrently, the Fund did not always enjoy good relationships with the General Assembly. When widows whose husbands had failed to make premium payments appealed to the General Assembly, they usually received a promise of intervention, which caused friction just as it had earlier with the synod. The case of the widow of John Carmichael, for example, dragged on for seven years. Carmichael's widow hired an attorney to seek from the Corporation annuity payments to Mrs. Carmichael and her family. After considerable discussion, "the trustees decided not to honor the request."[10] A series of charges were laid before both synod and General Assembly, and commissioners in 1793 decided to use their "influence with the corporation of the Widows' Fund in favour of the petitioners."[11] After more than six years of harassment and litigation, Corporation trustees reluctantly submitted to the General Assembly's wishes and granted Mrs. Carmichael a life pension of $93.33 a year. Five trustees, including Robert Patterson and treasurer John Ewing, voted against the exception to policy and expressed their displeasure with the assembly's interference with Corporation activities.[12]

Aside from denominational pressures, the Corporation had its existence threatened in the 1790s when circumstances produced the resignation and civil prosecution of its treasurer, and caused a prominent trustee to be jailed for bad debts. During Revolutionary War times the Fund made several extensive land purchases assuming that demand for undeveloped property would be heavy following cessation of hostilities. In 1793 some trustees felt that these landholdings should be liquidated in order to acquire needed capital. A newly appointed trustee, John Nicholson, at that time Comptroller-General of Pennsylvania, volunteered to purchase the land at 27s. an acre provided the Corporation would permit him to pay only interest on the investment until he could sell the land at a profit. The Corporation agreed and accepted as collateral other property believed to be in Nicholson's possession. Although Nicholson apparently never intended to defraud the Corporation, his careless business practices resulted in his inability to pay outstanding bills. At one point he gave the treasurer John Ewing a check for $2,000 that Nicholson's bank later refused to honor. Since there were no procedures for bankruptcy in the United States at that time, Nicholson eventually was sentenced to debtors' prison where he died in 1800.[13]

In an effort to recoup some of its losses, the Corporation tried to resell the land it had turned over to Nicholson. Because of the complexity of his land speculation, however, the State of Pennsylvania published a caveat against the purchase of any land formerly associated with Nicholson, which included much of the land owned by the Corporation. "This alarming publication excited great anxiety," Robert Patterson reported in 1804, "and it was long before the minds of the committee were relieved."[14] Only after protracted negotiations was the Corporation able to establish an undisputed claim to the property in question and in 1805 dispose of its land at one dollar an acre to Philadelphia businessman, J. B. Wallace. Nevertheless, parts of the land remained in dispute for many years.[15]

In addition to the unfavorable publicity generated by Nicholson, the Corporation became embroiled in a related controversy with treasurer John Ewing, renowned Presbyterian minister and former provost of the University of Pennsylvania. During his long tenure as treasurer, Ewing had steered the Fund through some treacherous financial times. In his later years, however, he grew increasingly irritable, autocratic, and independent as treasurer. He made some land investments without first consulting the board and entered Nicholson's worthless $2,000 check on his books as an asset. A committee appointed to investigate Ewing's records held him accountable for the $2,000 and ordered him to make restitution. Ewing refused to acknowledge any culpability in mismanagement of Corporation funds.[16]

Negotiations with Ewing lasted several years. In the meantime, Ewing resigned as treasurer and requested the Corporation to accept a mortgage on some of his property as security for his alleged financial discrepancies, which it refused to do. A special committee reported in 1799 that it had unsuccessfully made "several attempts to have an amicable suit entered" with Ewing. The Corporation sued Ewing for mismanagement of funds and falsification of books. The court ruled in its favor and forced Ewing to sell his family home and other assets in order to make recompense. Regardless of the legal victory, the Ewing scandal greatly affected the Corporation's ability to attract membership.[17]

When Robert Patterson succeeded Ewing as treasurer in 1798, he inherited chaotic records and financial conditions. Despite Ewing's assurance that Corporation finances were "in a flourishing situation," Patterson appraised them much less optimistically. Unpaid interest from Nicholson's loans amounted to more than $12,000. Other funds were tied up because of the litigation against Ewing. In addition, some lands had been sold at auction because of unpaid taxes, thus depriving the Fund of potential revenue. For several years Patterson borrowed money in order to honor annuity payments and on several occasions contributed his personal funds. It took Patterson more than a decade to achieve fiscal stability and to improve the company's public image.[18]

In addition to internal troubles, a variety of external factors affected the Widows' Fund. Most Presbyterian ministers continued to be grossly underpaid in relation to other professionals and consequently were reluctant to channel their limited funds into insurance premiums. Moreover, periodic economic fluctuations resulted in "panics" that conditioned people to be cautious about long-term investments, such as insurance policies, that might well be eroded by inflation and overvalued currency. Many unregulated insurance companies collapsed in the 1830s and aroused public suspicion about the industry's ability to deliver what it promised. People with money to invest sought safer, more predictable sources of retirement income.[19]

Looming beyond these economic realities were cultural and religious factors that mitigated against successful insurance programs, even ones with a specialized clientele like the Presbyterian Widows' Fund. Indeed, these non-economic factors perhaps were more determinative in restricting the growth of insurance companies than all of the economic conditions combined. In recent years economic and business historians have identified such religious and cultural attitudes as being crucial to a proper understanding of the relatively slow growth of the American insurance industry.[20]

A *New York Times* article written in 1853 expressed a commonly held evaluation of life insurance: "He who insures his own life or health must indeed be a victim of his own folly or another's knavery."[21] With this view many Presbyterians concurred. The editor of *The United Presbyterian Magazine*, himself an advocate of life insurance, acknowledged that life insurance savored somewhat of "impiety" to many devout Christians.[22] Another Presbyterian writer commented on "the inveterate prejudices in the minds of godly men" regarding life insurance and "a general distrust of the scheme as a mere human invention."[23] A contributor to *The Southern Presbyterian Review* in 1869 expressed his opinion of life insurance and the Widows' Fund in these terms: "The Widows' Fund was originally a charitable institution but ceased to be either charitable or Christian when it incorporated the principle of 'Life Insurance' in its terms."[24]

Some writers depicted the growing insurance industry as a calculated movement to rationalize and commercialize the management of death. To place a monetary value on life, they asserted, undercut the Judaeo-Christian principle of the ultimate dignity of human life and turned a person's worth into an "article of merchandise." Women in particular were sensitive to this argument because traditionally they were the benefactors of insurance payments. According to some insurance brokers, women frequently referred to life insurance proceeds as "blood money" and rejected "such sordid calculation of [their husbands'] future expectation of life."[25]

Insurance agents tried to diminish female antagonism to life insurance by "educating" them about basic business principles. Richard Clark, an Equitable Life agent, wrote a weekly column in *The Herald and Presbyter* entitled "The Insurance Department" in which he affirmed that "nearly all the prejudice existing against life insurance is the prejudice of women." Clark illustrated the folly of this attitude by quoting poignant letters from distressed widows who had opposed insuring their husbands' lives and later regretted it. After her husband had died suddenly and left her destitute, one widow penned these words: "I was inexperienced and imagined that he was going to die, and that he was aware of it, or why should he insure his life? My anxiety and nervous excitement increased to such an extent that he finally said, that since it worried me so much, he would not be insured." She pleaded for other wives not to make the same mistake.[26]

Perhaps the most frequently proffered argument was that life insurance indicated a rejection of trust in God's providential care. One Presbyterian minister said, "The system invades the prerogatives of the Lord of Life. ... God holds in his own hand the life of each individual of the race. ... Yet here is a soulless corporation, which affects to reverse the decrees of God or of fate, and promises life or its equivalent to both saint and sinner, disregarding all limits except those that are found in its statistical records."[27] Another writer contended that since God holds in his own hand all human life, the proverbial expression, "No person can die until his time comes," refutes the basic premise on which life insurance is based.[28]

In her popular novel, *The Shady Side: or, Life in a Country Parsonage*, Martha Stone Hubbell captured in colloquial language this argument. As the women's sewing circle is discussing ways of raising money for the minister's salary, one woman innocently suggests that they should purchase a life insurance policy for their pastor.

> "But that would not help him anyhow," said Mrs. Rogers.
> "It would provide something for the family," said Mrs. Brown, "if he should be taken away."
> "Get his life insured did you say?" ejaculated an old lady, looking over her spectacles; "never heard of such things 'mong Christian folks. I should call that tempting Providence."
> "I think," said a pert young miss, "that ministers ought to lay up something for old age."
> Hester's lip curled, and she said, "Ministers ought not to live to be old."
> "What do you mean?" said another.
> "They ought to *wear out*, first," was the reply.[29]

George Duffield, pastor of the Pine Street Presbyterian Church in Philadelphia, illustrates the "God will provide" syndrome. Duffield's congregation had failed to make salary payments, and he and his family could barely cover their necessities. At some point, when all of his resources had been consumed, he received an unsigned envelope containing enough money to sustain his family for a period of time, confirming his belief in the Lord's will. Ironically, Duffield had been a charter member of the Widows' Fund, but could not make insurance payments when little or no income was available to the family. His policy lapsed, so at his death his survivors received no benefits.[30]

Opponents of life insurance also argued that if taking out a policy tempted Providence it also weakened human responsibility. To rely on life insurance proceeds, they contended, had a debilitating effect on human resourcefulness and jeopardized the principle of self-help. Viewed from this perspective, life insurance was "a scheme by which lazy men could shift the burdens of their own responsibilities upon the shoulders of other people."[31] One Presbyterian minister said that the programs "contemplate placing the insured in a position in which he shall, or may at some time in his life, receive more than the legitimate return for what he has done, or the money he has paid." Life insurance, he reasoned, "is the use of means for the extortion from one to supply another."[32]

Another common objection represented life insurance as a form of gambling. An early treatise observed that to insure one's life "looks like a wager, a bet, or that appealing to the doctrine of chance, it partakes of the nature of gambling."[33] One clergyman called life insurance a "mean, low lottery game, yea, in fact worse than such for one places his life at stake."[34] A Presbyterian journalist informed his readers that an insurance company relies on its actuarial tables and bets each client that the promise of the tables will be fulfilled. He concluded, "It can never be moral to lay wagers upon any contingency, and the very idea of gambling upon a man's own chance of life is simply horrible."[35]

Deep-rooted suspicions about the morality of life insurance gradually receded in the nineteenth century because of a barrage of insurance company propaganda as well as the assistance of liberal clergy who defended it on practical and theological grounds. Henry Ward Beecher, Charles H. Spurgeon, and Charles Hodge, among others, endorsed life insurance. Spurgeon informed his parishioners that he had insured his own life for $5,000 and based it on his interpretation of Matthew 6:34. "Now I know how to practice Christ's command of 'taking no thought for the morrow.' I pay the policy money once a year and take no further thought about it, for I have no occasion to do so now, having obeyed the very spirit and letter of Christ's command."[36] Beecher once told his congregation that "We have no right to trust God for anything which he has enabled us to obtain by our own skill," and urged men to purchase adequate protection for their families.[37]

Commercial insurance companies frequently paid ministers to write pamphlets extolling the virtues of policyholding. One such publication, entitled *The American Manual of Life Assurance Answering All Questions Necessary To A Full Understanding Of The Whole Subject* and written by a "Clergyman," listed all the popular objections to life insurance and then refuted them point by point. In his expose of the "God will provide" argument, the author told of a minister who had taken out a $5,000 policy on his life and was rebuked by an elder who said that this "practically contradicted all the teachings of his ministry among them, on the subject of trusting Providence implicitly to take care of our interests here and hereafter." A few days later the minister saw the elder putting up a lightning rod on his house. "What!" said the pastor, "Cannot you trust Providence that He will not allow the lightning to strike your building?" The elder saw the logic of the lesson, and his opposition to "Life Assurance" vanished.[38]

Changing attitudes toward life insurance encouraged officers to maintain their commitment to the Widows' Fund. During the first half of the nineteenth century two men in particular rendered exceptional service to the Corporation. Both serving as treasurers, Robert Patterson and his son, Robert M. Patterson, provided sound fiscal management and steady leadership during troubled times and enabled the small company to experience a modest growth.

Robert Patterson's mathematical interests led him to devise the rate table used in the Plan of 1792. Among other prestigious positions, Patterson served as Vice-Provost of the University of Pennsylvania, director of the United States Mint, and president of the American Philosophical Society. For nearly fifty years a ruling elder in the Old Scots Presbyterian Church in Philadelphia, Patterson became a Corporation trustee in 1785 and served continuously until his death in 1824. Patterson was succeeded by his son, Robert Maskell Patterson, M.D., whose career accomplishments rivaled those of his father. Patterson held the post of professor of Natural Philosophy and Mathematics at the University of Pennsylvania and for a time served as Vice-Provost. After a short time on the University of Virginia faculty, he returned to Philadelphia to become director of the mint, a position he held until shortly before his death. Father, son, and grandson Robert Patterson II together served eighty years as treasurer of the Widows' Fund.[39]

Under the senior Patterson's guidance (1798–1824) the Fund gradually erased its deficits and accumulated a substantial balance. He eschewed undeveloped land investments and unsecured mortgages and invested Corporation capital in government and other secured bonds that yielded 6 to 8 percent interest annually. He also insisted on a policy of "a speedy collection of debts due to the corporation, and a rigid enforcement of punctuality in future payments."[40] Because of these procedures, Patterson reported in 1813 a brighter financial picture than was possible a decade earlier. The Corporation had a capital fund of $3,000 and a surplus of $600 after paying all the widows' annuities. Membership consisted of eighteen ministers who made annual payments, three churches which had made a permanent deposit for their pastor, and four individuals who had made a similar deposit. Reviewing the Fund's history, Patterson noted that thirty-six "extinct contributors" had paid in a total of $9,746.67, and their families had received $46,337.75, nearly five times the amount paid by the policyholders. Families of sixteen contributors still receiving benefits had garnered $15,719.42 from payments amounting to only $8,030.37. The total amount paid to families of deceased contributors since the Fund began in 1759 was $62,057.17. Acknowledging that "apprehensions that the fund would afford but a precarious security may have deterred some," Patterson distributed these statistics to commissioners at the General Assembly hoping that they would "render the fund more extensively beneficial."[41]

In 1820, Patterson proposed adding to the Fund's policies a modest annuity for "that portion of the clergy who may survive the period of active labour, in their sacred vocation." Assisted by a committee composed of Patterson's son, Archibald Alexander, Jacob J. Janeway, and Ashbel Green, Patterson drafted the "Plan of 1824" shortly before his own death in that same year.[42] The new plan offered to ministers who survived to age sixty-five an income of $100 a year if the applicants had at age twenty-five made a one-time payment of $100. By doubling the initial investment, they could receive $200 and by trebling the sum receive a maximum of $300 a year for life. Participants joining later in life paid correspondingly higher premiums based on revised actuarial tables. In addition, the Plan of 1824 offered the usual widow's pension with premiums modified to reflect longer life expectancy.[43]

Patterson's living annuity proposal demonstrated his awareness of a social revolution that had been gaining momentum since the time of the French Revolution. Between 1790 and 1820 American legislatures began to require retirement for public officials at a predetermined age, usually sixty or seventy. First introduced for New York judges in 1777, retirement law of some type was in effect in at least eight states by 1820. The term "superannuated" took on new connotations in the nineteenth century. Earlier it had referred to people of various ages who were disqualified from some particular service or activity because of age. Young boys who had passed the age for school admission were commonly referred to as superannuated. In the nineteenth century, however, the term increasingly referred to men and women in their sixties or above who were unable to perform assigned tasks. At the same time, new words which denigrated old age crept into the American vocabulary: codger, fuddy-duddy, geezer, galoot, old-timer, and similar references.[44]

Widows' Fund Secretary Ashbel Green explained the philosophy undergirding the Plan of 1824 in an "Address to the General Assembly" published in that same year. Green noted that from its inception the Corporation had been empowered to distribute money to needy clergymen, some of whom may never have been contributors to the Fund. Owing to various "disasters and embarrassments" under which the Fund had labored, no such distributions had ever taken place. Instead of random charity, Green argued that it was better "to establish a distinct fund for superannuated ministers." This marks the first usage of "superannuated" in the Corporation's literature and indicates a sensitivity to changing social values.[45]

In the lengthy "Address" Green urged young ministers to make "one vigorous exertion while in their prime, to secure a comfortable provision for old age which will not be subject to the vicissitudes of other possessions." He also challenged congregations to care for their ministers in old age by purchasing an annuity as an appreciation of services rendered. Such foresightedness, Green argued, would enable congregations to pension a pastor "who is no longer able, with advantage, to fulfill the duties of his office, stands in the way of one who is capable and active, and hangs like a dead weight on the church."[46]

Green anticipated opponents would argue that the plan would not benefit anyone who died before age sixty-five. On the one hand, he suggested that "annuitants and pensioners live longer" because they are free from the fear and "corroding anxiety" of facing old age with no visible means of support. On the other hand, Green appealed to a "Spirit of Christian benevolence" which looked beyond personal comfort to the wider community of faith. "And what happier destination could a servant of Jesus Christ give to a small portion of his property," Green asked, "than to make it subservient to the comfort of those who have not only borne the heat and burden of the day in the vineyard of the Lord, but have continued to labor until the eleventh hour?" The address concluded with a call to "the pious females of the congregation" to involve themselves in such a worthy project.[47]

Green's logic apparently made little impact on young Presbyterian ministers and their congregations. In a period of ten years only three policies were taken out and by 1854 only two contracts were still in effect. Lack of a death benefit, failure of congregations to assume annuity obligations, and the inclination of younger ministers to invest their meager savings in less expensive death benefit protection adversely affected the Plan of 1824. Neither congregations nor clergy were ready to accept the premise that Presbyterian ministers should retire.[48]

Although Corporation directors were disappointed at this poor response, they were satisfied with the company's overall financial health. The long period of deficits seemed to be over. In 1837, just before the Old School-New School division, the treasurer reported a balance of $5,768.04, a figure that continued to rise throughout the century.[49] Moreover, opposition to life insurance was moderating, and some of the denomination's most respected ministers held policies in the Widows' Fund. Among them were Albert Barnes, Charles Hodge, Archibald Alexander, and John Breckenridge. The Ewing-Nicholson affair was a fading memory to older ministers and an unknown event to a rising generation of potential policyholders. Having survived seventy-five difficult years, the Widows' Fund hoped to play an increasingly prominent role as insuring agents for Presbyterian ministers and their families.

Chapter 3
The Presbyterian Annuity Company

We believe that the management of our body has been on the whole such as has truly carried out the objects of our incorporation and that the Presbyterian Church has no reason to regret that it gave birth to this, certainly the oldest institution for Life Insurance in the United States.

—*Letter to the General Assembly*, 1881

The financial panic of 1837 caused by speculation and erratic governmental fiscal policies resulted in bank failures and depression. The Widows' Fund survived the immediate impact of these national monetary problems, but it had limited resources. Simultaneously, the Fund was involved with the struggle between Old School traditionalists and New School modernists that had been simmering since early in the century. These struggles would have a long-lasting impact on the Fund's future.[1]

The ecclesiastical controversy peaked at the General Assembly of 1837, which was controlled by a conservative majority. Abruptly those called Old School abrogated the Plan of Union (1801) with the Congregationalists, a program they called "Presbygationalism" and opposed as an abandonment of Presbyterian principles. They severed four western synods that had evolved from the Plan. As a result, 553 churches, 509 ministers, and between 60 and 100,000 members were dropped from assembly rolls. Opposing ministers, termed New School, organized a rival denomination right after the assembly.

The two factions operated independently until 1870 when a new generation negotiated a reunion settlement.[2]

Desiring to maintain neutrality between Old and New School General Assemblies, the Widows' Fund modified its rules to permit "any minister of the Presbyterian Church in the United States" to become a policyholder without denominational qualification.[3] Despite this gesture, the Fund maintained strong Old School associations. When a young minister who had been educated and ordained by the Presbyterian Church but who had accepted a call to a Congregational church in Vermont applied for membership, the directors tabled the request for a year and then resolved without any detailed explanation "that this measure is not at present expedient."[4] Throughout the schism the Old School General Assembly minutes continued to list the Widows' Fund as an "official institution" of its General Assembly, and the Fund's officers and virtually all of its policyholders were Old School members.[5]

The Old School conservatism influenced the Fund's operations. It offered only two types of policies, neither of which had ever greatly appealed to Presbyterian ministers. With no field agents and virtually no advertising procedures, most ministers who knew anything about the Corporation were from the Philadelphia vicinity. The Fund's ponderous title, "The Corporation for Relief of Poor and Distressed Widows and Children of Presbyterian Ministers," was reminiscent of a bygone era, and its volunteer board and annual meetings seemed incongruous alongside the commercial insurance industry. Although a balance in 1837 of some $5,700 "in favour of the Fund" and forty-five policyholders, out of a potential 2,000 who were eligible, represented an improvement over previous deficits, this hardly connoted a thriving institution.[6]

During the 1840s the Widows' Fund struggled against denominational indifference and economic malaise. Between 1840 and 1850 only seventeen ministers took out policies. In the economic sector, banks in Philadelphia, New York, Baltimore, and other eastern cities periodically suspended specie payment. Many insurance companies went out of business, but the Widows' Fund managed to survive. In 1841 the treasurer reported that the Corporation had assets of $55,600 consisting of "properly secured bonds," including State of Ohio Canal Sixes, Schuykill Navigation Sixes, Bank of America stock, and $33,500 in Lehigh Coal and Navigation Company bonds. Because at least the latter company was in financial trouble and offering coal rather than cash to its investors, the treasurer recommended that they reduce their investment as quickly as possible. The Fund subsequently formed a Finance Committee of five members with the president ex officio "to advise us in all sales, purchases, and changes of investments."[7]

Archibald Alexander recommended major changes to enable the Fund to adapt to current conditions. Alexander, professor of theology at Princeton

Seminary, had been a policyholder since 1798 and a trustee since 1808. One of the Old School's most respected members, he spoke and wrote in defense of life insurance in general and the Widows' Fund in particular.[8] Knowledgeable about commercial life insurance through family connections with the Equitable Life Assurance Society of New York, Alexander wrote President John K. Kane in 1851 urging that the Fund revamp its operations "to conform more closely to the terms of ordinary Insurance Companies" and to "increase its usefulness."[9] Among other things, Alexander suggested that the company modernize its name, adopt more aggressive advertising and promotional techniques, hire field agents, and offer a variety of competitive insurance programs including a "Division of Profits" or dividends similar to those available in mutual companies.[10]

Alexander's suggestions coincided with the appointment of a new treasurer, Robert Patterson II. As mentioned earlier, he was the third family member to serve in that capacity. Upon assuming office on May 21, 1852, he was placed on the committee to consider Alexander's proposals. Correspondence suggests that Patterson did the bulk of the committee's work. In a letter to Kane, chairman of the special committee, Patterson offered an extensive analysis of the company's financial status and policy offerings. Patterson opposed Alexander's dividend idea, but he advocated a number of modifications compatible with Alexander's other proposals.[11]

The Plan of 1852 offered potential policyholders three choices. The first option was a modified version of the traditional widows' annuity with premiums scaled according to the minister's age. The annuity, rather than being quoted in a multiple of the annual premium (i.e., five or six times the annual premium), was fixed at $100. Increased contributions could raise the annuity as high as $250. Second, the Corporation ventured into the field of ordinary life insurance by offering a policy not to exceed $3,000 that had a cash surrender feature and rates competitive with other Philadelphia insurance companies. To promote the new policy, the Corporation hired an agent to be compensated on the basis of ten percent commission of the first year's premiums. Third, the Fund sold a retirement annuity with an added option of maturation at age sixty or sixty-five. It also provided for an initial fixed payment, an annual premium, or a permanent deposit by a church or educational institution.[12]

In addition to these features, the Corporation changed its name to "The Presbyterian Annuity Company." The new name became official May 16, 1856, following court approval in Philadelphia.[13] The Company also broadened its potential market by adopting a more ecumenical definition of "Presbyterian" to include "all Presbyterially-governed bodies such as German Reformed, Dutch Reformed, Associate Reformed, Associate, Cumberland, or Reformed Presbyterian." The Company sent representatives to both Old and

New School General Assemblies to promote the advantages of insuring with the Presbyterian Annuity Company.[14]

Initial response to the Plan of 1852 was encouraging. In a new record for one year, 33 ministers took out policies in 1853 to raise the number of subscribers to 76. The Company experienced a modest annual growth until 1861 when membership peaked at 145 policyholders. During the 1860s, however, the trend reversed and by 1870 only 120 members remained on the rolls, some of whom subsequently surrendered their policies. The annuity policy generated virtually no interest either among clergy or their congregations, with only 3 ministers taking out retirement annuities despite repeated promotional efforts.[15]

Such statistics occurred in part because of the Company's inability to break fully from its conservative past. When its first field agent died shortly after his appointment, the trustees failed to appoint a successor. Moreover, despite Robert Patterson's well-founded actuarial objections, the Company continued to offer a widows' annuity based on unpredictable variables of second and third marriages and the number and ages of children. This, in turn, meant higher rates, a fact that did not go unnoticed in denominational papers. A contributor to the *American Presbyterian Review* characterized the Company's conditions and rates as "illiberal, arbitrary, impertinent—such as ordinary companies would not think of exacting, and such as few ministers are willing to subscribe to." He supported his accusations by comparing Presbyterian Annuity Company rates with those of some large eastern insurance firms. The writer also criticized the Company for its lack of business enterprise and competitiveness. "It is left mainly to run itself. There is no one whose brain and energies are wholly given to it. Little effort is made to bring it to the notice of churches and of ministers, and keep it before them." He concluded his analysis on a pessimistic note. "We have a noble ship, strong and freighted with a precious power; but it is *stranded*, and nothing less than a 'tidal wave' of new life and enterprise will lift it from the beach and speed it on its mission."[16]

External conditions also diminished the potential effectiveness of the heralded Plan of 1852. Burgeoning commercial competition encroached on its limited ministerial market. In 1840 there were only fifteen major life insurance companies in the United States with an estimated five million dollars worth of life insurance. By 1859, however, forty-three companies had in force almost two hundred and five million dollars worth of life insurance.[17] The Presbyterian Annuity Company also felt the impact of religious insurance agencies such as the Clergymen's Mutual Insurance League which permitted any clergyman over forty-five years of age and in good health to become a member. When a member died, everyone in the League contributed an assessed sum to the widow. Other mutual insurance organizations created by the Reformed Church (Dutch) of America and the United Presbyterian Church of North America filtered out ministers who might otherwise have insured themselves with the Presbyterian Annuity Company.[18]

Furthermore, the Presbyterian Annuity Company was adversely affected by the development of organized programs by both Old and New School General Assemblies that would assist retired and disabled ministers. These new funds tended to diminish the attraction of buying an insurance policy. As early as 1849 the Old School denomination had created a Fund for Disabled Ministers, enlarged it in the 1850s, and initiated a supplemental endowment fund. New School commissioners followed their counterparts with a Ministerial Relief Fund that distributed small grants. In establishing this Fund, the New School rejected the use of life insurance, claiming that "the wants of the great majority of those who most need this provision cannot be met by any practicable use of the principle of Life Insurance."[19] Largely because of these attitudes, when the Old School and New School Assemblies united in 1870, only 120 out of a potential 4,238 members held policies issued by the Presbyterian Annuity Company.[20]

Throughout the last half of the nineteenth century, the Presbyterian Annuity Company endured what might well be termed "an identity crisis" regarding its relationship to the Presbyterian church. Since 1789 its status with the General Assembly had been based on tradition and sentiment rather than law. Although at times it was treated by the assembly with benign neglect, it nevertheless had experienced no internal competition. With the establishment of denominational relief funds, and later, in the reunited church, a Board of Ministerial Relief, the future of a company whose well-being depended on the cooperation of Presbyterian ministers appeared uncertain. Some Company officials, predominantly laypersons, thought that to survive depended on opening up insurance coverage to a much wider clientele. Others, including many of the ministerial trustees, felt that any significant deviation from the original charter would endanger the company's status as a charitable organization and would adversely affect relations with the General Assembly.

During the 1860s, problems raised by the Civil War somewhat diverted the company from the question of denominational status to the issue of insurability. Initially the Company stated that insurance contracts "were not in any manner impaired by the Political circumstances of our Country," but it later decided not to insure ministers who were in military service "or in districts where controls dependent on life are more than usually hazardous."[21] Toward the end of the war, however, it permitted ministers considered to be special risks to acquire coverage by paying increased premiums. The Company also supported the Union cause by purchasing $25,000 in government bonds although it kept the investment a secret until after the war had ended.[22]

During the war years, the Presbyterian Annuity Company was challenged by the Old School General Assembly over certain funds being held. In 1863 the Board of Publication (O.S.) had undergone a thorough financial examination because of alleged mishandling of denominational funds. In the course of its audit, the investigating committee noted that the board had made a permanent deposit with the Presbyterian Annuity Company to provide life insurance for its corresponding secretary. The committee thought that such a payment was inappropriate and "liable to objection, or at least of misconception, far beyond its value to him." It recommended that the deposit be withdrawn.[23] When the General Assembly demanded a refund, company officers convened a rare special meeting and after "due deliberation" phrased an appropriate response. The company stated its unanimous opinion "that this corporation have no authority to restore the Board of Publication the fund deposited for their secretary." On that negative note, the matter was dropped.[24]

Upon Old and New School reunion in 1870, the question of the Company's relationship to the new denomination received considerable attention both in denominational newspapers and on the floor of General Assembly. Many church leaders thought that life insurance should be utilized either to supplement or to replace the inadequate relief pensions. Some even suggested that the Presbyterian Annuity Company had the assets and abilities to provide the denomination with a comprehensive relief program.[25] Responding to these indications of interest, President Charles Macalester released another "Address" to the General Assembly in 1871 in which he described "the objects and advantages of contracting with the corporation." The Company offered the church ordinary life insurance premiums with annual payments and annuities payable at ages fifty-five, sixty, or sixty-five. Macalester's plea for acceptance concluded with the hope that "through the sympathy and patronage of the church, its ministers, and laymen, our objects can become more widely known and our sphere of usefulness enlarged."[26] Again, the address had little influence on Presbyterian ministers. During the next three years only nineteen clergy applied.

When J. Ross Snowden, lawyer and director of the United States Mint, became president in 1874, he and the directors attempted to establish closer relationships with the General Assembly. Snowden appointed a committee "to consider the propriety of extending the benefits of this Institution, so as to meet the growing demands of the Church" and to cooperate with "any measures which that reverend body General Assembly may inaugurate."[27] Its answer came in May 1876, when the General Assembly established the Presbyterian Board of Ministerial Relief and committed itself to support retired and disabled ministers through voluntary offerings from the church-at-large. Regarding its relationship with the Presbyterian Annuity Company, the assembly ruled that it "ought not, even seemingly, to lend its name and influence to any such purely business projects."[28]

Although the Company would try again to win the endorsement of the General Assembly, for all practical purposes the issue was settled. The Company changed its name to the Presbyterian Annuity and Life Insurance Company and offered insurance policies to ministers, laymen, and families, including denominations of a similar polity. In effect, the Company was prepared to insure "all human beings" and intended to compete with commercial insurance firms. It hired an actuary who doubled as a sales agent, formed a Finance-Executive Committee for increased efficiency, and moved into new offices instead of sharing space with the Presbyterian Board of Publication.[29]

The venture into the commercial insurance field was short-lived. After initial aggressive activity, business declined because of poor economic conditions and because of the intense competition from established insurance firms. In 1880 the company reversed itself and again limited its coverage to Presbyterian ministers. Its new president, John Welsh Dulles (grandfather of former Secretary of State John Foster Dulles and Professor Avery Dulles, S.J.), made one last effort that proved fruitless to link the company with the PCUSA General Assembly. While thanking God for the benefits of life insurance programs, the assembly believed that the future usefulness of such programs must depend upon "the continuance of wise and judicious management rather than on the approval of the General Assembly."[30]

Following this rejection by the General Assembly, the Company vacillated on the scope of its programs. At first it expanded by successively adding foreign missionaries (1881), theological candidates (1886), and wives, widows, and sisters of Presbyterian ministers (1887). In 1888 it assumed a new name, The Presbyterian Ministers' Fund, which continues in use to this day, and in 1892 it expanded its market to include all Protestant evangelical ministers and laymen. Two years later, however, after extended debate, board members voted once again to limit insurance coverage solely to Presbyterian ministers.[31] Even this action proved to be only temporary. In 1906 the company widened its base to accept all Protestant evangelical ministers and from that time on has become increasingly ecumenical in membership. In 1967 it voted to admit any clergy who were employed by "a recognized religious body."[32] Its modern advertisements stress its inclusivity rather than denominational particularity.

In 1900 the Presbyterian Ministers' Fund was still a relatively small company by commercial insurance standards with only 3,002 policyholders and assets of $5,626,992. Under the entrepreneurial leadership of Perry S. Allen (1909-1930) and Alexander Mackie (1936-1963), however, the Presbyterian Ministers' Fund gradually emerged as a progressive, independent company with a national constituency. In 1980 it boasted assets of $233,547,830 and more than one billion dollars worth of insurance in force. It continues to utilize the leadership of Presbyterian ministers and laymen (the incumbent president, Robert J. Lamont, is an ordained Presbyterian minister) but functions independently of church structures and programs. Those interested in the fund's modern history are referred to *Horn of Plenty: The Story of the Presbyterian Ministers' Fund*, written in 1982 by John Baird.[33]

One final note regarding the relationship between the Presbyterian Ministers' Fund and the Presbyterian Board of Pensions warrants attention. Both groups have claimed 1717 as the origin of their respective organizations. From time to time these claims have evoked controversy and on at least one occasion resulted in a written protest from the Presbyterian Ministers' Fund to the Board of Pensions. Although neither group appears to be completely correct in all its assertions, some historical perspective on the subject makes it possible to understand the rationale of both positions.

In its earliest "addresses" and other literature, the directors of the Widows' Fund did not use 1717 as a founding date. In describing their origins, they referred either to 1755, the date when the Synod of Philadelphia created the Fund, or to 1759, the date in which it was incorporated, usually the latter. Although writers occasionally mentioned the Fund for Pious Uses as a predecessor of the Widows' Fund, we have not found any documents prior to the 1890s in which the Presbyterian Ministers' Fund used the date 1717. About that time, Company literature began to employ the terminology, "Founded in 1717 and Chartered in 1759." Although not always consistent in its usage, this practice became more common during the tenures of presidents Allen and Mackie in the twentieth century. In 1938, for example, Mackie released a brochure that featured a facsimile of the Fund For Pious Uses on its cover and proclaimed in eighteenth-century script, "The Presbyterian Ministers' Fund had its beginning in the 'Fund For Pious Uses' of the Philadelphia Synod in 1717." It was Mackie who challenged the Board of Pensions's right to use 1717 in advertising its own program.[34]

A survey of denominational reports and other official documents indicates that the Board of Pensions and its predecessor organizations frequently referred to the Fund For Pious Uses in recounting the church's interest in ministerial relief. The point was usually made that one of the Fund's first disbursements was to a minister's widow. Nevertheless, there is no evidence to indicate that the PCUSA claimed that its Ministerial Relief Board was "founded" in 1717. On the contrary, church executives carefully avoided such a claim. A history of ministerial relief work published in 1889, for example, says only that the early synod minutes "show that the *object* for which the present 'Board of Relief' was established, early occupied the attention of our Church."[35] There is evidence that the references to 1717 and the Fund For Pious Uses appeared in the 1920s when Henry Master, executive secretary of the Board of Pensions, employed such terminology in his reports. For four years (1935–1938), Master actually modified the traditional numbering of his board's reports to reflect the 1717 date. Although his successor discontinued this practice in 1939, the board reports frequently used such language as "founded in 1717" or "marking the 221st anniversary of the beginning of the work now carried on by this Board."[36]

In 1951 the Board of Pensions issued a pamphlet entitled "A Fund For Pious Uses in 1951" which contained the following paragraph:

> Two hundred and thirty-four years ago, in 1717, Presbyterians started to provide relief for ministers of the Church and their widows, calling their first project, "The Fund For Pious Uses." Later the name was changed to "The Widows' Fund," and then to "The Board of Ministerial Relief and Sustentation," and finally, in 1928, to the "Board of Pensions."

Alexander Mackie took sharp exception to the historical claims made in the pamphlet. In a letter to Sherman Skinner, president of the Board of Pensions, Mackie argued that the board had no right to use 1717 because it was not the legal descendant of the Fund for Pious Uses. Nor, he insisted, was the Board of Pensions legally connected with the Widows' Fund, chartered in 1759 as an independent agency. In addition, Mackie noted that the present Board of Pensions was not incorporated until 1876 as the Board of Ministerial Relief and that its historical roots went back no farther than 1849 when the Old School General Assembly created a Fund for Disabled Ministers.[37]

In one sense Mackie had both history and logic on his side. The Synod of Philadelphia and New York gave the assets of the Fund For Pious Uses "in trust" to the Widows' Fund in 1760 to be administered by Corporation trustees until its resources were exhausted. Nevertheless, the Widows' Fund existed as an independent insurance organization with no official relationship to the church after the formation of the General Assembly in 1789. Moreover, the Presbyterian Ministers' Fund did not exist as an insurance company until 1759 when it received a charter to issue policies. (Business historians employ that date.) On the other hand, the Board of Pensions can also trace its work back to 1717 though not in the same sense as the Presbyterian Ministers' Fund. It was *the church* that initiated the Fund For Pious Uses and also underwrote most of the initial capital necessary to put the Widows' Fund into operation. In other words, concern for ministers and their dependents dates back to the origins of the denomination. The Board of Pensions is a modern (if not legal) extension of this same concern. Indeed, virtually every other modern church board—Missions, Christian Education, Publication—can in this sense use 1717 because the Fund For Pious Uses embraced all of the activities later undertaken by these organizations.

Perhaps the fairest resolution of this subject is to leave it in a both/and tension rather than an either/or posture. The Presbyterian Ministers' Fund can clearly trace its lineage to 1717 even though its insurance history did not begin until 1759. The Board of Pensions, however, is also a continuing work begun by the church (not the Widows' Fund) in 1717. Although it is inaccurate to say that the Board of Pensions was "founded in 1717," it is correct to state that 1717 "marks the beginning of work now carried on by this Board." Both the Board of Pensions and the Presbyterian Ministers' Fund, therefore, are outgrowths of the Fund For Pious Uses.

Chapter 4
The Fund for Disabled Ministers

> The church has no right to inflict martyrdom on these servants of the Lord. Because they trust in God for daily bread, the church cannot leave it to the ravens to feed them.
> —*The American Presbyterian*, 1866

Although the Widows' Fund attempted to address the problem of the financial plight of aged ministers and their dependents, it never won favor among the clergy. Consequently, the Presbyterian church relied on another form of support, termed "ministerial relief." This program provided small assistance grants from synods or presbyteries when funds were available from those judicatories. More typically, the aid came directly from local congregations in the form either of cash or of food, clothing, and shelter.

Between 1789 and 1837 the General Assembly made only one overt effort to establish a national relief program. In 1794 the General Assembly referred for presbyterial vote a plan "to make provision for the support of invalid Presbyterian ministers and the distressed families of any ministers in our communion who may die in destitute circumstances." According to this plan each minister who had an annual salary of £80 or more was to contribute 30s. to a presbyterial treasurer who in turn would forward the money to the General Assembly "as a fund for charitable purposes to be applied to the relief of distressed Presbyterian ministers and their families." Unlike the Widows'

Fund, however, this proposed relief fund was to be available both to contributors and noncontributors on an equal basis.[1]

In 1795 a committee reported to the General Assembly that although presbyteries had "approved of the object, they considered the plan inexpedient and improper to be adopted." Along with its negative vote, however, Philadelphia Presbytery offered a substitute proposal. It recommended the General Assembly incorporate so that it could "secure and improve all such funds as they do at present or hereafter possess" for the cause of ministerial relief. This legal measure, the presbytery stated, would "encourage persons by devise or otherwise to intrust them with estates, real or personal, to be applied to pious or charitable uses."[2] The assembly approved the recommendation and appointed a committee to supervise the chartering process, which was completed in 1799. Trustees were then elected to serve as administrators of the fund.[3]

When this fund for "pious or charitable uses" reported in 1800, General Assembly minutes made no explicit reference to ministerial relief or to the support of widows or orphans. Records state that the fund was to be used for evangelizing Native Americans, instructing Blacks and "those who are destitute of the means of grace in various parts of this extensive country," purchasing and distributing religious literature, and educating candidates for the ministry. In other words, its scope was almost identical to the previous Fund For Pious Uses (1717) that had been absorbed by the Widows' Fund (1759). Although the trustees spoke vaguely of using money "for such other pious and benevolent purposes as may hereafter be deemed expedient," their records do not provide any concrete evidence that they disbursed funds to widows or orphans. For nearly fifty years, General Assembly minutes do not indicate any national efforts to care for indigent ministers or their survivors.[4]

In practice, this responsibility lay in the hands of local congregations with whom ministers and their families related. This "extended family" concept was particularly strong in agricultural communities in which ministers settled on a small plot of land and eked out an existence. Indeed, for many church members, an argument against either life insurance or a national relief program was that both deprived local churches of opportunities to extend Christian charity. One minister contended, for example, that "God would visit with a righteous retribution any church that would allow her ministry to live neglected and destitute."[5] Notices in church newspapers suggest that some local congregations were attentive to their retired ministers. When Eli Cooley of Trenton, New Jersey, ended his pastorate, *The Presbyterian* noted that he retired "to abide in the midst of an affectionate people who cannot and will not forget that he has given to them the strength of his manhood, and the maturer wisdom of his advancing years."[6]

Occasionally presbyteries intervened to insure that local congregations "did their duty." When James McRea announced his impending retirement to New Brunswick Presbytery, the judicatory negotiated with congregational representatives before dissolving the pastoral relationship. The presbytery observed that since McRea had "spent the vigor of his days in this place and is now come to the decline of life, it is reasonable that the congregation should contribute something annually for his support in the remaining part of his life." Parishioners acknowledged their willingness to cooperate, but qualified the precise nature of their commitment to McRea. "We do not mean that the whole of his salary shall be continued," they responded, "but only a part of it ... we are incapable to ascertain the annual sum; and we know that members are opposed to fixing a sum at all, tho from their former conduct and present declaration, we are very certain they will treat Mr. McRea kindly in this sense."[7]

McRea's case apparently was more of an exception than a rule. An examination of more than a dozen presbytery books for the period 1800–1830 did not provide a single comparable example. Although this does not prove that retired ministers were abandoned by their congregations, it does indicate that most presbyteries had no formal retirement procedures.[8]

Apart from occasional resolutions supporting the Widows' Fund, the General Assembly left the responsibility for ministerial relief in the hands of lower judicatories.[9] The subject surfaced for the first time at the Old School General Assembly in 1842 when several presbyteries requested that the General Assembly articulate a policy regarding the care of "aged and distressed ministers and their destitute families." In response to these overtures, the assembly resolved that the denomination should not pass the responsibility for such assistance to charitable or governmental agencies. It urged presbyteries to "take the subject under serious consideration, and take such action as may seem proper to them." The recommendation contained no call for a national organization, however, nor did it provide any machinery to monitor presbyterial response.[10]

Apparently, only a few presbyteries responded. The Presbytery of St. Clairsville in Ohio acknowledged its duty "to contribute as liberally as God in His providence may enable them, for the support of aged and distressed ministers and their widows and orphans, while they may reside in our bounds," but its records contain no reference to a specific program.[11] A few presbyteries, however, did take action. In 1848 Transylvania Presbytery formed an "Association for the Support of Superannuated Ministers" with an initial balance of $20. Two years later it reported assets of $142.77 but shortly thereafter the association ceased to function.[12] The Synod of South Carolina formed in 1854 a "Society for the Relief of Indigent and Superannuated Ministers," an organization that survived well into the twentieth century.[13] Nevertheless, such programs, limited in scope and size, were unable to deal with the overall problem of ministerial relief.

When the Old School General Assembly met in 1849, the Presbyteries of Steubenville and Elizabethtown again confronted commissioners with overtures requesting a national effort on this issue. The former asked the assembly "to take immediate measures . . . on terms within the reach of all," and the latter suggested that the Board of Publication be authorized to contribute $2,000 annually to a general fund from which presbyteries could request aid.[14] In response, the General Assembly directed synods and presbyteries to take up annual collections "for distressed ministers" and turn in the receipts to assembly trustees. The money received would then be disbursed by the Board of Publication based on recommendations from individual presbyteries. In addition, the assembly approved the establishment of an endowment fund derived from special contributions and legacies as an additional source of income.[15]

During the next two years General Assembly minutes gave no indication of any progress in developing the two funds. In 1852, however, the Board of Publication requested that the responsibility of receiving and distributing relief funds be transferred wholly to the assembly trustees. The assembly concurred and appointed a special committee with Thomas L. Janeway as chair and George Van Gelder as treasurer. The latter served as fund treasurer until the Old and New Schools united in 1870.[16] The committee held its first meeting in 1853 and appropriated funds totaling $675 to two widows and six ministers. At the same time the assembly elected Joseph H. Jones as an assembly trustee and appointed him to be chair of the fund, a capacity in which he served for fifteen years.[17]

Although the Fund for Disabled Ministers had been organized without any apparent controversy, it originated at a time when the General Assembly was studying its chaotic benevolence procedures. Offerings for denominational causes were uncoordinated and competition among board agents for congregational support fierce. One minister complained that board representatives descended upon congregations like the frogs of Egypt and disrupted the routine of worship with their impassioned pleas for money.[18] The General Assembly had appointed a Special Committee on Systematic Benevolence in 1853, but it produced no answer that satisfied the interested parties. This situation continued until later in the century when the church finally accepted the principle of a unified denominational budget.[19]

In this context, the Fund made its report to the General Assembly in 1856. The report triggered an extended debate that received front-page coverage in *The Presbyterian* and several other denominational papers. Ebenezer P. Rogers, chair of the Standing Committee on Ministerial Relief, chastised the denomination for its inadequate support of the Fund For Disabled Ministers. Contributions had amounted only to $1,580, less than seventy-five cents for every congregation in the PCUSA. Only twenty people had received assistance during the year although many others needed help. The highest grant was $100 and the lowest $35. Rogers charged that the assembly could generate pious resolutions but not tangible results. He also singled out several prosperous presbyteries "who did not send a penny to our Treasury" yet requested $300 in relief funds. Rogers said, "The time has come for the church to take this issue seriously."[20]

According to *The Presbyterian*, Rogers departed from his prepared speech and "pressed the whole subject with great earnestness for some further action."[21] Another eyewitness reported that Rogers had "much animation in the pulpit, both in voice and gesture. . . . Many of his gestures were particularly vehement, such as uplifting his hands toward heaven, etc."[22] With dramatic flair, Rogers concluded his remarks with a series of rhetorical questions:

> What has the minister received in return for his labours, his tears, his anxieties, his mental toils, his life-long devotion of himself to the interests of the Church? He has received a salary less than that of a third-rate clerk in a merchant's counting house, a competent overseer on a southern plantation, a clerk on a Mississippi steamboat, or a bar-keeper in a fashionable hotel. . . . But who can estimate the worth of his life to the Church and to the world? . . . What have the sympathies been worth which have drawn from his heart's deep stores by hundred of tried and endangered souls? What has it been worth to the mother, as in speechless anguish she bends over the beautiful corpse of her darling babe, to hear the accents of the man of God, saying, in solemn tenderness, 'It is well with the Child?' . . . What are the ten thousand varied and diversified labours of the ministry in behalf of every interest of this life and of that which is to come, worth to the world?[23]

The assembly referred his report to a committee of three ministers and two laypersons with Rogers serving as chair. The committee later proposed the creation of a permanent ministerial relief fund with monies derived from two sources: (1) from ministers who would give the equivalent of 5 percent of their annual salary (1 percent over a five-year period), and (2) from congregations who would make a single deposit of 20 percent of their minister's salary that would secure coverage for a succession of ministers. Only participating ministers "*and none others*" would be eligible for assistance from the fund. A minister would qualify for aid "when disabled from active labour by age, bodily infirmity, or other Providential hindrance not affecting his moral character." Requests would be made through presbyteries, and the amount received was not to exceed the average salary of ministers in the same presbytery. The committee also recommended that the General Assembly confer with the Presbyterian Annuity Company to see if it could make its fund "a nucleus of a suitable and permanent fund." The assembly approved the report "in general" but placed it on the docket for further discussion.[24]

Opponents of the proposal unleashed a barrage of objections. All the commissioners who spoke against the fund were clergy. Epenetus Patterson rejected the idea that ministers were financially overburdened and economically depressed. "There might be exception by accident, by disease, by particular providence," he asserted, "but as a whole the ministry are happy." According to Patterson, "the oldest men in the ministry were the richest men because instead of having dependent children they had grown families to support them."[25] A seconder to Patterson's speech denied the need for any national fund: "A minister ought to preach as long as he is able to stand, and then lie down and die."[26]

Some ministers objected to the manner in which relief funds would be dispensed. In an age when the ideals of self-sufficiency and independence ranked so high in American life, they argued, few ministers would bear the public shame involved in revealing their financial problems. One minister claimed, "It is disagreeable to any man of proper feelings to have his pecuniary circumstances made the subject of an exact scrutiny." He recommended as an alternative the purchase of an annuity similar to one offered by the Presbyterian Annuity Company and other commercial life insurance firms.[27] From another angle, some ministers opposed the fund's financial arrangement because of the dangers of mismanagement involved in such large sums of money. As one speaker warned, "It introduces a centralization of wealth and power, and a temptation to abuse which had better be avoided."[28]

A succession of persons continued the argument. One affirmed that each generation should bear its own burdens and that the present generation had no obligation to provide for the future. When Jesus said, "Give us this day our daily bread," a minister concluded, he meant "that this generation ought not to be burdened with the support of the future indigent.... Contingent necessities should always be met with contingent appeals."[29] Other speakers reaffirmed that responsibility for aged and infirm ministers should be vested in local congregations rather than in an impersonal national committee. "If you have a permanent fund," a commissioner said, "you will also have to provide a national almshouse for retired clergymen." Rejecting that possibility, he insisted "let each church say, no aged indigent minister shall be found within our bounds."[30] Finally, some opponents argued that any effort to alleviate poverty and hardship might prove to be counterproductive for the recipient's spiritual welfare. James H. Thornwell, prominent educator from South Carolina, believed that "heroism, courage, and energy" are produced by economic suffering. "Let us not take these means of hardening our ministry for the warfare away from them. It is a principle laid down by the Master, that hardship is absolutely necessary to form the highest grade of character."[31]

In sharp contrast most laymen endorsed the proposal and applauded any effort to relieve the economic burdens of parish ministers either before or after retirement. John Fine, a New York judge, commented, "Some of the ministers are of the opinion that it is wrong to depend on any human means. They imagine that they must live altogether by faith." Another speaker said, "The present state of things is a disgrace to the Church. . . . The poor have nothing but poverty before them without resources." Judge H. H. Leavitt from Cincinnati affirmed that unless the denomination quickly developed a reasonable program for ministerial support only a few wealthy young men would choose the ministry for a profession.[32]

The laity also stressed that such assistance should not be viewed as charity but as a reward for service. Speakers frequently invoked the precedent of government pensions for military personnel. One elder said, "The government has provided for her old soldiers and the Church should do the same for her aged soldiers of the cross." Noting that much of the opposition to a permanent fund derived from the stigma of receiving charity, a commissioner said, "Are the widows and orphans of our military and naval officers paupers because they receive pensions? It is a simple principle of justice, that when a man devotes himself to the service either of the Church or State, he should be sustained while able to work, and provided for when disabled."[33]

After both sides had defended their positions, commissioners voted on the proposal *ad seriatim*. The initial "general approval" quickly evaporated. Motions to table the matter indefinitely and to "receive" the report without any specific recommendation failed. Finally, commissioners agreed on a compromise. The assembly simply accepted the report and appointed a committee "to digest and report to the next General Assembly, a scheme for future operations." Chaired by Judge Leavitt, the committee was composed of three laymen and two ministers.[34]

The General Assembly's inability to agree on a unified approach to ministerial relief reflected a wider societal ambivalence about national welfare projects in general. No single point in the committee's report received unanimous approval, not even the basic premise that ministers deserved some kind of special financial assistance. A correspondent for *The Central Presbyterian*, who heard the debate in its entirety, analyzed the assembly's shifting moods: "The Assembly acted very carefully on this plan and when it had thus substantially committed itself to the whole, it seemed suddenly to find out that it did not like the plan, that there were several points about it which needed adjustment, and in short, it was doubtful whether it liked the principle of the thing at all."[35]

The ambivalence was still present when Leavitt's committee reported to the General Assembly in 1857. During the interim, Leavitt had queried each presbytery about the number of ministerial families within their bounds who had financial needs. Only 61 out of 144 stated clerks responded. Their replies indicated that there were eleven ministers, twenty-one widows, and thirty-six orphans who needed assistance. Extrapolating from this information, Leavitt estimated that about thirty ministers, fifty widows, and eighty children could be helped by a ministerial relief fund. Although he admitted that these were imprecise figures, Leavitt generalized, "With very few exceptions the Synods and Presbyteries have adopted no efficient and systematic action for the relief of their indigent and suffering within their limits."[36]

Beyond these observations, however, Leavitt's committee could reach no unanimity. Instead, it offered four alternatives for consideration: (1) create a permanent fund supported by voluntary donations; (2) establish a permanent fund raised by ministerial and congregational assessments; (3) make local congregations and presbyteries solely responsible for ministerial relief within their own areas; (4) reaffirm what had been approved by the General Assembly in 1849—presbyterial contributions administered nationally and a small endowment fund. In a lengthy summation, Leavitt listed arguments for and against a permanent fund. While he personally was not opposed to the plan, he felt that the denomination was not philosophically or financially prepared to support it. Noting that the attention given to ministerial relief in 1856 had spurred presbyteries to treble their annual giving, Leavitt suggested that "there is just ground for the expectation that the churches will . . . furnish a sum adequate to meet all demands upon a just and liberal scale." As a result, the assembly without a dissenting vote reaffirmed its actions of 1849 and recommitted itself to raise money for ministerial relief.[37]

The Fund For Disabled Ministers disbursed small relief grants annually until 1870. From its meager beginnings in 1853 when only $675 were dispensed, by 1870 the Fund aided 168 families with a total of $28,502. The number of contributing congregations also increased from fifty in 1849 to more than a thousand in 1869. The permanent endowment fund, which opened with a $13 contribution in 1851, reached $77,551 in 1870.[38] To heighten the Fund's importance, the General Assembly in 1861 instituted a permanent Standing Committee on Ministerial Relief and approved a special column in the annual statistics to list relief contributions. In the same year, the assembly approved the appointment of Joseph H. Jones as chairman of the Fund and its full-time promotional agent, the first such position in American Presbyterian history. From 1861 until his death in 1868, Jones visited synods and presbyteries, spoke in local churches, and corresponded with denominational leaders to encourage their wider participation in this enterprise.[39]

New School Presbyterians developed a comparable program for ministerial relief. In 1861 the Presbytery of Columbus presented an overture "with regard to a fund to be raised for the purpose of rendering aid to Disabled Ministers and their families."[40] Not until 1864, however, did New School commissioners approve of "The Ministerial Relief Fund." In an exhaustive report covering more than six pages of General Assembly minutes, a special committee recommended a plan of voluntary collections derived from local congregations because "the Church of Christ needs the frequent repeated appeal in behalf of Christ's poor, as one of the most effective means of developing a practical Christ-like spirit." Following the Old School pattern, the committee also favored a standing request for special contributions to create a small permanent fund whose interest could be used for unanticipated emergencies.[41]

The Ministerial Relief Fund similarly provided financial assistance to any disabled minister of good and regular standing and his survivors. The New School assembly appointed Charles Brown, a Philadelphia pastor, as the Fund's first secretary in 1864. In his first annual report, Brown announced that he had made appropriations to two families for a total of $250, and that $3,638 had been raised from the annual collections.[42] The following year contributions almost doubled but the number of recipients rose from two to thirty. Overall denominational support of the Fund, however, was limited. In 1866 only 130 out of 1,147 churches contributed and in subsequent years the percentages were not much better. Between 1864 and 1869 the Fund received only $51,734 and aided about two hundred people. In 1870 the Ministerial Relief Fund reported an income of $13,690 with seventy-eight families receiving financial assistance.[43]

Both Old and New School General Assemblies remained firmly committed to their voluntary relief programs. They required no assessments, no dues, no life insurance premiums, and no elaborate ecclesiastical machinery. Each channeled local offerings to a general treasury out of which voluntary staffs administered aid based on presbyterial recommendations. While rejecting the concept of a large endowment fund, both denominations encouraged the gradual accumulation of special bequests and legacies to supplement annual offerings. Most church leaders seemed satisfied. As one report concluded, "The experiment of another year has greatly deepened the conviction that this mode is the best."[44]

Not unexpectedly some laypersons did not share this opinion. In their estimation, neither fund had been able to deal realistically with ministerial poverty. This dissatisfaction emerged from time to time at General Assembly meetings of both denominations. In 1869 Old School ruling elder Theodore Strong challenged a glowing report made by George Hale, secretary of The Fund For Disabled Ministers. "The very fact that our Church raised for this fund less than $33,000 during the last year is sufficient proof that the machinery is inadequate to the work." Speaking from the perspective of a minister's son who knew about economic deprivation, Strong criticized the current plan because "we have no *system* in this important matter." Ministers and their families, he asserted, cannot live off spontaneous offerings. "We do not recognize their *legal and logical claim* upon the Church for a comfortable support. It is not *charity* to give them bread. It is what they have a right to. This is the fault of this Committee. They go upon the principle that it is a *scheme of benevolence*. It is not so. It is a *right*, such a right as the ministry has a right to demand."[45]

Strong recommended that elders be organized to raise an endowment with an initial goal of $100,000. He also urged that a minister's standing in presbytery partially be tested by proof that he had promoted and raised money for ministerial relief. Although Strong's proposal generated discussion, the assembly made no significant changes in its existing structures because of the prospect of reunion with the New School denomination. The assembly received the report of The Fund For Disabled Ministers and urged the church to "prosecute the scheme vigorously and sustain it liberally."[46] Nevertheless, by challenging the Fund's overall effectiveness, Strong indicated that the controversy surrounding ministerial relief had not ended. Indeed, it would continue on an ever larger scale than before.

PART II
Denominational Boards and Agencies
1870–1930

Chapter 5
The Board of Ministerial Relief

Prosperous Presbyterians may be expert in solving the problems of high finance; but it takes more than genius to get along on $342 per year. It takes grace!
—*The Assembly Herald*, 1912

Reunion between the Old and New School denominations occurred on November 10, 1869, and the new denomination assumed the name it had held prior to the schism—The Presbyterian Church in the United States of America (PCUSA).[1] Its General Assembly in 1870 endorsed a national relief fund called "The Relief Fund for Disabled Ministers and the Widows and Orphans of Deceased Ministers." This Fund was to be managed by a secretary and treasurer, elected annually, and a committee of four trustees of the assembly. The previous Old School (George Hale) and New School (Charles Brown) secretaries were retained as administrators, and the Board of Trustees of the General Assembly were to receive and disperse funds.[2]

The new Relief Fund was no more successful than its predecessors. Lacking sufficient endowment income and dependent on freewill offerings, the Relief Fund could not assuage the ministerial poverty that existed in post-Civil War America. A survey in 1871 indicated an average salary among the 61,000 clergymen in the United States of $700 a year. If one deducted salaries paid by major metropolitan churches, average salaries were less than $600 with probably more than one-third of American ministers receiving less than $500 a year.[3] Consequently, ministers could neither save for old age nor afford life insurance premiums. Relief Fund administrators acknowledged that disbursements to families in need failed to alleviate the conditions under which many Presbyterian ministers and their families lived.[4]

In the early 1870s, as before, most people agreed that ministerial support had merit but differed on how such aid should be administered. A considerable number now criticized making grants upon individual application, urging a more professionalized system, such as an insurance program with the Presbyterian Annuity Company or a so-called "parish" plan as represented in the Society for Promoting Life Insurance Among Clergymen. Others resurrected the argument that local congregations were responsible for assistance. Still others advocated the creation of a Sustentation Fund that would supplement salaries of *active* ministers rather than supplying "relief" to retired or disabled clergy.[5]

Despite these differing views, the assembly continued to manage the Fund through its trustees. The committee met once a month to conduct business. During its first year, using interest from its permanent endowment fund ($85,000) and offerings from presbyteries, local churches, and individuals, the Fund disbursed $67,371 to 108 ministers, 144 widows, and the orphans of 15 families.[6] Economic conditions such as the "Panic of 1873," which led to a dramatic fall in security prices and created widespread unemployment, prohibited the continuation of that level of aid. In 1874 the Relief Fund carried over a $15,684 debt from 1873, which meant that regular appropriations were cut in half and applications discouraged.[7]

Even given the economic variabilities, administrators of the Fund feared the implications of recommendations before the General Assembly that would create a central denominational treasury and consolidate various boards and agencies. George Hale argued on the assembly floor that such actions would "give a blow to the cause of benevolence which it has never felt since the foundation of the Church."[8] Hale particularly protested the merger of the Board of Education and the Ministerial Relief Fund, endorsing a resolution of the Presbytery of Westminster that pointed out "the sacred character of the ministerial relief cause and the just claims it holds on the most tender sympathies and liberal support of the church."[9] Others argued that the responsibilities of Education and of Relief differed so greatly that the incentives to contribute to one would not be the same as to the other. Although the General Assembly approved some minor board readjustments in 1874, the Fund remained intact as a distinct organization.[10]

Having avoided this merger, the administrators pressed for board status. The General Assembly in 1876 approved a recommendation from a special committee that the Ministerial Relief Fund be "clothed with the dignity of a separate Board of the Church, with incorporated powers."[11] The newly named

Board of Relief for Disabled Ministers and the Widows and Orphans of Deceased Ministers obtained a charter from the Commonwealth of Pennsylvania on October 21, 1876. The charter gave Relief administrators the power to receive bequests, provide releases to executors, and hold invested funds and real estate. (The Board of Trustees of the General Assembly for the Relief Fund had formerly been awarded these powers.) Villeroy D. Reed, a member of the General Assembly in 1849 when the Fund began, was elected board president, George Hale continued to serve as corresponding secretary, and Charles Brown became treasurer and recording clerk.[12]

The new board not only required careful presbyterial documentation of financial need before disbursing any funds, but also itself considered each request for aid on its individual merit. Since limited funds and increasing applications were annual occurrences, the board frequently had to deny or to reduce disbursements.[13] In all decisions, the board operated on a strict policy of confidentiality, because it was "unkind and inexpedient to personally expose the condition of our brethren whose poverty compels them to seek assistance from the board."[14]

Although most applications were routine, the board occasionally took up exceptional cases. When the Presbytery of Chester requested funds to assist two orphans, the board "granted no appropriation to these ladies who are aged 57 and 63 respectively."[15] One widow received no help because she had become a member of the Roman Catholic Church.[16] When one woman informed the board that she had recently married another Presbyterian minister who was receiving relief grants, the board informed her that she would not be eligible for aid a second time should her new husband precede her in death.[17]

The board rejected several applications because the requests did not meet with its criteria. One minister was turned down because he had given "eighteen years of the best years of his life to secular employment, at the same time utterly ceasing to exercise the functions of the Christian ministry."[18] Another received similar treatment because his ministerial labors had not been formally recognized by any presbytery.[19] At times the decisions bordered on legalism. The board refused to pay for support of two orphans because they were children of a second marriage.[20] Another time the board reduced a woman's semiannual allotment check by 25 percent because her husband had received a payment shortly before he died. In the board's estimation, she had been overpaid for five months.[21]

In fairness, the board's adherence to rules often yielded to expressions of compassion. When a minister returned his $100 relief check because he refused to accept charity, the board investigated, reissued the check, and enclosed a letter assuring him that the money was recompense for service to the church.[22] A widow received a supplement because of "the extra expense of the last sickness and funeral of her mother," and a minister was given additional funds because he had no money to travel from his house to the retirement home in Perth Amboy, New Jersey.[23]

The difficulty of deciding on recipients was insignificant alongside the board's tenuous fiscal situation, which was chronically marked by insufficient funds and increasing applications. In 1880 it refused new applications and reduced payments by 25 percent. During an extended economic depression in the 1890s, reduced grants were the rule rather than the exception. On an average those who qualified for relief funds received an insufficient sum of less than $300 a year.[24]

Board leaders issued emotional pleas for financial support, using sermons, speeches, letters, and reports. According to one observer, Relief ran primarily on "water power," meaning that its promoters elaborated on such dire need until their audiences were on the verge of tears, and then they would call for a collection. Benjamin L. Agnew, secretary of the board from 1897 to 1912, was masterful at this money-raising technique. Occasionally, however, ministers complained that Agnew's poverty stories were humiliating both to them as individuals and to the church at large. To these complaints Agnew would reply, "Then we say in God's name, remove the facts!"[25]

Beyond such informal fundraising, William C. Cattell, secretary of the board from 1883 to 1898, persuaded the General Assembly to authorize a campaign to raise a one million dollar endowment as a part of the centennial year of American Presbyterianism observances. The assembly of 1887 appointed George P. Hays, a former college president, well-known pastor, temperance activist, and champion of women's rights, as chairman of the Centenary Fund. Hays and his committee organized large public meetings that described the cause and indeed raised funds. In addition, presbyteries and synods made local appeals, while the Board of Ministerial Relief distributed nearly a million and a half circulars and placed promotional articles in dozens of church newspapers. Although the centennial campaign never realized its goals, it added $606,266.25 to the endowment fund and helped the board meet expenses for a few years.[26] Paradoxically the financial success of the Centenary Fund had negative long-term effects on the board's ability to raise money. Because $600,000 seemed a large figure in the nineteenth century, many people thought of the board as "small and rich and self-sustaining," while it very much needed the annual contributions as well. As late as 1904, Agnew admitted that his pleas for contributions encountered a lukewarm response because of a widespread perception of the board's financial solvency.[27]

The Centenary Fund Campaign reinforced an observation that the best way to raise money for needy ministers was through the eldership. At General Assembly meetings, the board held sessions to educate ruling elders about the scope of ministerial poverty and to discuss fundraising techniques. On a number of occasions the elders sent resolutions to the General Assembly supporting the work of ministerial relief and directing ministers to preach at least one sermon a year on its behalf. Even though the laity displayed concern, however, their efforts were sporadic and uncoordinated, and the board appeared unable to utilize effectively one of its most valuable financial resources.[28]

The Relief Board also enlisted the support of churchwomen, whose abilities to raise money and goods had been recognized since the early part of the century.[29] The first reference to the "ladies of the church" assisting the Board of Relief came in 1876 when Cattell thanked women for supplying boxes of clothing for the needy.[30] In 1883 the board noted that the women had sent out eighty boxes valued at $10,000 during the year and extended "to these earnest helpers—the ladies—sincere thanks for this good work."[31] By the end of the century, however, women were not contributing to the board nearly so much, partly because they were engrossed in the development of their own Home and Foreign Missions Boards, and partly because of economic conditions during the 1890s. Repeated efforts of Relief Board leaders to enlarge the participation of women were largely unsuccessful.[32]

To a great extent, the board's failure to generate substantial support could be traced to the conviction already discussed that in the eyes of the clergy relief represented charity, a distasteful concept to many. A special committee of the Synod of Philadelphia in 1880 reported that "the whole scheme is founded in charity to the needy" and that many ministers "shrink from the necessity of receiving aid" because of this. They further charged that "There is certainly no reference even remotely to a reward of service."[33] On a more personal note, a minister wrote to the editor of *The Presbyterian*, "We don't want to be looked upon, and thought of, and perhaps slyly whispered about, as supported by public collections, taken up after sermon on a designated day. It may be pride, but we do not think it a bad kind which stimulates the ministry to rise and keep above that style of life."[34]

Because it was sensitive to these feelings of the clergy, the board tried to soften aspects of its application procedures that seemed offensive. In 1890 the General Assembly approved its request to allow applicants over seventy years of age to receive stipends without annual renewal by their presbyteries. According to the initiators of the policy change, "the new rule ... renders more dignified and independent the position of many worn-out pastors and missionaries upon our roll."[35] As a consequence, during the next two years the board received seventy-seven new applications for assistance, the largest increase in any similar time period since the creation of the Relief Fund.[36]

That the board resisted other initiatives that addressed this issue was clear in its response to an overture from the elders of the Presbytery of Baltimore in 1891. This overture recommended that the General Assembly substitute the word "Pensions" for "Relief" in the board's title "with a view of removing the charity thought from its appropriations." They argued that this would make it easier for elders to seek funds both from church members and from prominent benefactors disposed to reward service. The board responded that while it agreed that appropriations should be considered on "equity and justice," it was not prepared to abandon the Relief designation because it embodied the principle on which the board functioned.[37]

In addition to its public relations problems, the board continued to struggle financially as well. Reviewing twenty-five years of operation in 1901, the Board of Ministerial Relief acknowledged that it could not provide adequate funds for worthy recipients, now including foreign and domestic missionaries as well as pastors, stated supplies, and dependents. The board asked the General Assembly for permission to borrow money so that it could dispense relief checks.[38] In 1902 the board reported that Presbyterians averaged only six cents in annual contributions to the work. As late as 1924 ministers with more than thirty years service received an average annual pension of only $376, widows received $244 yearly, and orphans were awarded only $184.[39] One board executive described the situation of retired clergy in these terms: "Prosperous Presbyterians may be expert in solving the problems of high finance; but it takes more than genius to get along on $342 per year. It takes grace."[40]

In another attempt to provide for dependent clergy, the board added a new area to its work in 1883 when it assumed responsibility for the management and maintenance of a ministerial retirement home. Although the board felt that children should bear the primary responsibility for sheltering aged parents, it acknowledged that some individuals had neither family nor friends who could provide them a home. Early in the century, "old age homes" had begun to be founded by religious and fraternal organizations to care for those constituents who had no residential options. By 1900 the Episcopal Church was operating eight homes in New York City alone, and other Protestant denominations were equally active. Presbyterians opened a Home for Aged Women in New York (1869) and another Home for Widows and Single Women (1874) with funds raised by women's societies. This trend was apparent in nonreligious associations as well, such as the Elks, Odd Fellows, Brotherhood of Railroad Trainmen, and the Machinists Union of Printers, who sponsored retirement homes where people of similar backgrounds and work experience could live.[41]

In 1883 the board accepted a bequest from Alexander M. Bruen conveying to the board a property at Perth Amboy, New Jersey, covering eleven and a half acres with a large house designated to provide a residence for aged ministers, widows, and orphans. The Perth Amboy mansion had a colorful history. Built in the colonial period, its massive walls were constructed of brick imported from England and its large public rooms, twenty-foot wide halls, and spacious verandas were surrounded by trees in a park-like area. In 1774 it had been the official residence of Governor William Franklin (under whose auspices New Jersey Presbyterians secured a charter to create a fund for the support of aged ministers and their dependents). Soon after the Revolutionary War, the mansion was acquired by the Bruen family.

When the Board of Ministerial Relief accepted the property in 1883, it secured authorization from the New Jersey legislature for tax exemption as a church facility.[42] The Perth Amboy property also functioned as a short-term recuperation facility for ministers and missionaries with physical or mental problems that did not require hospitalization. Applicants were accepted on a space-available basis and expected to pay a small fee for meals and services. Unsolicited letters to the board suggest that participants found their stay at the home to be helpful. One minister wrote, "I commend the Home to brethren suffering from nervous prostration, as I was, and needing rest. It is a good place to recuperate the overtaxed brain or body—because it is located in a retired, quiet place, free from noise and bustle."[43]

Even though early occupancy rates were promising, the Ministers' House at Perth Amboy placed heavy financial burdens on the board's already inadequate budget. Trustees spent $12,000 to refurbish and maintain the premises and provide services. Residents paid no fee but relinquished their annual pension of approximately $300. In 1886 Cattell suggested an endowment be raised for the house, pointing out that a Baptist home in Germantown, Pennsylvania, had recently received a $300,000 gift.[44] When this first attempt to secure an endowment was unsuccessful, in 1887 Cattell raised the question again, noting that another home in Montgomery County, Pennsylvania, had been similarly endowed.[45] By the centennial year of the General Assembly in 1888 he concluded, "But the Centennial summer is ended, and this appeal has not yet reached the heart of any Christian disciple to whom God has given the ability to do this great work for His ministers."[46] Thus, because of insufficient funds, in 1901 the board asked the General Assembly to close the Perth Amboy facility and return the property to its original owners.[47]

In documenting this request, the board reported that it spent an average of $5,000 more per year to house residents there than it would have had it paid them their $300 annuity. The inadequacy of such an annuity was not the issue; what was important was that the board was spending a large sum of money to maintain a few people while others were subsisting on a meager amount.[48] Despite attempts to attract guests by advertising in church newspapers, writing letters to presbytery committees, and personally contacting pensioners, the board concluded that "There is an ineradicable reluctance in the hearts of our annuitants toward availing themselves of the privileges of a ministerial home."[49]

Prominent among the reasons that people did not want to move to Perth Amboy was that perennial fear of potential residents that it appeared to be a public charitable institution, such as an asylum for the poor or mentally ill. Some presbyteries reinforced this notion, refusing to recommend occupants on the basis that they would help them at home rather than send them to "The Presbyterian Poor House." At one point an outcry against the name, The Ministers' House, caused the board to change it to Westminster House. Even so, applications did not increase.[50]

This dread of spending one's life in the local poor house was not unusual among nineteenth-century Americans. Tracts, magazines, and newspapers described the fear of separation from familiar surroundings. According to one story, an eighty-seven year-old widow with no family spent the last few weeks of her life in the local poor house braiding straw in order to pay for her funeral. "She shrank with pain from the thought of being buried at the expense of the town."[51] When Will Carleton published his poem, "Over the hill to the poorhouse" on the front page of *Harper's Weekly* in 1871, it touched a sensitive nerve. Letters to Carleton from managers throughout the country indicated that many children withdrew their parents from institutions as a result.[52]

The board also recognized that its constituents, along with many others in society, did not want to give up their privacy and independence. They not only wished to stay around acquaintances but in some instances they did not want to relinquish financial assistance claimed from congregations. Some ministers could also secure additional income from occasional preaching or other part-time employment that was not possible if they moved into a home.[53]

Based on their experience at Perth Amboy, the board had no plans to continue or expand its work in this area. It turned down offers of properties ostensibly suitable for use as retirement facilities. In one case the board explicitly stated that "the experience of this Board in conducting Homes given to it has made it manifest that the cost of maintaining a beneficiary in a Home is greatly in excess of what is allowed for the support of ministers and their families."[54] As early as 1896, Cattell informed the General Assembly that he thought that retirement homes should be established under local presbyterial and synodical control, citing the Mercer Home in Ambler, Pennsylvania, and the Downer Home in Milwaukee, Wisconsin, as examples.[55]

Despite these reservations, the board accepted a bequest in 1901 from Henry W. Merriam of a substantial residence in Newton, New Jersey, located in an attractive suburban setting in the hill country of that state. Although the board contemplated refusing, it reconsidered when it became evident that rejection endangered possible future income from a family trust fund. Unlike Perth Amboy, however, the Merriam property was in excellent condition and had a $30,000 endowment fund for maintenance. In addition, the local presbytery volunteered to assist in its management.[56]

The board launched a campaign to encourage pensioners to apply. Promotional materials focused on the "homelike" interiors, the spacious grounds, and the salubrious climate. Agnew described the Merriam Home as "not only tastefully, but luxuriously furnished, the walls adorned with handsome pictures and costly paintings, and the entire residence has the air of refinement and comfort throughout."[57] To further entice, the literature pointed to "Beautiful country! Beautiful Home! Air pure and fragrant as if it had been wafted down from the mountain of spices. . . . Everything that conduces to health, the enjoyment of the beautiful and the comforts of home this place is a step higher."[58] All this could be enjoyed in lieu of the annual relief pension of $300.

Favorable response to the Merriam Home encouraged trustees to accept additional bequests of property. The Thornton Home in Newburg, Indiana, operated previously by the Cumberland Presbyterian Church, became the board's responsibility following the PCUSA-CP union in 1906. Later, the board opened the Merrill Home in Saginaw, Michigan (1917), the L'Amoreaux Home in Ballston Spa, New York (1918), and the Haywood Home in Sharon, Pennsylvania (1925). Following the latter, the board added no new homes for about twenty-five years. In the meantime, it closed the Merrill Home in 1921 and transferred its guests to the Merriam and L'Amoreaux residences. Few homes were ever filled to capacity and even with endowment support they continued to be costly.[59]

Beyond financial considerations, the board found that group living with its regimentation and loss of privacy necessitated tact, patience, determination, and, above all, a commitment of time and energy. Sometimes residents had to be removed either because they were physically or mentally incapable of caring for themselves. Such decisions were difficult, and board officials proceeded cautiously before evicting anyone. One minister, however, was asked to leave because he "treated the superintendent in an unkind and ungentlemanly manner."[60] Another man who reportedly had "some degree of mental aberration" was referred to a committee with power to remove him "if such a course in their judgment seemed wise."[61] When a local physician recommended the removal of a deaconess whose health had deteriorated, the board decided to continue her residence "until we receive further information as to her resources or plans."[62]

Gradually the board tightened admission policies and would not admit annuitants who required constant oversight or skilled nursing.[63] The board also periodically reminded presbyteries not to recommend "persons who may be physically undesirable."[64] Nevertheless, borderline cases were difficult to adjudicate, and because there usually were rooms available the board apparently tolerated marginal health more than it might otherwise have done. In a number of cases considered "exceptional," family members were given free room and board in order to care for an ailing parent or relative. The daughter of one widow, for example, was admitted to the Perth Amboy Home without charge "to care for her mother who is sickly."[65]

The board endeavored to make its homes as safe and as comfortable as its limited funds provided. Board representatives inspected the premises so that they could better evaluate needs and problems. After one such visit, the board approved the installation of fire escapes and passed a resolution banning unvented kerosene and gasoline stoves in private rooms.[66] Sometimes board representatives would provide guests with diversion or entertainment. Agnew described a visit in 1897 when he took the residents at Perth Amboy for a boat ride in the bay and a picnic. Agnew felt that it provided "great joy."[67]

The inspections also offered residents an opportunity to voice complaints. One woman told Agnew that her room had "rather gloomy wallpaper." She received board approval to redo the room "in a cheerier color."[68] Another inspection revealed that residents were unhappy about the food services. They complained that they had meat (usually stew) only once a week, and sometimes even less frequently. The board agreed that such a menu was too limited and it took on supervision of the monthly menu, ordering that steak, chops, or chicken be served once a week. The board also ordered the large dining room table removed and replaced with smaller ones so that residents could have a more intimate atmosphere in which to eat.[69] The board also purchased a "Victorola" for $150, $50 worth of records, and provided a monthly budget of $5 to buy records, because "of the lack of entertainment for our dear old guests, and consequently a considerable discontent."[70] Every year the board appropriated "pin money," usually a few dollars a month, for personal needs. On special occasions, such as Christmas, the board awarded $5 instead of the usual $1.50 so that the guests could purchase gifts and send cards.[71] At a later date the board purchased an automobile for the Thornton Home to transport residents from home to church, "*and for no other purpose.*"[72] After an extended discussion, the board also instructed a committee "to consider the wisdom of purchasing an electric washer as it seems a necessary investment."[73]

Through the administration of its homes program the Board of Ministerial Relief became involved in medical care for retired persons. In some instances the board sought Presbyterian physicians willing to donate their time to the church, but the demands necessitated a formalization of medical arrangements. The first salaried doctor at the Perth Amboy Home received $150 in 1892.[74] As the cost of medical care rose in the twentieth century, the board found it less expensive to pay by the visit rather than with an annual contract.[75] The board did not include dental and eye care as a valid medical expense. When a dentist submitted a bill for $77 for treatment of patients at the

Haywood Home, the board reluctantly paid but sent a memorandum to all residents informing them that in the future such bills would not be honored.[76]

In 1914 the Board of Ministerial Relief and Sustentation, as it was designated after a yoking of the Sustentation Fund and Relief Board in 1912, expanded its health care program. It assumed responsibility for the Ministers' Memorial Cottage in Albuquerque, New Mexico, a facility that accommodated about a dozen ministers or dependents suffering from tuberculosis. The cottage was an adjunct of the Southwestern Presbyterian Sanatorium that had been built with Presbyterian money to assist tubercular cases. In order to provide accommodations specifically for clergy (the sanitorium itself was usually filled), the board raised approximately $15,000, most of which came from ministers themselves. Board reports indicate that the facility was utilized extensively.[77]

Admission policies to the Ministers' Memorial Cottage were relatively simple. Any minister, minister's widow, or dependent who had contracted tuberculosis submitted an application accompanied by a physician's certificate stating that the individual appeared to be curable and would benefit from a stay in New Mexico. After approval by the chair of the presbytery relief committee, the application was forwarded to the board. The sanatorium furnished food, nursing, and basic supplies, and local physicians donated their services. The board paid the expenses of annuitants' care (about $400 annually) at the cottage. If the individuals could not afford the railway fare to Albuquerque, the board even purchased the tickets for them.[78]

After the end of World War I, the board attempted to extend its involvement in health care. Noting that the denomination's retirement homes could only assist people in reasonably good health, board secretary Robert Hunter expressed what he termed "the imperative need" for a thoroughly equipped medical infirmary. Although the board maintained a small infirmary known as the Phelps Cottage at the Thornton Home, its facilities were inadequate to meet the growing demand for health services. In 1919, Hunter suggested that there was ample ground at the Newburg, Indiana, home for an infirmary and stated that he had "the faith to believe that in view of the abundant wealth which has been entrusted to Presbyterians, there is somewhere a very generous person or group of persons, who will contribute the necessary funds for the realization of this vision."[79] Two years later, with no response from Presbyterian philanthropists, the board secured permission from the General Assembly to conduct a $300,000 campaign to raise money for a modern hospital. This never materialized for several reasons, two of which were that Hunter died unexpectedly, and the denomination was engaged in other matters. As a result, the hospital program was disbanded. Nevertheless, the General Assembly enjoined the board to gather information about how homes and hospitals could be developed locally by presbytery, synod, and private agencies and to encourage participation in such projects. Despite overtures from time to time requesting that the board cultivate more health care programs, it was not until after World War II that the board created a special department to monitor and promote the growth of denominational homes and hospitals.[80]

In retrospect, the board's venture into the area of home and health care reflected the ambivalence of denominational leaders who questioned both if and how the church should involve itself with such projects. It also demonstrated a more general reluctance toward institutionalizing social responsibility beyond the boundaries of local, personal agencies. The board's position was further reinforced by its precarious financial status. Nevertheless, these early experiments provided the board with experience and established a precedent that would enable it to take on a range of social services beyond that of administering retirement pensions.

Chapter 6
The Board of Ministerial Relief and Sustentation

It is pathetically plain that the present system is not an adequate one, and never has been!

—Henry B. Master, *The Presbyterian Magazine*, 1924

Americans heralded the arrival of a new century with optimism, envisioning an era of ever-expanding political and economic influence both at home and abroad. Religious observers anticipated the unfolding of a "Christian century" in which foreign missionaries would evangelize the world and domestic missions would deal with societal ills that had emerged from urbanization and industrialization. In a move consistent with virtually all Protestant denominations that were supporting new programs and organizations, the PCUSA General Assembly endorsed the Twentieth Century Fund, a nationwide campaign to raise money so that its boards and agencies could meet the challenge of the twentieth century.[1]

Benjamin Agnew and the Ministerial Relief staff saw little change in their operation, noting deficits, reduced pensions, and inadequate endowments prominently in annual reports and church newspaper articles. As in the past, the board relied on emotional and personal appeals. "Should the Old Minister Be Shot?" queried Agnew when reporting in 1900 that inadequate contributions had forced a 20 percent reduction in pensions averaging less than $300 a year. With sarcasm Agnew suggested that the church might provide an ecclesiastical "glue factory" where worn-out clergy, like worn-out horses, could be disposed of with economy and efficiency. In his more serious statement, Agnew suggested no new solution but urged church people to be more responsive. In particular he challenged wealthy constituents; "Cannot our millionaires come to our relief?" he asked. He received no answer.[2]

In all its reports and promotional articles the Board of Ministerial Relief took little note of a burgeoning pension movement in the business world. In 1900 there were approximately sixty corporate and industrial plans in operation. In the decade following 1910, about twenty-one new plans were established a year. Most of these were encouraged by government policies and the social attitudes of the Progressive Era. The pension movement received a further boost in 1916 when the tax system permitted corporations to deduct as "ordinary and necessary expenses" payments to retired employees or their families and dependents.[3]

One of the most publicized pension programs began in 1901 when Andrew Carnegie gave five million dollars in bonds to be spent on libraries, injured employees and their dependents, and on pensions for those employees, who in Carnegie's words, "After long and creditable service, through exceptional circumstances need such help in their old age and who make good use of it."[4] In 1905 Carnegie created the Carnegie Foundation for the Advancement of Teaching, a fifteen million dollar pension plan which later became known as the Teacher's Insurance and Annuity Association of America (TIAA). Carnegie defended retirement programs, arguing that they were humanitarian and promoted better morale and work habits among employees. John O. Pew, president of the Youngstown Iron and Steel Company and an active Episcopalian layman, contended that what corporations were doing "the Church must do, not as charity, but as an investment for 'efficiency.'"[5]

By the turn of the century not one major Protestant denomination had seriously discussed the possibility of instituting some contributory pension scheme. In 1901, however, the same year that Carnegie instituted his plan, a Presbyterian minister from Burlington, Iowa, John R. Sutherland, proposed a service pension plan to the Synod of Iowa. Sutherland wished to remove "the taint of pauperism" inevitably attached to "relief." He believed that ministers themselves should bear a proportionate share of the cost of a pension or annuity during their years of active service. Sutherland cited Carnegie as a precedent, calling him "the prince of American philanthropists" whose five million dollar contribution for aged and disabled employees constituted "a practical illustration of justice and liberality which our church would do well to emulate."[6]

Sutherland's so-called Sustentation Plan received an enthusiastic endorsement from the General Assembly in 1902.[7] A committee was appointed to work out actuarial details and promotional plans. In the meantime, the General Assembly approved the following principle in 1905: "The adequate maintenance of the aged and disabled ministers of the Presbyterian Church, and the dependent families of the same, is to be regarded as much a moral obligation upon the Presbyterian Church at large as the payment of salaries by particular churches."[8]

Sutherland's initial proposal with actuarial modifications received approval in 1906 and marked the first of a number of ventures into pension programs for clergy and church employees. The Sustentation Fund envisaged an annuity of $500 at age seventy (later reduced to sixty-five) for ministers who had at least thirty years of service within the denomination. If they retired or were disabled before reaching seventy, the Fund specified a reduced annuity of $100 for the first five years and $10 for each additional year of service. The Fund did not *require* retirement at age seventy. Indeed it assumed that most ministers would continue to work and would use the $500 as supplementary income. Before issuing a certificate of membership, the Fund required that individuals be verified by the presbytery and undergo physical examination by a certified medical doctor.[9]

Designers of the Sustentation Fund also carefully devised what they considered to be a viable plan for financing the new program. The statistical and actuarial work was done in the office of the Fidelity Mutual Life Insurance Company of Philadelphia. George A. Huggins, who assisted in the calculations, later became prominent as an architect of denominational pension programs. Based on the age one entered the Fund, participants made an annual payment sufficient to pay one-fifth of the expense of a $500 annuity. The other four-fifths were to be raised from benevolences. Although the Sustentation certificates specified that the only "guaranteed" income was that derived from the individual's contributions, many members understood the certificate to be a contract binding the church to raise the other four-fifths.[10]

Proponents of the Sustentation Fund emphasized that every participant would get the same pension. Service, not congregational size or affluence, was to be the determining factor in calculating the annuity. References to "democratic Presbyterianism" and "ministerial parity" abound in early Sustentation literature. On a number of occasions, Sutherland told his audiences that "any plan that depends on assignments graded according to the minister's salary, would not be suited to the needs and temper of the Presbyterian Church."[11]

Ministers began to enroll in the Sustentation Fund even before it was formally chartered in 1909. By 1911 it had approximately 640 members and assets of $90,000 in cash and $115,000 in time-payment pledges. In addition, a number of wealthy individuals reportedly had made substantial bequests payable to the Fund in their wills.[12] At the same time Sutherland announced that the Fund was already paying annuities to ten widows and to five disabled ministers. Although the payments were only 25 percent of the contemplated benefits, Sutherland hoped that the full amount could soon be paid.[13]

Agnew and the Board of Ministerial Relief did not assess the Sustentation Fund positively. Although Agnew publicly accepted it, he privately resisted the integration of the work with his board. At a conference held in 1903 with the General Assembly's Sustentation Committee, Agnew testified that he did not think his board's charter could be amended to accommodate a pension program and requested more time "to consider issues intelligently."[14] Following the General Assembly's ratification of the Sustentation Fund in 1906, Agnew took a harder line toward merger. The proposed union, Agnew argued, would "tend to embarrass the simple and radical work of Relief . . . and introduce the disturbing element of insurance with its yearly payments and possibly lapsing policies." The Board of Relief wanted not consolidation, "but a freer hand and a fuller treasury."[15]

Forced to compete with agents of the Sustentation Fund canvassing for contributions and faced with increasing pressure from the General Assembly to combine Relief and Sustentation, Agnew and his staff launched a counterattack. Convinced that the board's financial problems could be remedied by increasing the permanent endowment fund, Agnew rallied his supporters to organize a nationwide campaign to raise ten million dollars.[16]

To promote the campaign, the board hired five field agents as moneyraisers. In addition, Agnew hired a specialist to write "short, crisp articles as 'reading matter'." In militant language, Agnew pleaded with his staff "to man the guns" and "to keep up the fire all along the line." Through his extensive contacts, Agnew secured 1,600 laypersons who promised to help make the ten million dollar endowment a reality.[17]

As agents from both the Board of Relief and the Sustentation Fund canvassed congregations in search of donations, their competitiveness generated controversy and confusion. Pastors and laypersons were bewildered by the two programs, each claiming to represent the solution to ministerial relief. Some clergymen closed their congregations to one or the other of the two groups. Tempers flared, and correspondence between the Board of Relief and the Sustentation Fund indicates that rival agents exchanged harsh words. Relations between Agnew and Sutherland deteriorated as both sought to maintain the autonomy of their respective organizations.[18]

A key item on the agenda of the 1911 assembly affecting both Relief and Sustentation was the report of the Executive Commission on Administrative Agencies. Not least among its recommendations was the proposed merger of The Board of Ministerial Relief and the Sustentation Fund. At well-orchestrated pre-assembly conferences, each group secured prominent Presbyterian spokespersons for its side. The Board of Relief had addresses by two former moderators, Henry C. Minton of Trenton, New Jersey, and Mark Matthews of Seattle, Washington.[19] Not to be outdone, Sutherland recruited a former parishioner, William Jennings Bryan, whom *The Presbyterian* described as that "good Catholic Presbyterian elder." Interrupted by numerous standing ovations, Bryan defended both the morality and the practicality of the Sustentation Fund.[20]

On the assembly floor the Executive Commission presented its reasons for uniting Sustentation and Relief, such as common constituents and goals, and savings in administrative costs. Representatives of the Board of Relief argued for an independent operation. One speaker claimed that "Relief is the ambulance at the foot of the hill of dependence and Sustentation is a fence around the top of the hill of disability. . . . They are two separate and distinct causes."[21] According to the editor of *The Presbyterian Banner*, it was Agnew himself who "succeeded in turning the tide" so that the assembly did not approve consolidation.[22] The General Assembly reaffirmed its endorsement of the Board of Relief's ten million dollar endowment fund campaign and instructed the Executive Commission to ensure that there would be "no conflict and no clashing of agents in the field and that peace and harmony would remain."[23]

Additionally, the Executive Commission appointed a committee that would attempt to end the divisiveness between Relief and Sustentation. A poll of church members affirmed that conditions were intolerable. After several unproductive conferences, the Executive Commission recommended to the General Assembly in 1912 a federated organization in which Sustentation and Relief each performed distinctive tasks under a central leadership.[24]

Agnew protested, arguing that by this action the Executive Commission had overstepped its mandate. In a report distributed to commissioners prior to the 1912 Assembly, Agnew documented the board's displeasure with the procedures and conclusion of the commission. Agnew announced, however, a policy change that he thought would "safeguard the delicate feelings" of relief applicants. The board would receive recommendations without requiring the description of individual circumstances in front of presbytery. Moreover, Agnew also proposed an alternative annuity program, conducted under the auspices of the Board of Relief. Termed the "Ministers' Accumulative Fund," it would have had each minister contribute 1 percent of the salary annually to the Board of Relief and receive at retirement a sum equal to the amount of contributions and accumulated interest.[25]

Sutherland avoided public debate with Agnew and his supporters. Although he defended his agents against charges that they were using unfair or unethical tactics, he told the Executive Commission that he did not oppose federation "provided it were feasible and did not impair funds already in the custody of either agency." Nevertheless, he felt the long-range effect would negate the good results accomplished by his staff. If the Sustentation Fund succeeded, there would be no need for a Relief Board except to dispense interest from its permanent funds.[26]

After having listened to both sides, assembly commissioners voted for a federated Board of Ministerial Relief and Sustentation Fund and called for an election of new officers. As future policy, the assembly recommended that all ministers "be encouraged to identify themselves with the Sustentation Department" and that the Relief Department provide for those disabled ministers who had not participated in the Sustentation Fund or who required support. It also proposed a financial campaign with receipts divided equally between the two departments.[27]

To implement federation, the directors of both organizations resigned. The Executive Committee nominated twelve persons to the new board, most of whom had been members either of Relief or Sustentation. The board then selected staff, appointing William H. Foulkes as general secretary and John Sutherland as associate secretary. W. W. Heberton, long-time Relief treasurer, continued in that capacity. Agnew resigned. The board appointed him a consultant; he was, however, no longer involved in the decision-making processes of the board.[28]

The Board of Relief and Sustentation had strict rules of protocol. One month Relief met first and conducted its business. Then, without adjourning, the members convened as Sustentation and transacted its business. The following month Sustentation met first. Although tension between the two departments inevitably remained, a new generation of leadership ameliorated relationships. As general secretary, Foulkes restored loyalty and cooperation among staff members. Two years after the merger he reported, "Whether in the matter of advertising and general publicity, extensive and intensive campaigns, field work or general office administration, there has been heartening harmony."[29]

Despite the growth of combined financial assets from two million dollars in 1912 to more than seven million in 1918, Foulkes saw federation as only one step to promote both causes. In a policy statement presented to the board in February 1918, Foulkes called for a merger of Sustentation and Relief with the former having precedence. "The growth of the Sustentation Department is the imperative need of the Church. While the Relief Department must be maintained intact, it is not to be our effort to build up that Department except by annual contributions." He also urged the board to "increase our propaganda among people of means" and recommended hiring additional field agents on a trial basis at a salary of $150 a month. Foulkes suggested that the board employ a woman, preferably one with missionary experience, to "cultivate" Ladies' Aid Societies which would "open up a lucrative field for seed-sowing and harvest."[30]

Although the General Assembly approved the merger of Ministerial Relief and Sustentation in 1918, Foulkes's plans were never implemented. Foulkes himself soon thereafter left the board to head up the New Era Movement, an effort to revitalize church boards and agencies following World War I. His successor Robert Hunter lived only one year. Moreover, an economic slump in post-war America not only hampered expansion but again forced the board into a struggle to survive.[31]

When Henry B. Master took over the Board of Ministerial Relief and Sustentation in 1919, he attempted to both increase relief pensions and save the Sustentation Fund.[32] Initially he concentrated on saving the Fund. In a series of articles published in the *Assembly Herald*, he reported that membership in the Fund had reached 2,500 and was growing. Master also promoted the board itself by producing a movie entitled "Soldiers of the Cross," which could be rented at a minimal cost.[33] In 1922 he announced a comity agreement with Congregationalists and Southern Presbyterians whereby ministers transferring from one denomination to another could carry their pension rights and credits. In the same year, Master held the first of a series of meetings and rallies prior to the opening of the General Assembly which featured the board's programs and activities. At the assembly, Master successfully lobbied for the appointment of a layman, Nelson H. Loomis, general solicitor of the Union Pacific Railroad, as chair of the Standing Committee on Ministerial Relief and Sustentation, a position that had previously always been held by a minister.[34]

Nevertheless, in the 1920s, the Sustentation Fund was in trouble. In 1907, when the Fund began soliciting members, the average salary of a Presbyterian minister was about $600 a year. By 1923 the average was more than $1,800. An annual pension of $500, adequate in 1907, promised little more than marginal existence in 1923. Benevolence contributions from the denomination never fully materialized; the Fund was so close to collapse (with a deficit of more than two million dollars) that it requested emergency funds from the 1923 General Assembly to meet its current obligations, although no funds were available to reduce the deficit. After the board's public admission of financial problems, enrollment rapidly diminished. Reluctantly the board announced that after October 1, 1926, no new members would be admitted. Although the board acknowledged a moral responsibility to Sustentation members, it reminded people that it had no legal obligation to pay anyone more than what he or she had personally contributed.[35]

The Sustentation Fund had always experienced deficits both in its reserve funds to underwrite long-term actuarial obligations and in its collections of contributions to augment participants' payments. In the case of the reserve funds, the problem was not acute at the outset because few people were retiring. By the 1920s, however, many members were disabled or reaching the age of seventy, and the deficit became unmanageable. The amount of benevolences from voluntary gifts was unpredictable, fluctuating, and inadequate to keep the fund solvent. These two factors also influenced similar programs in other denominations patterned after the Presbyterian Sustentation model.[36]

Although the Sustentation Fund lasted fewer than twenty years, it marked the first step away from the traditional relief principle and aligned church pensions more closely with those of business and industry. Moreover, it accustomed ministers to the notion that they should contribute to their own retirement annuities, thus assuaging the idea of charity so long identified with relief. Even though many clergy refused to participate in the Sustentation Fund, more than 2,500 ministers belonged to the Fund when it closed in 1926, a figure that represented about one-fourth the eligible clergy at that time.[37]

The Presbyterian Sustentation Fund also served as a model for other Protestant denominations. George Huggins credited the Fund's early success as being an important factor in the proliferation of similar programs during the first two decades of the twentieth century. The Methodist Episcopal Church established the Conference Claimants Plan in 1908 that combined offerings received from congregations and interest from endowment funds to provide small annuities for retired ministers and their dependents. Congregationalists approved an annuity fund in 1913, and the following year the Northern Baptists instituted a pension program modeled almost entirely upon the Sustentation Fund. In 1917 the Protestant Episcopal Church created the Church Pension Fund, the first denominational program to feature a reserve pension plan with contributions and benefits related to salary and service. The Episcopalian Pension Fund in turn provided the basic ingredients for what later would become the Presbyterian Service Pension.[38]

Another ecumenical effect of the Sustentation Fund was the formation in 1915 of the Interdenominational Secretaries Conference, an organization committed to the development of sound, adequate pensions for Protestant church employees, both lay and clergy. At the urging of Huggins, leaders from the major Protestant denominations first met in 1915 to confer on mutual problems, to share information, and to learn more about investment policies, market values of securities, and the general business outlook. The interdenominational group changed its name in 1931 to the Church Pensions Conference and continues today as an informational and promotional outlet for denominational pension policies and programs.[39]

Long before the collapse of the Sustentation Fund, many Presbyterians had criticized the board's dissension over priorities of relief and sustentation and its inability to develop denominational interest in pensions. Despite repeated pleas for contributions, the board could only provide an annual pension of approximately $350 per year for ministers and missionaries who had at least thirty-five years' service. Others challenged the board to encompass all church employees, lay and clerical, in a comprehensive pension program including a retirement stipend, medical care, and housing where necessary.[40]

These negative feelings about the Board of Relief and Sustentation surfaced clearly during committee hearings dealing with the process of reorganization of General Assembly boards and agencies between 1920–1923. By 1919 the denomination had twenty boards in addition to a number of permanent committees, all of which reported annually to the General Assembly. After several abortive attempts to modify what many leaders considered to be an unnecessarily complicated and ineffective administrative structure, the General Assembly in 1920 appointed a committee chaired by John Timothy Stone (referred to popularly as the Stone Committee) to consider possible ways in which boards could be consolidated. Reorganization compressed existing groups into four major boards: National Missions, Foreign Missions, Christian Education, and Ministerial Relief and Sustentation.[41]

On several occasions the Stone Committee interrogated Master about the role of the Board of Relief and Sustentation in the proposed new structure. The committee pressed Master sharply about the program, especially in the areas of medical care and adequate pensions. More than once committee members accused the board of being insufficiently aggressive and poorly organized. One exchange between Master and Stone went as follows:

Stone: We think the matter of Relief is one of the great activities of the Church and it has not had the commendation of the Church. Instead of your Board doing less, you ought to have a great more to do. Don't you think there is an enlarged opportunity for your work?
Master: Undoubtedly, if the Church will give us funds. Opportunities are simply endless.
Stone: You have no objection to taking up other relief work if you have the funds?
Master: No.
Stone: I don't think you have a great enough appeal. There is no appeal that I have heard that touches the ordinary laymen sufficiently. There ought to be emphasis placed on the sick missionary. It is not emphasized.
Master: Yes it is. But you don't let us in.
Stone: A great many criticisms come in that the relief agencies are not big and broad enough. I know of one appeal that was made and got a check for $50,000 because an only child died of tuberculosis. I think the work of relief is bigger than we have anticipated.
Master: It is bigger than you know now.[42]

The Stone Committee, while commending the board for its past accomplishments, called for enlarged relief and pension systems to include college professors and other ordained clergy working in church-related institutions and the promotion of the establishment of hospitals, homes for the aged, and orphanages. The committee criticized the board's policy of soliciting funds through field representatives as "inadequate and unsatisfactory from every point of view." It recommended that the General Assembly appoint a special lay committee to construct a comprehensive pension program and to organize a nationwide financial campaign to underwrite its implementation.[43]

The committee's report to the General Assembly in 1922 left the Board of Relief and Sustentation essentially intact except for the mandate to "enlarge the scope of its activities" as described above. Two changes in board composition, however, were approved: the board would expand its membership to include representation from other geographical areas than Philadelphia and its vicinity and should appoint three women to serve as trustees.[44]

Before the 1922 General Assembly had ended, Master was working to stimulate interest in a new service pension program. He urged prominent laymen to submit overtures to their presbyteries requesting that the General Assembly modernize its existing pension structures. As a result, the Presbytery of Elizabeth (New Jersey) and the Synod of Southern California endorsed overtures calling for the creation of a lay committee that would formulate and seek funding for a new pension plan. By the time the 1923 General Assembly convened, 200 presbyteries and 9 synods had endorsed the overtures. The assembly appointed the committee, which included Richard B. Mellon of Pittsburgh, Fred G. Weyerhauser of Minneapolis, Senator William B. McKinley of Champaign, and the Honorable Will H. Hays of Sullivan, Indiana.[45]

At its initial meeting the Laymen's Committee elected as chair Hays, who was traveling in Europe at the time. An active layman and the grandson of a Presbyterian minister, Hays had given an impassioned speech on behalf of a pension system to the 1923 assembly entitled "Justice for the Minister." Hays, who served as Postmaster General in the Harding administration and resigned in order to become a motion picture czar and the self-appointed guardian of cinematic morals in the so-called Hays Office, initially declined the nomination and had to be persuaded by George Francis Greene, president of the board, that his leadership was essential to the project's success. "I told Greene at the time that I would do it," Hays recalled, "provided that I could 'raise a little hell'. He said that was just what they would like to have done."[46]

The Laymen's Committee held its first meeting on September 18, 1923. At this time it invited members of the Board of Ministerial Relief and Sustentation to discuss plans and procedures for a new pension program. After soliciting information from more than 7,000 ministers and missionaries, the committee worked out the major outline of a program. This program was submitted to the Prudential Life Insurance Company of Newark, whose president, Edward D. Duffield, was a Presbyterian elder. Duffield expressed Prudential's approval, saying, "Put it in operation, and you will have something as sound as the Rock of Gibraltar."[47] The 1924 General Assembly, after a three and one-half hour discussion, approved the Service Pension Plan and authorized the committee to raise the money necessary to put it into operation.⁴⁸

The new plan would be contributory as was the case in most secular programs, thus making the minister a participant rather than a recipient and placing at least part of the burden for promoting the program on the clergy itself. Large reserve funds would be required to undergird the venture. The Service Pension Plan would go into effect only when three conditions were met: (1) 4,000 churches or other salary-paying organizations must be committed to participate; (2) 4,000 individual ministers, missionaries, or other employees must be willing to contribute; and (3) adequate reserve funds must be available to underwrite the project.⁴⁹

The Laymen's Committee arrived at a figure of fifteen million dollars as the sum needed to give the pension plan stability. Included in this figure were two million in reserve for clergy who would be sixty-five at the time the plan came into operation and thus would make no contribution to the program; another eight million were included to care for ministers who had only a few years to serve under the new plan; and five million were designated to honor the Sustentation Fund obligations. The projected campaign was the largest ever undertaken by any single denomination up to that time.⁵⁰

The Service Pension Plan (SPP) offered a guaranteed minimum pension of $600 for ministers and other eligible church workers, such as missionaries, college professors, and deaconesses, who had served at least thirty-five years. Increments above this minimum would be determined by the number of years the participant had paid into the new plan and his or her average salary during those years. The money would be derived from annual payments of 10 percent of one's salary, 7½ percent from the church or employing agency, and 2½ percent from the member. The anticipation was that a person who participated in the plan a full thirty-five years would receive a pension equivalent to one-half of one's average income (1¼ percent of each year's salary for which the 10 percent was paid). The maximum pension was initially set at $2,000 with the understanding that it would be increased when it was deemed actuarially sound to do so.⁵¹

Other features of the plan included an allowance for "total and permanent disability" calculated at 40 percent of the salary for the five years preceding the disability. Initially the board could not promise more than $600 until it was actuarially sound to increase the amount. The plan also provided a widow's benefit of one-half the sum to which her husband was entitled. (Females in the plan had no survivors' benefits.) The proposed minimum was $300, which would be increased as conditions warranted it. The final benefit was an annual allowance of $100 for each minor child of widows with a proviso that the total amount received should not exceed the total pension the participant was receiving or to which he or she would have been entitled at the time of his death.[52]

Promotional literature repeatedly stressed that retirement was not a prerequisite in order to receive a pension. Unlike the Church Pension Fund of the Episcopal Church that required retirement at sixty-eight, the Presbyterian model both permitted and encouraged ministers to keep on working. Master reported, "Our plan provides a pension at the age of sixty-five IN ORDER TO PREVENT RETIREMENT."[53] The board based this feature on studies of ministerial salaries which indicated that incomes peaked about age forty-nine and then dramatically declined. Larger churches wanted young ministers, so older ministers were faced with taking smaller churches that offered reduced salaries. The pension, therefore, was designed to provide supplementary income for active clergy when their resources became inadequate.[54]

The nonretirement feature reflected a long-standing attitude that clergy should continue in the ministry as long as health and strength permitted. It is doubtful if the plan would have been approved had it specified retirement as a precondition for a pension. General Council member Mark Matthews made it clear that he backed the Sustentation Fund and the Service Pension *only* because neither legislated retirement. At a pre-assembly conference on ministerial relief, he said:

> I take the position that the Church has no right to create a deadline for me, and say, because you are sixty-five, seventy or eighty years of age, you are retired from the active duties of the Christian pulpit, and I want to say to you right now that as long as God Almighty gives me health there is no Church on earth that will make a deadline for me. I will never be retired until I lie in the little bed that God has placed beneath the green sod for me. It is a mistake to think that the gospel has been entrusted to young hands and young voices only, and as long as a man can preach and give advice and wisdom he ought to be permitted to occupy the active plan on the platform of that pulpit.[55]

A decade later when the board required retirement at sixty-five, it engulfed the denomination in controversy.

Taking a new direction, the plan dealt with ministers collectively rather than as individuals. Although each participant earned pension credits based on his/her income, the maximum pension of $2,000 meant that those whose salaries generated credits above the maximum were contributing to help others who had lower salaries. That income, said Master, "is spread over all the other members of the group to which he belongs. It goes to provide additional benefits for the men in the smaller and the smallest churches. It goes to pension the men and women who break down early in life and have no resources at all."[56] Expressed in theological terms, the group concept meant that "The strong must help to bear the burdens of the weak." Some ministers in large congregations, however, opted not to enter the program because of this provision or stopped making payments when they reached the $2,000 maximum pension.[57]

With the main features of the SPP worked out, the Laymen's Committee set out to raise the fifteen million dollar reserve fund. Hayes had enlisted Secretary of the Treasury Andrew W. Mellon, a Presbyterian, to be acting honorary treasurer, reasoning that he would signify stability and security. Every check, whether for fifty cents or fifty thousand dollars, would be made out to him. Mellon also promised a gift of two hundred thousand dollars and the same from his brother Richard. Given this impressive beginning, the committee intended to raise the entire amount from fewer than 2,000 wealthy Presbyterian families known to be sympathetic to benevolent causes. The results, however, were discouraging, forcing the committee to take another course of action.[58]

At this juncture Hays convinced the committee that it needed a professional fundraiser. Although some board members questioned employing business techniques for a "spiritual cause," Hays hired Arnaud C. Marts, president of Marts and Lundy of New York, Inc., to revive the fund drive. Marts launched a campaign utilizing slick brochures and catchy phrases ("Religion is the one essential industry of the world. The management of that industry is in the hands of ministers.") He organized a series of nationwide inspirational rallies that Mellon and others underwrote. Marts formed a "National Committee of 100" (later increased to 200) of laypersons from every presbytery in the denomination. He instigated a competitive program of benevolence among four regions of the country. Within a year the campaign had reached a successful conclusion.[59]

According to the final report, $15,045,000 had been subscribed. The top four presbyteries of New York, Pittsburgh, Chicago, and Los Angeles together raised more than three million dollars. The Madison Avenue Church in New York ranked highest among congregations with $443,000. Altogether, 110,000 families contributed to the reserve fund with pledges ranging from twenty-five cents to $300,000. Hays himself contributed 10 percent of his total assets to the reserve fund. Even non-Presbyterians participated. Will Rogers gave $100, a Baptist layman in Washington State sent $5,000, and a Roman Catholic from California mailed a check for $50.[60]

When the 139th General Assembly convened in 1927, the Laymen's Committee was prepared to announce its victory. The moderator, Robert E. Speer, recognized Master who introduced Hays. In his address Hays summarized the committee's efforts, describing how the campaign had been organized in successive zones beginning on the Atlantic seaboard and working westward to the Pacific. "And we conclude this morning the laymen's westward march to the sea. We take the hand of every minister in the denomination and with him look to the rising sun of a new day." Then, pausing for effect, Hays announced, "The necessary amount has been raised!" The assembly gave Hays a standing ovation and after sustained applause spontaneously sang the Doxology.[61]

Hays had one more item on the agenda. He turned to Speer and announced that the Laymen's Committee wanted to pay tribute to Christ's ministry in the Presbyterian church. As he spoke, aides removed a large American flag from the side of the platform and there in large letters stood the announcement: VICTORY—$15,000,000—THE LAYMEN'S COMMITTEE. According to an eyewitness, commissioners sang the Doxology a second time and recited the Twenty-third Psalm "with tremulous voices." For the first time in denominational history, women voted in the General Assembly by standing with their husbands in a vote of silent gratitude to the Laymen's Committee. In recognition of the event, the General Assembly instructed the board to change its corporate title to "The Board of Pensions of the Presbyterian Church in the U.S.A."[62]

Master reported to the General Assembly in 1928 that the SPP was operating and that membership was growing. Thus far 7,050 ministers and church workers were enrolled, and during the first year of operation 253 individuals had received pensions totaling $68,589. Two hundred and fifty-six presbyteries had adopted a "Stabilizing Resolution" that said in effect that presbyteries would not hereafter place a call in a person's hand unless it contained an agreement to pay a sum equal to 7½ percent of the salary in the Service Pension Plan. Although the resolution had an exception clause, "Nothing in this resolution shall be interpreted as abridging the sovereign right of the Presbytery to excuse a church or a cause," it made participation in the pension program the rule rather than exception.[63]

Implementation of the SPP, effective April 1, 1927, marked a new era for a board which for so many years had been associated with "relief" rather than "service." A major and irreversible step had been taken to combat a situation that had existed since colonial times. Master confidently extolled the reliability of the Service Pension Plan: "It is sound, it is safe, it is conservative."[64]

Chapter 7
Cumberland and United Presbyterian Traditions

We insist that Ministerial Relief is in no sense a charity; it is a debt due to faithful men who have devoted their lives to the self-denying work of the holy ministry, and to their families, when left in indigent circumstances.
—*UPNA General Assembly*, 1885

During the nineteenth century, two new Reformed denominations played significant roles in American Presbyterian history. Both groups eventually merged into the Presbyterian Church in the United States of America in the twentieth century. The efforts of both the Cumberland Presbyterian Church (CP) and the United Presbyterian Church of North America (UPNA) in addressing the needs of the aged and incapacitated paralleled those of the PCUS and PCUSA denominations, although both the CP and the UPNA denominations had unique approaches to ministerial relief.

The Cumberland Presbyterian Church originated in Kentucky and Tennessee in the early nineteenth century. During these years revivalist and anti-revivalist factions in the Synod of Kentucky clashed over ordination procedures involving four men of the Cumberland Presbytery. The Synod of Kentucky dissolved Cumberland Presbytery in 1806 because it refused to submit the candidates for reexamination and accept the *Confession of Faith* in its entirety. On February 4, 1810, Samuel McAdow, Finis Ewing, and Samuel King reconstituted Cumberland Presbytery without synodical approval.

Although the trio apparently did not intend to form a new denomination, they were unsuccessful in their efforts to effect a rapprochement with the Synod of Kentucky or any other neighboring judicatories. Growing rapidly, the Cumberland Presbyterians formed a Synod in 1813 and a General Assembly in 1829. By the beginning of the twentieth century, the Cumberland Presbyterians numbered approximately 180,000 with 3,000 congregations scattered throughout the country.[1]

The United Presbyterian Church of North America traced its origins to Scotland where various groups had separated from the established church due to differing theological or political ideas. These dissenters, known as Covenanters and Seceders, came from both Scotland and Northern Ireland, settled in New York, southeastern Pennsylvania, and South Carolina, and later moved to western Pennsylvania, their eventual center of strength. In 1753 the Seceders organized the Associate Presbytery of Pennsylvania, and in 1774 the Covenanters created the Reformed Presbytery of America. After several unions and divisions, the main body of dissenting Presbyterians united on May 26, 1858, in Pittsburgh, Pennsylvania. The new United Presbyterian Church of North America had a membership of slightly more than 250,000, most of whom lived within a several hundred mile radius of western Pennsylvania. By the mid-twentieth century, the small denomination had churches stretching from coast to coast. In 1958, the UPNA Church merged with the Presbyterian Church in the United States of America to form the United Presbyterian Church in the United States of America (UPUSA).[2]

In the Cumberland denomination, a majority of ministers operated not in established congregations but in "missionating" or circuit-riding patterns in frontier settlements. Because of informal preaching arrangements and poor conditions on the frontier, the clergy were underpaid and with few exceptions engaged by necessity in other vocations, such as farming, teaching, and commercial trade. One historian calculated that of the early itinerants and circuit riders, approximately one-third received no remuneration, one-third received "some socks" and up to $20 a year, and the rest averaged no more than $20 annually.[3] Presbytery records confirm these generalizations. James Logan, a licentiate in Logan Presbytery, noted that from April 20 to November 12, 1826, he had traveled 1,038 miles, preached 161 times, and received only $27.25 for his services.[4] J. W. Smith of Little River Presbytery traveled 2,776 miles, preached 121 sermons, and collected $253.75.[5] Fortunately, few had the experience of W. M. Speegle of Elgin, Texas, who informed his presbytery in 1883 that he had "preached fourteen times at twelve different places and received one dollar and that too from a half-drunk man."[6]

Early in its history, the CP General Assembly expressed concern about its aged ministers, as well as individuals who needed assistance. In 1833 the assembly noted that Samuel McAdow, one of the three who organized the first presbytery, was "old and afflicted, and in circumstances quite necessitous." For several years commissioners raised money to assist him and his family.[7] On another occasion, the General Assembly procured funds to purchase a small farm for the widow and children of David McLin, whose sudden death had left the family without support.[8] From time to time the assembly exhorted synods and presbyteries for assistance. Although a few church courts responded, most judicatories were too weak and insolvent to render any significant aid.[9]

The General Assembly took steps to unify its approach to ministerial relief in 1880 when it appointed a "Committee on Sustentation of Superannuated Ministers" to draw up policies and procedures. The committee recommended a permanent committee of two ministers and two elders to serve as a general treasury and proposed that only ministers who had served their entire career in the Cumberland denomination would be eligible for aid. In addition, it advised that it would only consider applicants who had "neither property, money, nor income to support them, nor children who are able and willing to do so." As a final test, ministers had to present satisfactory evidence to the committee that "their manner of life [had] been frugal and not extravagant both with regard to their own habits and those of their family."[10]

A special committee reported to General Assembly in 1881 that only a strong, unified organization could adequately cope with the widespread ministerial poverty. "The Church cannot properly recognize its duty and acknowledge its obligations toward this class of ministers except through its highest judicatory, and by means of a general Board or Committee, organized and operating under its supervision."[11] The General Assembly established the Board of Ministerial Relief, to be located in Evansville, Indiana, and appointed William J. Darby, a pastor and advocate of a denominational relief program, as president. The assembly authorized this board to collect and disburse all contributions received either from congregations or individuals. The Board of Ministerial Relief also assumed the responsibility for seeking private contributions and bequests to provide capital for the creation of an endowment fund.[12]

In his initial report Darby expressed optimism that ministerial relief would "at once occupy a large place in the hearts of all the ministers and members of the church." Nevertheless, during the first year the board received only $598.61 from ninety congregations and eleven individuals. From these limited funds, it made appropriations to three ministers and one widow.[13] Both receipts and participation in the relief program grew, however, as board members mounted an aggressive publicity campaign. In 1890, more than 1,300 congregations and 200 individuals contributed $10,306.45.[14] Despite this increase, the rising number of applicants made it impossible to augment individual grants that averaged only about $200 a year.[15]

Darby's annual reports to the General Assembly frequently relied more on pathos than statistics, and the lower the annual offerings the more melodramatic they were. His narrative in 1890 described a young minister who was unable to work because of illness; in order to pay the rent, the minister's daughter had to leave home and teach school. Darby described the impact of this turn of events on the ailing clergyman:

> You observe this man leans on a staff and trembles, and tears trickle down his cheeks as he watches his frail daughter receding in the distance. "Why weep, O man?" "This is why," he says. "Did I ever think I would come to the point where my children would have to support me?" He turns to the house heavy at heart—he can not work—live he must—he has not laid by for this extremity—what must he do—simply sit down in his home, with all the desire of a good father to help his children crushed, and submit to being helped by the daughter and wife.

Darby concluded his story with a happy ending. The Board of Ministerial Relief sent a check for $200 that enabled him to contribute something to his family.[16]

The board also appealed to specialized constituencies, such as women of the church. "Christian women," a board report commented, "are peculiarly fitted for this form of benevolence, and we hope that through pastors and sessions they may be brought actively into co-operation with this Board."[17] In 1892 the board created a Woman's Department that would enlist "the ladies" to make donations of clothing, food, and household articles or cash. Darby's wife directed this auxiliary organization during its early years.[18]

Their annual reports enumerated contributions such as these: the ladies of Grace Church, San Antonio, Texas, gave cash for a suit of clothes; Miss Ella Kilbourn of Van Alstyne, Texas, provided one wheelchair; the ladies of First Church, Evansville presented one box of clothing worth $40; the ladies of New Florence, Missouri, sewed a quilt; and women from Selma, California, donated one box of fruit valued at $50. When the Board of Ministerial Relief opened a home for retired ministers in 1890, the Ladies Missionary Society of Evansville furnished one room and part of another at a cost of $120.[19]

Trying to reach the young, the General Assembly approved a denominational offering on the third Sunday in November as Ministerial Relief Day for Children. Although the board reported "a good measure of success," the total amount generated annually was usually less than $400. Efforts to elicit additional support from Christian Endeavor Societies produced annual offerings of less than $100.[20] A movement to introduce "Banner Presbyteries" in which every congregation and Sunday school contributed some amount no matter how small had equally disappointing results. Only a half-dozen presbyteries attained such a status.[21]

The board entered a new phase of its work in 1890 with the acquisition of property outside of Evansville to be used as a home for aged ministers and their dependents. Located on ten acres of ground in a rural setting, the home was described in 1891 as "a commodious and beautiful three-story frame home—plenty large for immediate purposes—comfortably and neatly furnished throughout, ready for occupants."[22] It was formally dedicated on November 27, 1890, as the Thornton Home, in honor of Emeline Thornton of Petersburg, Indiana. At the dedication, Darby, who had been instrumental in securing the gift, described the purpose of the home. "I can assure you that it is no thought of Mrs. Thornton that those who are sheltered beneath this roof should feel that they are pensioners upon her charity. It is the recompense of reward. The laborer receiving his hire. The balancing of the scales."[23]

The Thornton Home, equipped to shelter fifteen people, rarely ever reached capacity. People associated Thornton Home with a poor house. Others thought that the home was too expensive to maintain for such a small number of people, a fact that prompted Darby on a number of occasions to refer to the project as experimental. By 1906 the Thornton Home required more than a third of the total relief budget in order to care for fewer than a dozen people. Nevertheless, the board considered it worthwhile, noting that those who opted to live in the home found "an atmosphere of peaceful rest and quiet."[24]

In its campaign for the Thornton Home, the board employed natavist principles to defend its establishment. During a period of American history when many Protestant organizations espoused anti-Catholic sentiments, the board promoted the Thornton Home as an effective barrier against increasing "Romanism" in the United States.

> Protestantism is pitted against Roman Catholicism, and the cry is, "What shall we do to stop the onward march of this dangerous influence?" Then we madly rush forward to the platform and pulpit and cry out against the Roman Catholics. Judiciously done, it may be to a degree good, but there will come along two inoffensive "Sisters," and from the pockets of the Protestants get money to build a home for the aged, the poor, the homeless, the friendless, the orphan, and the sick. Then this very building speaks louder to the heart of man than any sermon or lecture.

The report ended with a challenge: "Go and do likewise, Churches of Christendom, and you will do more to raise the standard of the Cross to its true position, defeat Roman Catholicism, as well as attract many men who are making secret societies their Church."[25]

During the same years the Thornton Home was being established and defended, intense negotiations were taking place that culminated in 1906 with a vote by the Cumberland General Assembly to merge with the PCUSA. Those who refused to enter the united church constituted a denomination that exists today as the Cumberland Presbyterian Church. After extended litigation, the Thornton Home became the property of the united church as did most of the churches and schools belonging to the former denomination. The Thornton Home continued to operate until 1967 when it was closed and its residents transferred to the new Mid-Continent Home in Kansas City.²⁶

The United Presbyterian Church of North America developed its ministerial relief program along lines similar to the Cumberland Church. It first established a general fund and later raised it to board status. Like other denominations, the UPNA had an underpaid ministry. According to an editorial in *The United Presbyterian*, the average salary of UPNA ministers in 1868 was $794. Of the 541 ministers listed on General Assembly rolls, only forty received more than $1,000 a year. At the lower end, 172 received between $600–$1,000, 51 between $450–$600, and 278 between $300–$350.²⁷ Another report told of a pastor who in order to remain in the ministry supplemented his own salary at about $300 a year. The correspondent affirmed this was only one of many such instances in the United Presbyterian ministry.²⁸

In response to these conditions, the Board of Home Missions in 1861 requested and the General Assembly approved the creation of "The Aged and Infirm Ministers' Fund" with money to be raised by annual contributions from congregations. In support of its petition, the board appealed to the precedent of government pensions and warned that the church would lose potential ministerial candidates if remedial steps were not immediately taken. "It surely cannot be regarded as strange," the report argued, "if in many cases deserving and noble-hearted men will avoid entering a ministry which might have them placed in such a position."²⁹ Two years later the General Assembly extended coverage to include both widows and orphans. In keeping with contemporary language, the assembly entitled it, "The Fund for Superannuated and Disabled Ministers in Need, and for the Destitute Widows and Orphans of Deceased Ministers."³⁰

In 1864 the General Assembly approved in principle the establishment of an endowment fund to supplement the fluctuating receipts from annual congregational offerings.³¹ Because of poor response, a special committee recommended in 1869 that $100,000 be raised by requiring each congregation to contribute 5 percent of its minister's salary for a period of six years. The assembly concurred, and commissioners promised "to use our influence to promote this object in the presbyteries to which we belong."³² Their efforts proved insufficient, as presbyteries narrowly rejected the proposed assessment program.³³ The General Assembly later approved a $50,000 endowment fund campaign to secure voluntary contributions. After a slow start, the fund gradually reached and surpassed its goal. By the beginning of the century it had accumulated more than $100,000, most of which was invested in government bonds and Westinghouse Air Brake stocks. A unique feature of the UPNA endowment plan was its policy of laying aside each year a small percentage of receipts from congregational giving for investment in the fund. This money along with other gifts and bequests guaranteed a steady increase to the principal.[34]

To elevate the status of ministerial relief, a lay group from Philadelphia Presbytery, led by businessman James McCandless, petitioned the General Assembly in 1873 to create a Board of Ministerial Relief. The assembly approved, and the board was formally chartered in 1875. Serving on the board initially were ministers J. B. Dales and W. W. Barr and laymen John Alexander, William Getty, Henry Harrison, James Brown, J. P. Hanna, Thomas Stinson, and James McCandless, who became its first treasurer. The board commenced its work with $6,500 in its treasury.[35] Although at one point the balance fell to $500, contributions were sufficient to provide grants ranging from $100 to $250 annually. In 1895 the board reported that it had funded fifty-nine beneficiaries, twenty-one males and thirty-eight females.[36]

In its early years the board had to encourage presbyteries to identify possible recipients. Rather than being flooded by requests for relief funds, the board discovered, as had other relief agencies, that many potential applicants were unwilling to appear to be on the dole. In 1875 the board noted that "there is often a hesitancy on the part of those whose lives have been throughout nobly self-sacrificing to make application for their just share of that provision which the Church makes as a reward to the faithful rather than a gift to the indigent." Consequently, the General Assembly directed presbyteries to look carefully into the needs of their constituents "lest they be kept back by diffidence or lack of information or false notions of pride and propriety or by any other cause from seeking from this Board what is their due."[37]

Despite this invitation, the board had stipulations for grants. Any minister or widow with a family able to provide food, shelter, and clothing was ineligible.[38] In specific situations, the board adhered to its general policy. When the widow of Samuel Findley requested financial assistance in 1877, the board tabled action on her request because she had been offered a home with one of her sons and had declined to accept the invitation.[39] Another time it rejected a widow's request for funds noting that "it appeals to our sympathy" but was not consistent with board policies.[40] A retired couple asked the board if moving to a church-sponsored retirement home would affect their annual payment, and the board ruled that each case would have to be taken on its own merits.[41] Despite its apparent hard-line attitude, the board could be flexible when circumstances warranted. In 1884, for example, it gave the treasurer freedom to increase grants when necessary without consulting the entire board.[42]

In the 1880s women became important in the ministerial relief program. Even prior to the formation of the Women's General Missionary Society (WGMS) in 1883, the Board of Ministerial Relief was successfully soliciting assistance from local societies. In 1882 the board reported that a number of "Ladies' Societies" had distributed food and clothing and in several instances had sent money directly to the treasurer for distribution.[43] Later, the WGMS established a Home and Ministerial Relief Department which annually raised funds for the board. Throughout the nineteenth century, contributions from this department ranged from $600 to $1,000 in addition to food and clothing distributed at the presbyterial level. Through frequent reports and pleas for help in the pages of their monthly missionary magazine, UPNA women provided a steady source of support for the Board of Ministerial Relief.[44]

UPNA women were also instrumental in providing the denomination with its first orphanage, hospital, and retirement home. In October 1878, James M. Fulton, pastor of the Fourth U.P. church in Allegheny, Pennsylvania, assumed responsibility for a family of five small children when their mother, a widow, died suddenly with no next of kin. Fulton asked the women of his congregation for assistance, and they responded by organizing themselves into The United Presbyterian Women's Association. They rented a house to serve as an orphanage and raised funds to supply necessary staff. Later, the association raised $7,000 to purchase a larger residence to accommodate the growing number of children and in 1889 opened a fifteen-bed hospital to care for children who needed special medical attention. Their most ambitious venture commenced in 1892 when they purchased a large house in Wilkinsburg, Pennsylvania, which became the first United Presbyterian Home for the Aged. Although the Wilkinsburg Home was not officially under the aegis of the Board of Ministerial Relief, it accepted retired clergy and widows who had no families with whom to live. The Wilkinsburg home served as a prototype for similar retirement homes through the country, most of which were synodical projects.[45]

UPNA women were also successful through their national organization in securing equal benefits for incapacitated male and female missionaries. Single male missionaries disabled while in service were covered by provisions in the Board of Foreign Missions' manual. Single women, however, had no similar protection. The WGMS petitioned the General Assembly in 1897 to redress this inequity. After several conferences between representatives of the WGMS and the Board of Foreign Missions, the latter agreed to amend its manual to read: "This rule shall apply to unmarried missionary women, and to all other unordained missionaries." In case the disabled women did not remain on the missionary field, the WGMS or the Foreign Board were empowered to grant, if needed, an annual allowance equal to that given to disabled ministers by the Board of Ministerial Relief.[46]

In the twentieth century, the UPNA enlarged its programs beyond relief grants. Under the leadership of James Price, Robert W. Burnside, and Charles L. Hussey, the denomination developed a Retirement Plan (1910), a Ministerial Annuity Fund (1917), and a modern Pension Plan (1928). In each instance these programs were patterned after similar ones in other mainline Protestant denominations, especially the Presbyterian Church in the United States of America. Because these programs are discussed in more detail elsewhere in this work, only a brief account of their development will be included here.[47]

The Ministerial Relief Plan required each minister in active service to pay $10 annually and every congregation to contribute its full quota based on equal portions of a $12,000 appropriation. Payments to retiring ministers were limited to available funds. In actual practice, the grants ranged from $150 to $200. Widows received three-fifths of ministerial grants and each child under sixteen could receive up to $100 a year depending on resources available. The Retirement Fund, however, was not widely accepted. At the end of its first year of operation, fewer than fifty ministers had joined, and when a new program became effective in 1917, only ninety-one members were enrolled.[48]

In 1916 the Board of Ministerial Relief described what it termed "a growing demand" for a pension fund in which both ministers and congregations participated to provide increased annuities "irrespective of need."[49] The following year the General Assembly approved a Ministerial Annuity Fund with membership restricted to ordained ministers, commissioned missionaries, and lay missionaries of the Board of Publication who had served the board at least ten years. The Annuity Fund, modeled after the PCUSA Sustentation Fund, promised an annuity of $500 at age sixty-eight for a member who had at least thirty years of service in the United Presbyterian Church. One-fifth of that amount would be derived from ministerial payments based on age at time of entrance, and four-fifths would come from congregational contributions and endowment incomes. In order to put the fund on a sound financial basis, the General Assembly authorized the Board of Ministerial Relief to begin a campaign to raise a reserve fund of $500,000.[50]

Efforts to secure the $500,000 endowment were curtailed by the onset of World War I, an influenza crisis, and widespread denominational indifference to the project. By 1925 less than $300,000 had been collected for the reserve fund and younger ministers were hesitant to join a program with such questionable financial stability. Moreover, the $500 annuity that seemed sufficient in 1917 now appeared inadequate. Payments had never actually exceeded $400, a fact noted at General Assembly. When the Ministers' Annuity Fund closed in 1928, only 294 ministers and missionaries, fewer than half the eligible members, had participated. Nevertheless, in closing the Fund the committee stated that it was being supplanted "not because of failure, but only because its provisions are inadequate to present day needs."[51]

In 1927 the Board of Ministerial Relief recommended that the UPNA Church follow the example of the Episcopal, Congregational, Methodist, and

Presbyterian (USA) denominations by creating a modern service pension program. Under the actuarial guidance of George A. Huggins, the UPNA Church approved a pension plan that proposed an annuity on retirement at age sixty-five after thirty years of service which would amount to approximately one-half of a minister's average salary with a minimum pension of $600. The pension would be provided by the combined payments based on the minister's salary of 2½ percent (minister) and 7½ percent (congregation). Widows were to receive one-half the ministers' entitlement.[52]

The new Board of Ministerial Pensions and Relief launched its program at a most inauspicious time in America's economic history. With the stock market crash of 1929 and the ensuing Depression, it was impossible to raise more than about a third of the required million and a half dollar prior service fund. Consequently, the board had to reduce the estimated minimum payments to $400 and the widows' annuities to $200. Nevertheless, by 1930 more than 75 percent of the eligible members had signed up. By the 1950s participation had soared to more than 90 percent, and the financial base had greatly improved. In 1958 the board reported assets of $8,370,000 and an average ministerial pension of $867 per year. Although the plan had no medical or hospital coverage, it offered a total and permanent disability pension at 90 percent of the accrued pension. Union with the Presbyterian Church in the United States of America in 1958 brought added strength to the program.[53]

Chapter 8
Executive Committee of Christian Education and Ministerial Relief

Is it not a reproach to the name we bear, that so many of the beloved ministers of God, who once labored with us, are permitted to pine away in poverty and want, unpitied and unnoticed? Can the compassionate Jesus be otherwise than displeased with such unfraternal, unmerciful, not to say unchristian, neglect?
—*Southern Presbyterian Review*, 1869

Long before Confederate forces bombarded Fort Sumter on April 12, 1861, American Presbyterians had begun to divide along sectional lines. When commissioners in the New School General Assembly pressed the issue of slavery in 1853 and 1855, Southern constituents withdrew to form the United Synod of the Presbyterian Church in the U.S.A. For a time the Old School General Assembly maintained a tenuous official unity when it met in Philadelphia on May 16, 1861, even though all the Southern states except North Carolina and Tennessee had left the Union. In a highly charged atmosphere, Gardiner Spring of New York moved that a committee be appointed "to inquire into the expediency of making some expression of their devotion to the Union of these States." The assembly subsequently passed the "Spring Resolutions" endorsing the Federal cause. As a result, Confederate adherents renounced their allegiance to the Northern controlled assembly and formed what would become the Presbyterian Church in the United States (PCUS), a denomination of about 70,000 members and 1,000 ministers.[1]

Between 1861 and the end of the century, the PCUS had no formal ministerial relief program comparable to the PCUSA. The new denomination found itself almost totally absorbed in supporting war-related activities that tended to deplete both human and financial resources. Younger ministers served as chaplains or as short-term missionaries to soldiers and camp followers, while others entered secular employment to support the war effort and supplement meager salaries. Synods and presbyteries reported a general decline in church attendance, blaming the lack of interest on the wartime activities. Members of the Presbytery of South Carolina complained that ministers, elders, and church members of all ages felt the intensity of war so much that "comparatively few come to Zion's solemn feasts, and hence her ways do mourn."[2] The Synod of Georgia claimed that "Many of our people and churches are allowing the trials and troubles of our country to engross all their feelings, resources, and energies to the neglect of the salvation of the soul and the building up of God's kingdom in the world."[3] As the war intensified and Union armies penetrated farther south, many judicatories could not hold meetings, let alone maintain any active missionary and benevolent enterprises.

When peace returned in 1865, Southern cities were in ruin, much of the countryside was a wilderness, and river and rail traffic was largely at a standstill. Not only was currency valueless, but cotton crops had been destroyed. Church buildings had been burned, congregations scattered, and ministers exiled from their families and homes. The editor of *The Southern Presbyterian* described conditions based on information he had gathered from states in the former Confederacy:

> The condition of our church is one of great prostration and distress.... Hundreds of our churches, during the progress of war have either been destroyed, or rendered useless without a greater outlay in the way of repairs than our people can afford. Many of our best and most earnest preachers have been compelled to betake themselves to school keeping, or some secular employment, in order to provide the means of subsistence for their families.... The wheels of benevolence have been brought almost to a standstill from the want of funds.... Our condition is obviously one of great prostration.[4]

Along with inadequate financial resources, ministerial relief languished because the denomination did not want strong boards with powerful leadership. The oft-repeated warning of theologian Robert L. Dabney that the PCUS had to be vigilant lest it become a "secretaryatted Church" in which executives wielded too much authority seemed to have been heeded. Instead of boards, the denomination appointed executive committees from year to year, limited in power, and directly supervised and regulated by the General Assembly.

Although these executive committees eventually functioned as boards, for nearly one century PCUS leaders resisted changing the nomenclature.[5]

Because of its desire to keep denominational structures simple, General Assemblies during the nineteenth century elected not to grant executive committee status to ministerial relief. Initially ministerial relief was a subcommittee of the Executive Committee of Sustentation. In 1879 the assembly transferred this responsibility to the Executive Committee of Home Missions where it remained until 1902. With no full-time leadership and limited denominational visibility, the PCUS program lagged behind other Protestant denominations whose structures provided more ministerial aid.[6]

Concurrent with the widespread aversion to strong boards was a conviction that ministers should not receive special treatment when it came to facing old age and death. This perspective, which suggested that everyone was expected to lead industrious, frugal, and prudent lives, anticipated that God, in turn, would reward such qualities with ample material provisions. "There is no reason why ministers rather than other men should be exempted from such conditions," said one correspondent. On "occasional instances of destitution not caused by the sufferer," he concluded, "the proper provision is to be found in the personal benevolence of the individual Christians who are familiar with them."[7] John N. Craig, who served as secretary of the Executive Committee of Home Missions for seventeen years, acknowledged that in his travels throughout the South parishioners frequently complained that they earned no more than ministers and had no special fund available to meet their needs. Ministers, they told Craig, "should learn to lay up for old age like everybody else."[8]

Despite such attitudes, some PCUS ministers believed that a centralized agency should deal specifically with ministerial relief, and their efforts began to produce results. As early as 1863 the Presbyteries of Mississippi and Hopewell requested the General Assembly to devise a plan of assistance for disabled ministers and families of deceased clergy. In 1864 a committee appointed to study the overtures asked the General Assembly to send two resolutions to the presbyteries for ratification. The first proposed a change in the *Form of Government* pertaining to the section on pastoral calls to specify the obligations of the congregation to its minister. To the existing language a sentence was to be added: "And should you become disabled, or depart this life, whilst you are the regular pastor of this church, we hereby promise and oblige ourselves to furnish you, or, when you are dead, your family, with all proper support, including the education of your children." A second resolution recommended that the General Assembly raise a permanent fund by seeking donations and bequests, the interest from which would be used to support disabled missionaries and evangelists who did not have settled pastorates and ministers whose congregations were too poor to provide adequate salaries.

Commissioners decided, however, that wartime was not an appropriate occasion to undertake such ventures, so they tabled the proposal.[9]

After the war, the General Assembly again faced a similar issue. In 1867, J. T. Pollock requested the General Assembly to provide financial aid to a widow and her family who resided in his presbytery. The assembly authorized the Executive Committee of Sustentation to set aside 5 percent of its annual receipts to handle this and future requests with the provision that such a plan of operation not be continued longer than two years.[10] The following year the assembly introduced a new procedure that would prove to be the basis of its ministerial relief funds throughout the rest of the century. Instead of using 5 percent of the Sustentation Fund's collections, the assembly authorized an annual collection in July to be taken in each congregation and forwarded to the Sustentation treasurer for distribution. This offering, which subsequently became known as the Invalid Ministers' Fund, raised $3,624.26 in 1868 and was divided among fifty-seven families.[11]

Invalid Fund grants normally ranged from $25 to $200, most of which went to families of deceased ministers. Sustentation secretary J. Leighton Wilson used his annual reports to apprise church members of the growing needs of the Invalid Fund, especially as the roster of recipients increased. Wilson also described what he termed "the silent grief among the servants of God," aged and indigent ministers who although in extreme poverty would not make their needs public. He told of one minister who was found on the streets "in deplorable destitution, without suitable food or comfortable bedding, or even money enough to buy medicine for the alleviation of his sufferings." A small grant from the Invalid Fund enabled the man to meet some of his basic needs.[12] Even such stories of poverty and suffering, however, failed to generate much money for the Invalid Fund. This lack of response prompted Wilson to chastize his readers for their insensitivity: "It has been a matter of continual surprise and grief that so little interest is felt in this Fund by our ministers and people."[13]

Statistics confirm Wilson's observations about the Fund's mediocre support. For the first twenty years of its existence, the Invalid Fund rarely exceeded $10,000 and often its receipts were much lower. In 1890 the Fund was $700 in debt and had to reduce payments by one-third.[14] Although conditions gradually improved, the resources of the Invalid Fund were totally inadequate to meet growing requests. In 1901 a contributor to *The Christian Observer* reported that collections were so small that the average appropriation was less than twenty-six cents a day to furnish food, clothing, fuel, rent, education, and miscellaneous expenses for ministerial families.[15]

Several attempts to raise an endowment for the Invalid Fund failed due to poor economic conditions and to entrenched resistance to contributing money for benevolent purposes. In 1882 Stewart Robinson bequeathed $25,000 to the

FRANCIS ALISON: A native of Ireland, Alison came to America in 1735 and established himself as a prominent educator and theologian among his Old Side colleagues. He was the prime mover in organizing the Widows' Fund and its first secretary, serving until 1779.

CHARLES BEATTY: Elected a member of the Corporation in 1759, Beatty toured England and Scotland in 1762 raising funds to underwrite the Widows' Fund and to provide support for colonial missionary work.

ASHBEL GREEN: A prominent ecclesiastical figure during the early nineteenth century, Green was the founder of Princeton Theological Seminary, a trustee of the College of New Jersey, and president of Jefferson Medical College. Green served the Corporation as secretary 1794–1848 and helped to promote the Plan of 1824.

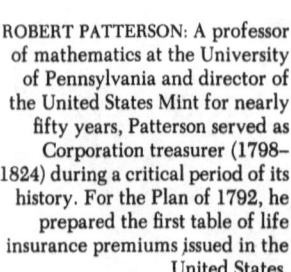

ROBERT PATTERSON: A professor of mathematics at the University of Pennsylvania and director of the United States Mint for nearly fifty years, Patterson served as Corporation treasurer (1798–1824) during a critical period of its history. For the Plan of 1792, he prepared the first table of life insurance premiums issued in the United States.

PATTERSON, M.D.: Patterson succeeded his father as Corporation treasurer in 1824. He resigned in 1828 to join the University of Virginia faculty but returned as treasurer 1836–1852. In addition to various professorships, Patterson also served as director of the United States Mint.

ARCHIBALD ALEXANDER: An ordained Presbyterian minister, Alexander was elected as the first professor at Princeton Theological Seminary in 1812 and taught all the courses himself. A policyholder and trustee of the Corporation, Alexander advocated a modernization of the Widows' Fund that resulted in the Plan of 1852.

CHARLES MACALESTER: A Philadelphia banker, active layman, and noted philanthropist, Macalester was president of the Presbyterian Annuity Company 1862–1873. In 1871 he made a gift of land for a college in St. Paul, Minnesota, which today bears his name.

JOHN WELSH DULLES: Dulles was the first ordained minister since 1779 to serve as president of the Presbyterian Annuity and Life Insurance Company (1880–1887). His grandson John Foster Dulles achieved prominence as Secretary of State during the Eisenhower administration.

ALEXANDER MACKIE: Mackie was president of the Presbyterian Ministers' Fund from 1936 to 1963 and led the company into a period of remarkable growth and expansion. A Presbyterian clergyman with a keen interest in history, Mackie wrote a definitive narrative of the company's early days.

WILLIAM W. HEBERTON: A graduate of Lafayette College and Princeton Theological Seminary, Heberton succeeded Charles Brown as treasurer of the Board of Ministerial Relief in 1883. He held that position for more than forty years until his retirement in 1925.

WILLIAM C. CATTELL: A graduate of Princeton University and Seminary, Cattell served as president of Lafayette College before becoming secretary of the Board of Ministerial Relief in 1883. During his fifteen-year tenure the Board raised nearly three million dollars for ministerial relief.

BENJAMIN L. AGNEW: After graduating from Western Seminary in 1857, Agnew served various pastorates in Pennsylvania before coming to the Board of Ministerial Relief in 1897 as secretary. A vigorous defender of the traditional relief principle, he unsuccessfully opposed the introduction of the Sustentation Fund and resigned in 1912.

JOHN ROSS SUTHERLAND: Referred to as "the father of the Sustentation Fund," Sutherland served pastorates including Pittsburgh, Pennsylvania, and Jacksonville, Illinois. In the latter congregation, William Jennings Bryan became a member and lifelong friend. From 1910 to 1918 Sutherland held the positions of head of the Board of Sustentation and associate secretary of the Board of Ministerial Relief and Sustentation.

WILLIAM H. FOULKES: A McCormick Theological Seminary graduate, Foulkes served several pastorates in the midwest before heading the Board of Relief and Sustentation from 1913 to 1918. During his tenure he worked diligently to heal the breach between the Sustentation and Relief factions. He was elected moderator of the General Assembly in 1933.

HENRY B. MASTER: As chief executive officer 1919–1937, Master presided over the creation of the Service Pension Plan and its early development in the Depression era. Elected as moderator of the General Assembly in 1936, Master also served the World Alliance of Reformed and Presbyterian Churches as secretary for twenty-two years.

WILLIAM J. DARBY: The first president of the Cumberland Board of Ministerial Relief in 1881, Darby served the Board in a number of capacities until union with the PCUSA in 1906. He was also instrumental in organizing the Cumberland Women's Board of Missions in 1880.

J. LEIGHTON WILSON: A pioneer missionary in western Africa before the Civil War, Wilson was appointed secretary of the Executive Committee of Home Missions in the PCUS. He devised the Relief Fund in 1870 as a means of caring for dependents of deceased clergymen.

HENRY H. SWEETS: For nearly forty years (1904–1943) he provided the PCUS with leadership in the fields of education and ministerial relief. Under his guidance the Ministers' Annuity Fund was created in 1940.

ALICE L. EASTWOOD: A graduate of Smith College, she was one of the first women to serve on the Executive Committee of Christian Education and Ministerial Relief. From 1923–1949 she chaired the subcommittee that had oversight of ministerial relief grants.

REID DICKSON: Associate secretary of the Board of Pensions 1925–1937, Dickson succeeded Master as general secretary in 1937. During his leadership the Board experienced a financial crisis that brought it under extended examination by the General Assembly.

Following the retirement of Henry H. Sweets in 1943, the following four men provided the Board of Annuities and Relief and its predecessor with nearly four decades of leadership as Executive Secretaries (left to right): Wade H. Boggs (1943–1954), Charles J. Currie (1954–1962), George H. Vick (1962–1976), and Charles C. Cowsert (1976–1982).

DONALD L. HIBBARD: For twenty-six years (1946–1972) Hibbard was the chief administrator of the Board of Pensions. During his era the Board introduced medical benefits, life insurance, and disability payments and greatly expanded the Homes Program.

ARTHUR W. BROWN: President of the Board of Pensions 1972–1980, Brown worked closely with the new Vocation Agency to implement denominational reorganization and to improve benefits of the pension plan.

ARTHUR M. RYAN: Elected president of the Board of Pensions in 1980, Ryan continues to serve as copresident of the Board of Pensions of the Presbyterian Church (U.S.A.).

J. PHILLIPS NOBLE: In 1983 Noble became executive secretary of the Board of Annuities and Relief. In the new structure he serves with Arthur M. Ryan as copresident of the Board of Pensions.

Portraits of relief recipients appeared in a booklet entitled "Heroes of Peace," published by the Board of Ministerial Relief and Sustentation in 1914.

Mrs. Mariah E. McCune, a resident of the Aged People's Home in Pittsburgh. Photograph from *Women's Missionary Magazine*, April 1908.

Seal used by the Board of Ministerial Relief and Sustentation. Photograph from *The Presbyterian*, 17 March 1927.

Invalid Fund with a stipulation "that the General Assembly shall encourage and organize an effort to increase the amount to one hundred thousand dollars." The General Assembly directed the Executive Committee on Home Missions to organize a campaign to raise $75,000 in order to meet the terms of Robinson's will.[16] The committee appealed for money in the religious press and sent letters to each synod and presbytery asking their cooperation. After one year they had raised only $177. One committee member suggested that agents be hired to solicit funds but the General Assembly was in no mood to adopt such secular methods. It simply requested the Executive Committee on Home Missions to make another special appeal for "this very worthy object."[17] In 1884 the General Assembly abandoned the endowment project because of insufficient interest.[18]

A second abortive effort to raise a small endowment materialized in the 1890s. The General Assembly in 1894 appointed an ad interim committee to report the following year "touching the advisability of creating an endowment, . . . or of inaugurating some other feasible plan to provide a support for our aged and infirm ministers, and the families of deceased ministers."[19] The committee recommended in 1895 that the Executive Committee of Home Missions be authorized to raise a small fund of $100,000 for such purposes. The proposal precipitated a heated debate in which traditional arguments against endowment giving were reopened. In language reminiscent of previous discussions, a minister said, "I am opposed to the principle of laying up endowments to deprive future generations of the privilege of supporting the Gospel."[20] A motion to table the proposal was only narrowly defeated (75–78). By a vote of 92–58, however, the measure finally passed with the details of fundraising left to the judgment of the Executive Committee of Home Missions "subject to the approval of future Assemblies."[21]

The committee asked ministers to set an example by subscribing to the fund in cash or installment payments. Only three presbyteries responded to the request and their replies were negative. According to Home Mission Secretary Craig, "ministers generally showed no interest in it."[22] Appeals to the laity were equally unproductive. By the beginning of the twentieth century, the church had raised only about $2,000 for the endowment.[23]

As early as the 1860s Secretary Wilson had recognized that the Invalid Fund could not cope with the growing number of ministerial widows, many of whom had young children. He also knew that many were too proud to accept what they considered charity from the church's Invalid Fund. To mitigate this situation, Wilson proposed in 1869 that the General Assembly institute a "Relief Fund for the Widows and Orphans of Ministers at their Decease" patterned after a program already being successfully employed by the Free Church of Scotland.[24]

According to Wilson's proposal, congregations could provide an annuity of

$1,200 to the widows and families of deceased ministers by making an annual contribution of $30.00. Higher annual payments would result in correspondingly larger annuities up to a maximum of $2,400. In the event that congregations did not wish to participate, ministers could pay their own individual premiums and provide their families with the same coverage. The voluntary scheme did not discriminate on grounds of age, health, or number of years of service to the church. No congregation or individual, however, could establish claim to a full annuity until four annual payments had been received. If death occurred before that time, the family would be entitled to one payment worth four times what had already been contributed.[25]

Although most commissioners acknowledged Wilson's good intentions, they were concerned about two aspects of this Relief Fund. First, when ministers transferred to other churches, they forfeited their claims and would not be covered unless their new congregations chose to participate, which involved another four-year qualifying period. Moreover, if a minister became disabled, the congregation would then be responsible for him as well as his replacement. Many people felt that the continuing movement of ministers and the problematic "health retirements" would ultimately make the plan impracticable. Second, the Relief Fund had all the earmarks of a life insurance policy that was based on a calculated gamble of average life expectancies and promised at least to some participants more than what was paid in annual premiums. This latter objection proved to be the Relief Fund's greatest obstacle and embroiled the denomination in an extended debate regarding the compatibility of life insurance and Christianity similar to the discussions of the same subject a decade earlier in the Old School General Assembly. Moving cautiously, the General Assembly of 1869 referred the Relief Fund proposal back to Wilson for "further investigation and with a view to the perfection of the plan" and docketed the subject for a full hearing and vote in 1870.[26]

During 1869 and 1870 Southern Presbyterians exchanged views about Wilson's proposal at presbytery meetings and in the religious press. At first it appeared likely to win support despite its alleged association with life insurance. A.D. Converse, editor of *The Christian Observer*, enthusiastically called Wilson's proposal "the best plan yet devised." Unlike life insurance companies, Converse pointed out, Wilson's Relief Fund involved no commissions, no profits, no overhead, and the money received would be invested wisely "by judicious Christian men as a sacred trust."[27] The editor of *The Southwestern Presbyterian* predicted that Wilson's scheme would be "received with great favor by the majority of our churches" and gave front-page coverage to articles written in defense of it. "Dr. Wilson is a safe guide and advisor," he wrote. "Give the Relief Fund a fair chance!"[28]

Wilson himself wrote a number of articles in which he clarified his purposes and explained how his proposal would alleviate ministerial poverty. In response to the life insurance criticisms, Wilson avowed that his proposal "eschewed altogether the principles involved in the working of all of the life assurance companies." In contrast, he argued, his plan contained no health or age restrictions and promoted the welfare of all participants. "The plan sets out the principle that our church is a united body, and it proposes, not to seek the welfare of any particular class of ministers but the highest mutual interest of the whole."[29] Wilson also stressed that the Relief Fund would be a positive factor in recruiting ministerial candidates. "Many of our pious young men are halting and hesitating about entering the ministry on account of the almost inevitable poverty in which it will involve them and their families."[30]

Opponents of the Relief Fund countered that the concept was both impractical and immoral. Although most writers focused on alleged flaws in the Fund itself, some attacked Wilson personally, accusing him of "riding a hobby" and using his reputation as a foreign missionary to stir up support. One writer said that Wilson lacked faith in the providence of God and was spiritually blind to the life insurance features of his relief proposal. "The simple and perfectly obvious principle on which the Fund is based is that each party is willing to risk money on the contingency of death. It seems to me that it is worse to bet on death than on cards."[31] Another correspondent claimed that congregations employed a minister only for the time of his actual services and did not owe him the assurance that his family should be provided for after his death. He called for total faith and trust in God for care of material matters and closed by asserting, "Every true minister of Christ is already insured!"[32]

As the debate continued in press and pulpit, Wilson maintained that the Relief Fund would be a boon for the denomination. He admitted publicly, however, that he had not anticipated the opposition that his proposal had engendered. "I do not know that I have ever looked into a subject which has suggested such un-numbered and unheard of objections as have sprung up from all parts of the country." He challenged his opponents to do more than simply pick flaws in the Relief Fund. "If anyone can bring forward another system simpler, more effective and more acceptable to the churches, I would like to see him do so."[33]

When the Relief Fund came up for consideration at the General Assembly in 1870, commissioners recited the same arguments. Following a "protracted debate," the assembly authorized Wilson to implement the Fund when a minimum of 100 churches and/or individuals had agreed to participate. As a concession to some objectors, the General Assembly specified that neither it nor the Sustentation Committee were legally bound to pay annuities. Everything depended on the faithfulness of participants to pay their pledges and the ability of invested funds to produce sufficient capital to meet demands for payment. In addition, the assembly, concerned about the possible accumulation of capital in such a mutual fund, ruled that it should not be allowed to exceed $100,000 unless subsequent General Assemblies raised that limit.[34]

Despite strenuous efforts to generate denominational interest in the Relief Fund, only a small percentage of congregations and individual ministers enrolled as members. By April 1873, only twenty-two churches were paying premiums for their pastors. Sixty-six members made their own contributions or were sponsored by other individuals. Wilson attributed the negative response to the poverty of many congregations, the confusion of the Relief Fund with life insurance, and the active opposition of secular life insurance agents.[35] Although the General Assembly subsequently modified the plan to conform more closely to actuarial realities, denominational support never materialized. In 1876 the Standing Committee on Sustentation expressed its "gratification at the satisfactory condition" of the Relief Fund but recommended that since it could be successfully operated without ecclesiastical supervision, it should be placed on an "independent basis."[36] After several delays caused by legal technicalities, the General Assembly handed over the Relief Fund to the Clergy's Friendly Society of Baltimore which transferred it to the Presbyterian Ministers' Fund in 1890. At that time it had a balance of $53,949 and thirteen members.[37]

Following the demise of the Relief Fund, the General Assembly in 1885 considered the possibility of a "benefit fund" for ministerial widows which would not compete with collections for the Invalid Fund. William W. Murray, a pastor from Suffolk, Virginia, proposed the fund to the General Assembly after the idea for the project originated with a group of local elders. Murray requested permission to form a benefit association managed by three or more elders, each appointed from a different congregation. Each of these elders would serve as an agent to solicit names of people willing to pay a small sum every time a Presbyterian minister died leaving a widow with minor children. On notification of such a death, the agents would collect the money and forward it to a central treasurer for disbursement to the widow. All agents and committee members were to work without pay, and with postage and stationery as the only paid expenses. Under this scheme, Murray said, "we promise no stipulated amount but leave it to the broad charity of the church."[38]

In the debate that followed, most commissioners expressed satisfaction with the Fund's general intent but pointed out a number of objectionable features. "It makes no distinction between rich and poor," said one minister who feared that money might go to widows who had other sources of income. Another raised the issue of life insurance. "The Presbyterian Church cannot run an insurance program." Others doubted the effectiveness of such an uncoordinated group of volunteers, no matter how well-intentioned their motives. Any hope of implementing the proposal ended, however, when Craig, secretary of the Home Missions Committee and guardian of the Invalid Fund, expressed his opinion. When the July collections are taken up, he predicted, people will say, "I have just given to a minister's widow. I'll give less to the Invalid Collection." He opposed the idea because it would "mar the church's regular work."[39] The assembly disposed of the benefit fund by voting to table discussion.[40]

As the nineteenth century drew to a close, the PCUS recognized that its ministerial relief programs were inadequate. The Invalid Fund offered only minimal financial support for a small number of families. Efforts to raise an endowment had proved unsuccessful and other experiments such as the Relief Fund or the Mutual Benefit Association failed to win denominational approval. In 1899 the Executive Committee of Home Missions recommended that an ad interim committee be appointed to devise "a more adequate provision" for ministerial relief. This proved to be a turning point. From that report would emerge the first Executive Committee on Ministerial Relief and an expanded program.[41]

The General Assembly of 1900 met in a spirit of optimism at Atlanta's historic Central Presbyterian Church. Robert Q. Mallard, editor of *The Southwestern Presbyterian*, projected a bright future for the "New South." Mallard interpreted encouraging agricultural, industrial, and business statistics as clear signs of God's providential hand working in Southern history to move the territory from economic chaos to prosperity. He also reported concurrent impressive gains in evangelistic outreach both at home and abroad; for the first time in more than a decade the church could point to increasing finances and a growing number of ministerial candidates.[42] A reporter who covered the opening session in Atlanta described it in these terms: "Seldom has the General Assembly of our Church met under such favorable auspices. . . . The work of the Church has prospered in many ways during the year and the good reports are a ground of joy and cheer."[43]

Unlike other aspects of denominational activity, the causes of Ministerial Sustentation and Relief had little to show that year. Statistics showed that ministers' salaries averaged only $755.33 a year ($2.07 a day), three cents less per day than the average pay of a railroad fireman. Contributions to the Invalid Fund were up slightly ($33,856), but with 149 beneficiaries, grants averaged less than $100. Because of increased applications for financial aid, treasurer John Craig reported that he could provide only 83 cents for every dollar requested by local presbyteries.[44] Such salaries and relief annuities, elder John Munce told commissioners, made provision for old age or illness a "manifest impossibility." He called for an endowment "organized on the most practical business lines, similar to the pension plans becoming so popular of late among the great corporations."[45]

On a more positive note, the ad interim committee appointed in 1899 presented a comprehensive report which described a variety of relief, pension, and insurance programs currently in use. Distributed to commissioners in pamphlet form and introduced by chairman Francis R. Beattie, professor of systematic theology at Louisville Theological Seminary, the report received favorable coverage in church papers and made ministerial relief a prominent issue on the assembly's agenda.[46]

Beattie presented three distinct possibilities for the PCUS to consider: (1) a pension program supported entirely by the church or complemented with ministerial contributions; (2) an annuity derived from some type of insurance policy either through a commercial or nonprofit organization; and (3) relief offerings based solely on need or with an added factor of years of service. In addition, Beattie suggested three ways of generating income for this cause: endowment funds, congregational collections, and ministerial contributions. Although his committee was not prepared to offer a definitive solution, it recommended further study of ways to upgrade the denomination's ministerial relief program. Commissioners unanimously endorsed the report and requested a presentation with specific recommendations in 1901.[47]

When the General Assembly met in Little Rock, Arkansas, in 1901, the ad interim committee presented fourteen resolutions, all of which were approved. Heading the list was a recommendation for an Executive Committee of Ministerial Relief with a full-time salaried administrator. For the first time ministerial relief would stand on its own rather than as an appendage to Home Missions. The report also specified that a majority of the new executive committee should be business people who could provide expertise and guidance. Other recommendations called for an endowment fund campaign and more formal application procedures including medical certification of disability and written endorsement from presbyteries. Finally, the report suggested consideration of a contributory payment scheme by which ministers could provide funds for death-benefit annuities but left the matter open for further discussion.[48]

The Executive Committee of Ministerial Relief opened an office in Richmond, Virginia, with Russell Cecil, pastor of the Second Presbyterian Church, serving as chair and Samuel H. Hawes, a local businessman, functioning as interim secretary-treasurer without compensation. Because of strong ministerial opposition, the committee abandoned plans for a contributory pension program and recommended instead that clergy who wished to provide annuities for their dependents should purchase insurance policies. It provided assistance for disabled ministers, lay missionaries (both male and female), and children of deceased ministers. The executive committee's *Manual of Operations* specified that ministers were not eligible for relief funds unless they had served the church at least thirty years and had been honorably retired by their presbyteries.[49]

The executive committee's initial report indicated that more than a name change was needed to overcome ingrained attitudes toward ministerial assistance. Following custom, the committee at first continued to rely heavily on requesting contributions through church papers or circulars. Chairman Cecil noted that a circular asking local churches to pledge ten cents a member per month for a period of five years had little impact. "The majority of the churches made no reply to the circular whatever." Several substantial individual donations raised the endowment to approximately $4,000 but annual offerings fell $6,000 short of what the General Assembly had requested. Cecil argued that the Executive Committee of Ministerial Relief would not be a viable force in denominational life until it secured a full-time secretary who could travel widely and promote its causes.[50]

In August 1902 the executive committee hired Isaac S. McElroy, pastor of the Maxwell Street Presbyterian Church in Lexington, Kentucky, to be its first salaried employee. McElroy had previously served as financial agent for the Synod of Kentucky and had led Louisville Seminary in a successful $100,000 endowment campaign. Full of energy and enthusiasm for his new position, McElroy made a positive impact on ministers and laypersons alike as he visited every synod and many of the presbyteries during his first year of service. Newspaper accounts attested to his effectiveness. A minister attending the Synod of Alabama reported that McElroy made "the best address I have ever heard from one of our Secretaries—he is the right man in the right place."[51] A commissioner at the Synod of Georgia called the new secretary "a live wire" who "smartly electrified us before he was through."[52] Within eighteen months McElroy had organized ministerial relief committees in virtually every presbytery, charging them to channel information to local members of the denomination and to promote financial responsibility.

McElroy's labors quickly produced results. Between 1902 and 1904 annual offerings increased from $14,000 to more than $20,000. The endowment, which totaled only $4,000 when McElroy assumed office, expanded to $20,000 by 1904. He also secured a number of legacies that promised significant sums in future years. Moreover, the secretary reported that he was mounting a campaign to enlist the aid of "well-known millionaire Northerners" on behalf of the endowment. Among his list of possible benefactors were John D. Rockefeller, Andrew Carnegie, "and a host of others."[53] His annual report in 1904 asserted confidently that "these figures furnish good reason for encouragement and for profound gratitude to Him who hath prospered and blessed this very important work."[54]

Despite these outward signs of success, McElroy's frenetic campaign to elevate ministerial relief provoked complaints, especially from other executive committees. During his travels McElroy complained that the Executive Committee of Ministerial Relief lost income because it had been allotted July for its annual congregational offering, a time when people either were on vacation or less inclined to support church causes. Acting unilaterally, McElroy called for a special November offering, a month traditionally assigned to the Executive Committee of Education, an action not unnoticed by education officers. Also at McElroy's urging, the General Assembly appointed a committee in 1903 to consider a revision of benevolent collections. The committee recommended that the Executive Committee of Publication be assigned July because it was "better able to stand that month of the year." Publication officials protested so vehemently, however, that the committee reconsidered and recommended that the Executive Committee of Education take July and give November to Ministerial Relief. This generated yet another prolonged debate. By a vote of 77–73 the status quo prevailed, but not without implications for McElroy and his executive committee.[55]

In the meantime, McElroy's assertiveness continued to arouse opposition. Samuel M. Neel, pastor of Central Presbyterian Church in Kansas City, spearheaded a movement to diminish McElroy's influence by consolidating the Executive Committees of Education and Ministerial Relief. Largely through his efforts, two overtures requesting consolidation came before the assembly in 1904, one from the Synod of Missouri and one from Hanover Presbytery. They were referred to the standing committees on Education and Ministerial Relief, whose majority report favored the continuation of independent executive committees. A minority report urged that Education and Ministerial Relief be immediately united. Citing high operating expenses in maintaining two offices, and "feeling further that there is a real unity between the two causes," the minority report concluded that consolidation could be effected without loss to either program.[56]

In the ensuing debate, supporters of consolidation concentrated on economic factors—two secretaries, additional traveling expenses, and office and staff costs. Advocates of separate committees reminded commissioners of how the Invalid Fund had languished as an adjunct of Home Missions and warned that yoking Education and Ministerial Relief would cripple both causes. The assembly decisively approved the minority report and selected Louisville as the new site of the Executive Committee of Ministerial Education and Relief.[57]

Although McElroy's supporters thought he should be retained as executive secretary, committee members decided to look elsewhere. They chose Henry H. Sweets, pastor of the James Lee Memorial Church in Louisville, noted as being "one of the most active and effective of the younger ministers" in the Southern Presbyterian Church. He had begun a seven-year ministry in Louisville with a mission located in a cramped and dingy storeroom. During his pastorate, this mission grew to a 300-member congregation with a debt-free building and a large annex which provided reading, recreation, and bathing facilities for low-income neighborhood residents. Sweets also wrote "Practical and Illustrative Notes" on Sunday school lessons which were published in the

Earnest Worker and studied by church members throughout the denomination. After twice turning down the secretaryship, Sweets relented and embarked on what would be a career of forty years as chief executive of the educational and ministerial relief work of the PCUS.[58]

Sweets's popularity minimized the potentially negative effects of consolidation on ministerial relief activities. By drawing on his seemingly unlimited energy, he cultivated and enlarged programs initiated by McElroy. Nevertheless, educational responsibilities consumed much of Sweets's time and attention, especially after 1910 when the General Assembly added Schools and Colleges to his portfolio and made him executive secretary of Christian Education and Ministerial Relief. Although his accomplishments in that area were significant, they are beyond the bounds of this study. Suffice it to say that Sweets played a major role in influencing his denomination's educational enterprises.[59]

Sweets possessed a social conscience and an ecumenical vision. His "institutional church" ministry in Louisville that had provided a full range of social programs foreshadowed concerns that he would study throughout his lifetime. Additionally, his commitment to ministerial relief was an extension of his concept of social Christianity. He participated in the formation of the Council of Church Boards of Education and was host for the first interdenominational gathering of ministerial relief secretaries in 1913, an organization which would later become the Church Pensions Conference. This conference today fosters ecumenical cooperation among major denominations to provide more effective pension programs. The PCUS acknowledged Sweets's accomplishments in 1935 when he became the first executive secretary to be elected moderator of the General Assembly.[60]

Sweets began his career as executive secretary in modest surroundings at 410 The Urban Building in Louisville. According to an inventory taken in 1905, his entire effects consisted of "one roll top desk, seven office chairs, one Remington typewriter, one ledger, one minute book, and miscellaneous pamphlets and stationery."[61] Early on, Sweets traveled extensively, mending fences between advocates and opponents of consolidation and seeking revenue for both education and ministerial relief. Within two years he reported that contributions had been received from 1,703 churches, an increase of ninety-three over the previous year, and an all-time high for the denomination. In addition, gifts to the endowment for 1906 totaled more than $25,000, the bulk of which had come from one donor whom Sweets had interested in supporting indigent ministers. With these encouraging statistics also came assurances that ill-feelings engendered by consolidation were subsiding. Sweets assured his colleagues that "we have been able to carry on a more aggressive work."[62]

The executive committee had only informal relief policies at this juncture. Presbyteries recommended applicants on the bases of need and length of service to the church. Sweets had discretionary power to allocate funds and consulted the full committee only when cases deviated from normal patterns. When one minister was reported to be "in a dying condition," the committee authorized Sweets to forward a special grant "if after investigation it was found needed." At the same time it allocated $75 for an operation "if the patient lived long enough to have it."[63] In another unusual situation, which involved an appropriation for a divorcee, the committee ruled that it had no authority to grant money to "one divorced from a Minister of the Church, and on the further ground that this lady has grown children who are able to support her."[64] In most instances, however, charity prevailed over rules. "On account of the feeble condition, advanced age, and entire loneliness of Rev. Brown," for example, the committee awarded him an annuity of $700, well above the average of other recipients.[65]

Sweets also had to deal with the problem of the college and the assembly's home and school at Fredericksburg, Virginia. In 1894 the General Assembly had endorsed a home and school to provide educational facilities for the children of deceased ministers and missionaries without charge and for local residents with a tuition charge. Alexander P. Saunders, a former missionary to Greece, served as its first principal and president. To house the school, Saunders secured permission from the Virginia legislature to assume control of the Female Orphan Asylum of Fredericksburg which had been erected in 1834 but had closed during the Civil War. The school opened on September 4, 1893, as the Fredericksburg Collegiate Institute (later called Fredericksburg College) with seven professors and one hundred pupils, most of whom were local residents.[66]

From the outset Fredericksburg Collegiate Institute had financial difficulties from which it would never fully recover. At the end of its first year of operation it had a deficit of $3,000 and had borrowed nearly ten thousand dollars to purchase more real estate and furnishings.[67] Although the General Assembly sold the property in 1897 to local residents who administered the institution, it continued to provide tuition grants for children of deceased ministers and missionaries. Gradually it became a practice for widows to purchase small homes nearby and receive $100 annually for each child who boarded with them. Institutional and educational expenses became so great that in many instances the church paid more than $900 a year to maintain one family. This practice, Sweets insisted, was unfair, uneconomical, and needed to be discontinued.[68]

For several years the General Assembly vacillated regarding its relationship to the college and home at Fredericksburg. After turning the college over to private management, it reversed itself and repurchased the buildings and grounds at a cost of $18,000 in 1910. The assembly took this action against the advice of Sweets who recommended that the college be closed. After a careful inspection in 1911, Sweets supplied the General Assembly with sufficient information to warrant abandonment of the college program. The college had an endowment of only $200, inadequate buildings that were also in disrepair, and a lien on the property of $12,470. Sweets reported lax supervision of students, uneven application of rules and regulations, and flagrant violations in intercollegiate athletics. Some football players apparently were not properly matriculated, and one professor frequently dismissed classes in order to travel with the team. Sweets reported, "It is the opinion of this committee that it is not wise for the General Assembly to undertake the conduct of a college at Fredericksburg, as we are convinced that debt and confusion will constantly arise from such an attempt."[69]

Although resistance from college trustees and members of the Synod of Virginia delayed implementation of the report, the General Assembly finally decided in 1912 to suspend operations and sell the property. The assembly also adopted an official policy drawn up by Sweets that guaranteed equity for all ministerial relief recipients. "The Policy of the church shall henceforth be to give equal aid to widows and families of deceased ministers when in need of financial assistance irrespective of place of residence or agency through which help of the church is extended. The aid in every case being, so far as the church can give it, in proportion to actual need."[70]

Sweets's experience with the Fredericksburg community convinced him that communal living for elderly people was neither fiscally nor psychologically advantageous. Although the executive committee subsequently discussed the possibility of providing homes for ministers and widows, none were ever authorized. In rejecting this concept, Sweets listed five arguments: families should live (1) where it is least expensive and most healthful and agreeable to them; (2) where they can be near friends and relatives; (3) where they can be "free from the depressing effects of living in a community in which so many are suffering from the same sorrow"; (4) where they can have the supervision of local sessions, diaconates, and presbytery relief committees; and (5) where widows and children can readily find employment.[71]

Freed from responsibilities for the Fredericksburg facilities, Sweets proved to be an effective fundraiser. When he assumed office in 1904, the endowment was slightly more than $20,000. By 1920 it topped the million dollar mark and increased significantly each year. Encouraged by Sweets's progress, the General Assembly set a new goal of $2,500,000 in 1921 and declared that the endowment should be regarded "as an opportunity for special liberality, rather than as part of the regular budget."[72] Three unusually substantial individual gifts abetted Sweets's quest for funds. In 1905, Hugh T. Inman of Atlanta gave $100,000 on the condition that the PCUS would contribute $125,000 in a three-year period. The Presbyterian portion was in hand long before the expiration date. In 1916 George W. Watts of Durham offered $68,000 if the church raised $136,000 within the calendar year; this accomplishment raised endowment assets to approximately half a million dollars. Finally, in 1920 C. E. Graham of Greenville, South Carolina, proposed to give $200,000 if the church would contribute $400,000 and invest the total $600,000 to purchase the Heard National Bank Building in Jacksonville, Florida, which Graham had recently purchased from receivership. After initial hesitation, the executive committee accepted the challenge and launched a campaign that reached its goal within the specified time span. Later known as the Graham Building, the property generated substantial income to the endowment.[73]

With a growing endowment and increasing offerings, the executive committee upgraded its ministerial annuities annually until the Depression reversed the trend. In 1900 the average grant to a retired or disabled minister was less than $100. By 1910 it had doubled and by 1929 it averaged about $550. A generally good economic situation following World War I helped to make such statistics possible, but two other elements were important. First, in 1911, the General Assembly revamped the traditional schedule for annual benevolence collections. It assigned Ministerial Relief the months of December and April instead of July. Second, churchwomen began to take an active part in ministerial relief. Although Ladies' Aid Societies had provided boxes of food and clothing for retired ministers and their families since early in the century, it was not until the General Assembly approved a Woman's Auxiliary in 1912 that women's organizations became a significant factor in denominational benevolences.[74]

In other mainline Protestant denominations, women had organized on state and national levels during the latter part of the nineteenth century. The PCUS, however, opposed such organizations alleging that they were unscriptural and an affront to traditional societal patterns.[75] Despite this opposition, local women's societies proliferated, and eventually, led by Hallie Winsborough, churchwomen successfully petitioned the General Assembly in 1912 to approve a Woman's Auxiliary, one that would not constitute itself as something of an independent benevolence organization as did the women's organizations of other denominations, but rather would promote all church agencies and causes.[76]

To achieve this end as well as to monitor women's work, the General Assembly appointed a supervisory committee composed of the four executive secretaries and representatives of women's synodical organizations. Sweets cultivated churchwomen's support for both Christian Education and Ministerial Relief. The Woman's Auxiliary designated several of their Birthday Gifts, an annual offering begun in 1922 to commemorate the beginning of women's work a decade earlier, to Ministerial Relief. In 1930 the Birthday Offering of $55,137 originated the Hallie Paxton Winsborough Foundation in the ministerial relief endowment fund. Four years later the same offering, taken in the midst of the Depression, produced $30,000 to be administered by the Executive Committee on Christian Education and Ministerial Relief for assistance of home mission families, and another $20,000 to supplement reduced annuities then being given to retired ministers and widows.[77]

In addition to their Birthday Offerings, churchwomen played a pivotal role in creating and sustaining the single most productive fundraising program ever directed under ministerial relief auspices. As mentioned above, in 1910 the General Assembly designated December as one of the months in which the executive committee could solicit congregational offerings. While this seemed to be a better month than July with its vacations and poor church attendance, December was not without its own difficulties. Presbyterians traditionally downplayed Christmas observance as a "Popish practice" and discouraged parishioners from having special celebrations. As late as 1899, the PCUS General Assembly stated that "there is no warrant in the Scripture for the observance of Christmas and Easter as holy days, . . . such observance is contrary to the Reformed faith, . . . and not in harmony with the simplicity of the gospel of Jesus Christ."[78] In this context, Sweets and his staff were unable to generate large offerings.

During the Depression of the 1930s, annual offerings declined sharply. In the summer of 1933, a number of executive committee staff members met in Montreat to plan new strategies for the languishing December offering. Among those present were Alice Eastwood, Cornelia Engle, Irene Hope Hudson, and Margaret Lane. All agreed that a distinctive name and theme for the Christmas offering would enhance its effectiveness and encourage colorful promotional materials. They agreed upon the title, "Joy Gift," and the executive committee presented its new theme in the October issue of *The Presbyterian Survey.* "The Christmas service is 'come of age'. This year it bears the name, 'And They Offered Unto Him Gifts,' and its theme is that of Joy." Along with a Joy Gift stocking and other leaflets, the Christmas package included a book of Christmas carols and pageants.[79]

In time the Joy Gift became one of the most effective programs in the denominational benevolence program. Beginning with modest offerings, it has in recent years topped the one million mark. Through the years the Joy Gift has provided about 85 cents of every benefit dollar distributed from relief funds. Much of the success of the Joy Gift can be attributed to the efforts of PCUS churchwomen.[80]

In 1923 the General Assembly added three women to each of their executive committees in recognition of the effective work of the Woman's Auxiliary, even though women technically could not serve on such committees since they could not be ordained as ministers or elders. The assembly's decision came after an extended and at times acrimonious debate. Conservative commissioners opposed placing women on administrative committees as being unbiblical and leading eventually to the "ungodly practice of female ordination." Proponents prevailed, however, by a vote of 139–50.[81]

The first women appointed to serve on the Executive Committee of Christian Education and Relief were Madeline Pegram, Mrs. J. Gault Fulton, and Alice L. Eastwood.[82] Eastwood's connection with the executive committee was particularly significant. A graduate of Smith College, Eastwood early in her career served as an officer of the Woman's Missionary Union of Louisville Presbytery (1904) and later as secretary of the Synodical Auxiliary of Kentucky. One of the staff members who participated in establishing the Joy Gift, Eastwood assisted in educational projects and for nearly twenty-five years chaired the subcommittee that had oversight of ministerial relief grants. According to associates, she kept meticulous records and displayed personal concern for families with whom she came in contact. When restructuring took place in 1949, Eastwood became a member of the new Board of Education.[83]

Despite the important contributions of churchwomen and the growth of income, Sweets recognized that these measures were only temporarily expedient. Largely through his contact with the Church Pensions Conference, Sweets decided that the PCUS should adopt a contributory pension plan similar to other mainline Protestant denominations. Because many ministers and elders opposed such programs, Sweets moved cautiously in order to avoid controversy and dissension.[84]

During the first two decades of the twentieth century, commissioners to PCUS General Assemblies displayed little interest in adopting a contributory pension program. When the Presbytery of Chesapeake proposed in 1909 that the denomination adopt a plan similar to the PCUSA Sustentation Fund, a committee recommended rejection of the proposal.[85] In 1911 another overture endorsing ministerial pension at age sixty-five met a similar fate.[86] Sweets himself made no public response to such overtures until 1918 when he launched a three-year program to raise the endowment and increase relief payments. At the same time, he acknowledged that something more needed to be done if the denomination intended to prosecute a "statesman-like handling of this sacred and binding obligation." Sweets told commissioners that while the relief program should be continued and expanded, it was not a long-term solution. "It has been clearly demonstrated," he asserted, "that no static fund, of moderate proportions, will adequately provide pensions or annuities for an increasing class of annuitants. *There must therefore be a contributory plan devised*" (italics added). He requested and received permission from the assembly to gather actuarial data relative to the costs of instituting a pension plan.[87]

After studying the data, the executive committee reported in 1919 that because the problem was so "broad and intricate" it could not agree on the form a pension plan should take. Indeed, because the costs appeared to be considerable, the committee suggested "that with the light we now have, it appears that this business could be better cared for by the Presbyterian Ministers Fund Insurance Company."[88] The board later reconsidered its decision and recommended instead a Deferred Life Annuity Bond which could be purchased by congregations or individuals and paid for on the installment plan to provide a pension of $600 at age sixty-five. The Standing Committee on Christian Education and Ministerial Relief rejected the annuity plan and called for more study "because of the importance of the subject and the difficulty involved."[89]

In 1922 Sweets's annual report to the General Assembly discussed both practical and theoretical problems of a ministerial pension plan. Among other things, he noted that a large reserve fund would be essential. In discussing the question, "Shall we have Pensions?", Sweets admitted that "the pension idea" had not been fully justified on social, economic, or Christian grounds and that such a program might possibly lessen the appeal of ministerial relief, "a method founded on Christian ethics." Nevertheless, he offered some "basic suggestions," should the General Assembly eventually opt to develop a pension plan: well-defined plans should be laid, adequate funds should be in hand, and care should be taken that the relief program not fall into abeyance.[90]

Having raised the possibility of a contributory pension plan for six consecutive years without any definite recommendations, Sweets presented in 1924 principles on which a pension program should be based. He proposed adopting "in principle" a Ministers' Annuity Fund (MAF) which would provide a minimum annual annuity of $600 (maximum $2,000) upon retirement at age sixty-five. Congregations or employing organizations would contribute 7½ percent of total salary and participants 2½ percent. Disability payments, widows' pension, and assistance to orphans were also included.[91]

Having received from the General Assembly approval "in principle," Sweets and his staff worked three years to perfect the details of implementing the Ministers' Annuity Fund. In 1927, the executive committee's report received endorsement from the General Assembly, nine years after Sweets had first discussed such a program. Because several colleges and seminaries were in the midst of endowment fund campaigns, the committee agreed to postpone its drive to raise a $3 million reserve fund until January 1, 1930.[92] That postponement stretched out some thirteen years. "Black Monday," October 29, 1929, plunged the United States into the Depression that changed the country's economic history. Sweets alone seemed optimistic that the PCUS would make the Ministers' Annuity Fund a reality. After five discouraging years, he concluded his report to the General Assembly in 1935 with a challenge: "This big thing must be done soon. It is our great UNFINISHED BUSINESS."[93] Many commissioners wondered, however, if they would live to see Sweets's desire become a reality.

Part III
*Modern Pension Programs
1930–1986*

Chapter 9
The Board of Annuities and Relief

The Ministers' Annuity Fund is a sane, equitable Christian business plan of meeting an obligation laid upon the Church by its great Head and recognized by the Church in all ages.
—*General Assembly Minutes*, 1931

Even for an optimist such as Henry H. Sweets, the 1930s promised more problems than possibilities. Despite efforts to proceed with a "Mobilization Day" in 1931 that would launch a three million dollar prior-service fund for the Ministers' Annuity Fund, the financial campaign never materialized. In the throes of the Depression, Southern Presbyterians were in no position to donate large sums to the proposed MAF. By 1935 only $500,000 had been received, and pledges made in good faith had to be abandoned because of economic conditions.[1] Between 1932 and 1937 the General Assembly suspended all moneyraising efforts for the MAF in order to channel benevolence funds into areas such as missions and education. For Sweets it was a period of "watchful and hopeful and prayerful waiting." He assured his executive committee that while the situation appeared discouraging, "he was not yielding to it."[2]

Sweets encountered other obstacles in his quest to implement the MAF. Since most Presbyterians had little experience with the intricacies of a pension plan, it required time, patience, and money to promote its adoption. Moreover, many were reluctant to modify the simple relief concept. Sweets and his staff made repeated trips to synods, presbyteries, and local churches to attempt to clear up misunderstandings about the MAF. Including the mailing of explanatory literature and the placing of advertisements in church periodicals, Sweets estimated that by 1940 the executive committee had spent more than $250,000 interpreting the MAF to the denomination.[3]

Some of those to whom Sweets appealed, however, were convinced that the MAF was unscriptural, inequitable, and financially unsound. Both ministers and laypersons mounted campaigns to scuttle the idea, at times using questionable methods. One anonymous individual mailed pamphlets to every PCUS minister and called the commissioners who had approved the MAF "knaves and fools" because they had been duped by "politicians and dictators of the General Assembly who wanted to feather their nests." The writer concluded, "If you do not quit trying to run God's Church with your natural minds, you will do just one thing too many and cross the dead-line of God's patience, and He will snatch you bald-headed and speed you away to Hell aboard some flying machine!"[4]

Even those who avoided such language could be devastating in their opposition. South Carolinian Robert W. Jopling typified the ministerial resistance that Sweets encountered. At the General Assembly in 1931, he contended that ministers should not receive pensions based on what they earned but on what they needed, supplied by voluntary contributions from local churches and not from a denominational fund. Jopling advised his colleagues to "stay out of the Ministers' Annuity Fund, and in that way either kill it or force it to be revised and brought into harmony with the Word of God." Insisting that there were no Christian principles in the MAF, Jopling concluded, "Be not taken in by the witchery of great names, or by the promise of a $600 annuity, dangled before your eyes and the airy hope that by and by the Fund will increase your annuity to meet all your needs! Fidelity to Jesus Christ is worth more than all annuities."[5]

Despite these and other attacks, Sweets declined to respond even though private correspondence indicates that his patience frequently wore thin. When a Richmond layman threatened the PCUS with a lawsuit unless it immediately dropped the MAF, Sweets provided him with requested information and remained conciliatory in every letter.[6] To a friend, however, he confided, "To my mind, these are the meanest and most harmful criticisms that have ever come to me or to our committee. I know, however, that hundreds like this have been whispered over the church since 1930."[7] Nevertheless, Sweets believed that when people thoroughly understood the underlying philosophy of the MAF opposition would cease and the plan would be implemented.

Although economic conditions improved in the late 1930s, Sweets found it difficult to marshall financial support. In fact, some contributors asked that their money be returned because the MAF had not commenced on schedule. Sweets attributed such requests not so much to direct opposition to the MAF but to a resentment of the government's Social Security Act of 1935.[8] At the same time, the PCUSA Service Pension Plan was under investigation by the General Assembly, and PCUS ministers heard stories about speculative investments, unexpected modifications in pension regulations, and dissension among Pension Board administrators and employees. These developments in a sister denomination cast a shadow on the proposed MAF and armed its opponents with arguments that large pension programs were subject to corruption and misuse.

Sweets nevertheless pushed forward. When the General Assembly voted in 1937 to resume the MAF financial campaign, he worked indefatigably to raise the $3 million reserve fund. "I often work sixteen hours a day lately," he confided to a friend, "however, it has been the joy of my life and I have gone to this work like my friends go to the golf course."[9] Aided by several substantial pledges, Sweets reported to the executive committee in February 1940 that he had $2,230,000 in cash and the rest in pledges. At long last, the MAF, delayed by more than a decade of theological opposition and financial chaos, could begin to function. On April 1, 1940, Sweets's long deferred dream became a reality.[10]

Almost singlehandedly he had nurtured and promoted the MAF through nearly two decades of turbulent times. Congratulatory letters arrived from every section of the church, acknowledging his unique contribution to the MAF and praising him for his perseverance in the face of considerable opposition. One minister wrote, "I feel that the success of the MAF has been due practically altogether to your earnest, consecrated effort in its behalf." Another said, "I have never known anyone to stick to an undertaking so perseveringly, so cheerfully, and with more faith in the face of one tremendous obstacle and setback after another." A layman from Virginia concluded his letter with this optimistic observation: "I feel that this is a great achievement for the Church as a whole and that it will bring new inspiration and courage to every other agency of the Church."[11]

When the General Assembly met in 1940, commissioners gave Sweets a standing ovation. Some had discussed informally naming the MAF in Sweets's honor, but he quashed the effort by insisting that it was a cooperative achievement and that no one name should be permanently associated with it. The assembly honored Sweets with a gift of silver and later authorized a commemorative plaque to be displayed in the executive committee's offices.[12]

Sweets also supervised the implementation of a retirement program for lay employees, mostly single females who did not qualify for participation in the MAF. As originally conceived, the MAF included nonordained employees whose qualifications and types of services were similar to those of ordained ministers. Largely from the pressure by Home and Foreign Mission executives who did not want to enroll their large lay staff, the General Assembly in 1930 deleted references to lay members and later specified precisely that only ordained personnel were eligible for membership in the MAF. To accommodate lay employees, the assembly in 1942 approved the formation of the Employees' Annuity Fund (EAF). Like a similar plan in the PCUSA, the EAF was a money purchase rather than a defined benefits plan.[13] Despite efforts over the years to improve the EAF, board reports annually noted that most secretaries, organists, and sextons in local congregations were not members.[14]

With both plans in operation, Sweets retired in 1943 after thirty-nine years with the executive committee of Education and Ministerial Relief. He continued to serve the executive committee as a consultant for six years and from 1949 until the day of his sudden death on February 25, 1952, he remained active as a teacher and minister. One of Sweets's lifetime friends described him as being like a man rushing to catch a streetcar—always busy. Alice Eastwood, who served twenty-six years on the executive committee, concluded her tribute to his ministry with these words: "To his co-workers he was a constant inspiration and challenge and a beloved friend. The generations yet unborn will profit from his labors."[15]

Wade H. Boggs succeeded Sweets as executive secretary in 1943 and served in that capacity for more than a decade. A graduate of Davidson College and Austin Presbyterian Theological Seminary, Boggs came from a pastorate at the First Presbyterian Church of Shreveport. In addition to his extensive pastoral experience, he had served on the executive committee for a number of years and had worked with Sweets in implementing the MAF and the EAF.[16]

Under Boggs's leadership, the MAF struggled with a variety of financial problems in its early years. For one thing, because pledges to the prior service fund came in much more slowly than anticipated, it was not possible to grant retirees the minimum $600 annuity as advertised. Only two-thirds of the required $3 million was in hand when the MAF opened and by 1948 the deficit still hovered at $900,000 with pledge money coming in slowly.[17] In addition, salaries remained low in the 1940s, so it was difficult for ministers to accrue more than minimal pensions. A survey taken in 1949 revealed that the average salary of a PCUS minister was $3,315.42, with 700 having incomes below that average and 75 earning less than $2,000. In some instances, clergymen reported that they had no set salary or that congregations were two to seven months in arrears in their payments.[18]

Particularly at a disadvantage were Mexican American pastors whose small rural congregations were unable to raise the 7½ percent necessary for inclusion in the MAF. In 1940 the Home Missions Committee of the Synod of Texas reported that twenty-one Mexican churches could not make adequate contributions to the MAF, that ten ministers were paying the full 10 percent, and that the other eleven were unable to participate in the fund. The highest salary was $1,470 and the lowest $460 without a manse. On several occasions the executive committee designated 50 percent of Joy Gift contributions in Texas to build up a reserve fund for Mexican American ministers. In 1946 the Synod of Texas included in its budget a sum sufficient to cover the MAF dues from congregations unable to pay.[19]

The board supplemented inadequate pensions by utilizing relief funds and permitting retired clergy to earn income. In 1946 it secured permission from the General Assembly to use available relief funds to supplement MAF grants.[20] It also approved in 1949 a "temporary modification" of MAF rules to permit retired clergymen at age seventy to be employed by local churches under certain conditions. Monthly salary could not exceed $125 and incomes from all sources could not exceed the salary received prior to retirement. Congregations employing such ministers agreed to make payments to the MAF, but their contributions went to the general treasury rather than being credited to the minister's individual account.[21] The board subsequently liberalized these restrictions by lowering the age limit and raising the permissible income level for ministers who wished to serve as stated supplies or in similar capacities.[22]

In its first year of operation the MAF had faced another type of financial crisis when the Secretary of the Executive Committee of Foreign Missions, C. Darby Fulton, informed Sweets that Fulton's committee would continue its established scheme of providing retiring allowances from its own funds which he termed "more economical and better suited to our needs" than the MAF.[23] Without participation of the entire PCUS ministerial membership, Sweets feared that the MAF would face adverse actuarial consequences. In an exchange of correspondence with Fulton and other Foreign Missions administrators, Sweets tried unsuccessfully to convince them that their participation in the MAF was essential to the ultimate success of the denominational pension program.[24]

It took nearly four years to negotiate a compromise between Foreign Missions and the MAF. At first, Fulton proposed that only ordained missionaries who were employed prior to April 1, 1940, would be enrolled in the MAF, thus meaning that older missionaries would place a heavy burden on the MAF. Sweets informed Fulton that he was prepared to take the issue to the floor of the General Assembly if Foreign Missions persisted in its limited participation in the MAF. In a counterproposal, which was finally accepted by both groups, Foreign Missions agreed to enter all its ordained personnel but maintained the right to supplement MAF benefits with cash payments so that retired missionaries would receive the amount promised in the Foreign Missions manual.[25] Foreign Missions subsequently modified this agreement by transferring funds to the MAF in 1954 to provide ordained missionaries with higher pensions and in 1958 made sufficient accrued liability payments to enter lay missionaries and other employees in the EAF. In 1966 the Board of World Missions contributed more than $800,000 to enlarge the participation of missionaries, staff, and employees in the MAF and the EAF.[26]

Beyond these initial difficulties, low status limited the MAF's growth. Yoked with Christian Education and Ministerial Relief, it had neither the full-time leadership nor the visibility needed to expand its outreach. For a number of years General Assembly Ad Interim Committees had been studying the denomination's various executive, administrative, and promotional committees with a view to simplification and efficiency. In 1947 the General Assembly appointed a single committee to undertake a comprehensive examination of administrative structures and make recommendations that would "simplify, coordinate, and generally make more effective the total work of the General Assembly."[27]

In 1949 the committee proposed a restructuring that would reduce the various General Assembly agencies to five denominational boards: Annuities and Relief, Church Extension, Education, World Missions, and Woman's Work. Noting that the title "Board" departed from PCUS tradition, the committee affirmed that change of terminology in no way implied that the General Assembly had abdicated its essential sovereignty in matters of supervision and control. The change would, however, bring the PCUS in line with other denominations, promote interdenominational cooperation, and reduce confusion among constituents of the PCUS itself. After considerable discussion, the General Assembly concurred.[28]

In arguing for an autonomous Board of Annuities and Relief, the committee contended that the functions of Christian Education and Ministerial Relief were not naturally related; that the operation of an annuity fund demanded business expertise; that growing relief responsibilities would need active promotion. "This area of responsibility deserves and needs the undivided attention and careful administration which cannot be provided by the Committee with its multiplied functions."[29]

In constituting the new Board of Annuities and Relief, the General Assembly specified that its membership be composed of eighteen members, at least nine of whom would be laypeople. For the first five years, however, the term laypeople apparently was interpreted to mean laymen, a fact that did not go unnoticed by PCUS women who by previous assembly mandate had been represented on the Executive Committee of Christian Education and Ministerial Relief. While not raising the issue publicly, they conveyed their displeasure to board officials who responded in 1955 by appointing the first woman board member. In a letter to the nominee, Miriam Schmidt of San Antonio, a graduate of the General Assembly Training School in Richmond, Virginia,

Executive Secretary Charles Currie acknowledged that women felt strongly that they deserved a place on the board because of their long history of support of board causes.³⁰

The committee also recommended that the new organization "explore the possibilities" of providing ministers and lay employees with additional benefits such as health and life insurance. Although the committee did not believe that the PCUS should itself venture into the life insurance business, it thought that the board might be able to purchase group insurance at lower rates than any individual congregation or agency. This recommendation marked the beginning of an expanding program of life and medical insurance programs made available through the auspices of the Board of Annuities and Relief.³¹

After considering various possibilities, the board approved in 1951 a group life insurance program underwritten by the Home Life Insurance Company of New York which offered ordained personnel $4,000 coverage at a cost of $50 annually and lay participants $2,000 coverage for $27. The plan went into effect in 1952 following approval by the General Assembly.³² The board later added a major medical insurance feature that provided $8 for hospital room, $160 for "extra charges," and $200 for surgical fees. Members paid $82.50 per year to qualify for these medical benefits.³³

From this beginning, the board periodically improved its programs in order to meet the rising costs of health care and to provide a wider range of benefits. In 1959 the board became a pacesetter in the church pension field by offering retired members, both ordained and lay, major medical benefits comparable to those of active members.³⁴ With the introduction of Medicare in 1966, the board assumed responsibility for payment of supplemental insurance with funds from the annual Joy Gift.³⁵ In 1973 the General Assembly approved major changes in the MAF which included provision for retirement at age fifty-five, increased lump sum death benefits, educational benefits for surviving children, and improved orphan and disability benefits. Disabled members were not required to pay dues during disability, and annuity credits continued to accumulate until age sixty-five.³⁶

Even as it expanded the scope of life and health insurance coverage, the board resisted pressure to sponsor retirement homes and hospitals. In the 1920s Henry Sweets had proposed that the executive committee raise money to build a cottage for tubercular patients at the Southwestern Presbyterian Sanatorium in Albuquerque at a cost of approximately $12,000. Shortly thereafter, however, the committee decided that the proposition was too expensive and that PCUS ministers could be cared for individually.³⁷ In 1949 Secretary Boggs raised the issue of retirement homes, describing them as a "pressing need" for older ministers and missionaries. The board encouraged him to study the problem and report his findings but no such report occurs in board minutes.[38] In 1954 the board responded to a request from Donald Hibbard, president of the PCUSA Board of Pensions to join with them in a study of needs in the area of retirement homes and charitable institutions by referring the letter to the Board of Christian Education "since this Board [Annuities and Relief] sustains no official relationship to such institutions."[39]

The board also significantly increased the size of its retirement annuities. Hampered initially by small reserves, low interest rates, and minimal salaries, and influenced by conservative investment policies including mortality tables and interest assumptions on which benefits were based, the MAF grew slowly. Despite their fiscal conservatism, those responsible for the growth of the annuity funds in the 1940s took account of variable economic factors by periodically reconsidering investment policies. In 1944, for example, although directors established a limit of not more than 20 percent of total funds in common stocks, they agreed to reevaluate that decision "in the light of changing conditions as they occur."[40]

During the 1950s a sharp rise in interest rates and more creative investment policies under the counsel of the Trust Company of Georgia, including placing an increased portion of its funds in equities or common stocks, produced earnings in excess of those required to meet the contractual obligations to its members. These changes enabled the board for the first time in 1964 to issue what it termed good experience credits to retired and active members as a cost of living increase. During the decade 1964–1974, the board added eight credits, ranging from 5 to 15 percent of accrued credits or annuities. Members of the MAF received an 80½ percent increase and EAF participants a boost of 41 percent.[41]

The 1950s saw other changes in the work of Annuities and Relief. Largely through the efforts of Charles Currie, the board moved its headquarters from Louisville to a new Presbyterian Center in Atlanta in 1954. A former manager for Mutual Life Insurance Company of New York, Currie had wished to centralize the PCUS general offices for reasons of efficiency and economy. In 1950 he located property on Peachtree Street that was on the market for what he considered a bargain price. Currie convinced forty Presbyterians to sign a note for $1,000 each to acquire the property and secured financial assistance from the Trust Company of Georgia. The investment resulted in a substantial profit when later sold and provided the nucleus for the Presbyterian Center.[42]

About the same time the board also adopted a new administrative system with committees assigned to various areas of responsibility such as Finance, Relief, Insurance, and Presbyterian Center. In addition, the board formalized its policies regarding relief payments by introducing in 1956 an Income Assistance Formula. Under this system, people completed a confidential information form that indicated all sources of income. Assistance was determined as the difference between the formula and the income from all other sources. In 1956 the base figure was $1,000 for individuals and $2,000 for couples. By 1973 the support level minimum income for retirees had been raised to $3,300 for individuals and $4,800 for couples.[43]

In the early 1960s, with competent professionals handling the financial aspects of its work, board directors decided that the executive secretary should be an ordained minister who could meet the following criteria: this minister should have administrative abilities, be well known, be acceptable to all areas of the church, and be able to interpret the work of the board. The executive secretary, therefore, was to be one who had "lived" with church courts at all levels and had an understanding of "preacher psychology" in order to deal with ministers and families who had little knowledge of either the MAF, EAF, or relief procedures.[44]

Based on these criteria, the Board of Annuities and Relief selected George H. Vick to succeed Currie in 1962. Pastor of the First Presbyterian Church of Charleston, West Virginia, for nearly two decades, Vick was widely known and respected throughout the denomination. He would serve as chief executive officer for fourteen years, the longest span since the days of Sweets. During Vick's tenure, the board continued to expand its pension plans including eliminating the $2,000 maximum for a retirement annuity, initiating the previously mentioned good experience credits, introducing vested rights (permitting a person to leave the program and maintain credits already established), and significantly raising the limits of life and health insurance coverage.[45]

After nearly three decades of existence, the Board of Annuities and Relief had established itself as an integral part of the denomination. Having begun in 1940 under financial exigencies and theological criticisms, the board had improved all aspects of its programs, especially the MAF and EAF. Through its cultivation of the Joy Gift and other benevolences, it had sustained and enlarged the relief program. Even so, the board could not remain aloof from the changes and controversies of the 1960s, especially in social issues. Although this will be discussed in the next chapter, one issue should be raised here. It involved denominational reorganization and the board's resistance to proposed changes in its relationship to the General Assembly.

In 1969 the General Assembly created the Ad Interim Committee on Restructuring Boards and Agencies chaired by William Fogleman. After extensive study, the committee proposed to the General Assembly in 1972 a plan which included a fundamental principle that the denomination should be managed by a single board, the General Executive Board (GEB) (later changed to the General Assembly Mission Board or GAMB) which would be accountable both to the General Assembly and the denomination as a whole. One element in this new plan was the creation of a Division of Professional Development within the GEB through which the committee intended to relate all functions of enlistment, training, placement, counseling, retraining, relief, and retirement as they related to the professional resources of the denomination.[46]

In justifying its inclusion of the Board of Annuities and Relief within the framework of the Division of Professional Development, the committee contended that the relief function of the board would benefit from the experience of and association with the placement, mental health, and counseling units of the division. Regarding the MAF, the committee noted that the pension program operated "without significant guidance from the denomination" and that there were no General Assembly policies regarding retirement age for ministers except compulsory retirement at age seventy. Moreover, the committee continued, the denomination had no uniformly accepted minimum income for retired ministers and no standards of mental or physical health permitting early retirement. Decisions regarding such matters, the committee concluded, should be made by the whole church acting through the Division of Professional Development rather than being delegated indirectly to the Board of Annuities and Relief.[47]

The board issued an emphatic negative response to the proposal that would place it under the direction of a program agency of the General Assembly. Vick said his directors were unequivocally opposed to such a drastic and unnecessary change. "The Board's present relationship of direct accountability and responsibility to the General Assembly for the dimensions and performance of its task has historically proven to be the best," Vick responded to Fogleman. "We have no reason to believe that your committee would be interested in changing a structure which has and can continue to serve so many so successfully."[48]

At the 1972 General Assembly meeting, commissioners debated various aspects of the proposed restructuring. After a minority report that would delay restructuring was defeated, Robert Strong, a commissioner from Montgomery, requested the assembly to exclude the Board of Annuities and Relief from the new arrangement. In the ensuing discussion, board chairman John A. Fulton argued that the dollars of the MAF and EAF were neither conservative nor liberal and that the board should be directly responsible to the General Assembly without any program responsibilities. In addition, Vick noted that the board was not asking for special treatment but he warned that "many people will have to pay a tremendous price if a mistake is made." He called for an objective study to be made of the board's status before the assembly reached a final decision. The assembly appointed a committee of "impartial professionals" to evaluate the board's operations and to make a report to the next assembly. In the meantime, the board was exempted from any organizational changes.[49]

Board members organized to make a strong case for independence, asserting that the board would be less effective if the proposed administrative change became a reality. *The Presbyterian Survey* published a number of supportive articles during 1972 and 1973, including announcements that the board intended to recommend much larger pension benefits to the next General Assembly because it had been so successful in its management of funds. Most impressive was an article written by Gene T. Harpe, business editor of the *Atlanta Constitution*, who extolled the virtues of the MAF. Citing assets of more than $90 million and a sound investment portfolio, including government and private bonds, preferred and common stocks, and mortgages, Harpe wrote that the MAF is "safe, secure, liberal in benefits, knowledgeable in investments, and cognizant of its trust relationship . . . it adds up to an excellent annuity program."[50]

By spring 1973 the special committee charged with evaluating the board released its conclusions, unanimously recommending that the board of Annuities and Relief be exempted from restructuring. It termed the proposal to unite the board with the Division of Professional Development "tantamount to mixing apples and oranges" and stated that it would be "fiscally hazardous to impose on the Board of Annuities and Relief changes that may be financially infeasible." The MAF, the committee declared, is "functionally incompatible with other areas of responsibility allocated to the new Division of Professional Development."[51]

In appraising the board's current operations, the special committee commended its directors and staff for administering a quality organization. It noted that the board had developed a sound annuity program with a variety of insurance programs and was pursuing an investment program that had achieved results superior to those attained by comparable private organizations. Moreover, it had a highly cost efficient management process that handled claims promptly and effectively. Sensitive to changing needs and problems, the board had from time to time suggested program improvements to the General Assembly rather than waiting on resolutions from the church at large. The only negative observation was that the board had not "sold" its insurance programs as aggressively as its annuity programs nor had it offered adequate coverage in the areas of group life, disability income, and hospitalization.[52]

By the time the General Assembly convened in 1973, thirty-three overtures from presbyteries opposed joining the Board of Annuities and Relief to the new denominational structure. The committee report passed without discussion. The only question addressed to the Standing Committee on Annuities and Relief related to the composition of board membership. The Rev. Jacqueline Rhoades asked why no women had been nominated, noting that of a board of eighteen members only one was a woman. Although the assembly ultimately accepted the nominations as presented, a lengthy debate over the question of equitable representative of minorities and women suggested that other areas of controversy awaited the board in the following decade.[53]

Chapter 10
The Board of Pensions
PCUSA

Is the Service Pension Plan in danger of collapse? With all solemnity and sincerity which are in our hearts may I answer this question with a strong negative—The Pension plan is not in jeopardy.
—Reid Dickson, *Report on the Service Pension Plan*, 1939

Although extended economic "panics" and recessions had affected the Board of Pensions and its predecessors, none matched the intensity and duration of the Depression of the 1930s. Stock prices fell a staggering $14 billion on October 25, 1929; American Telephone and Telegraph lost $449 million, and the net worth of United States Steel declined by $142 million. By September 1932, nearly 5,000 banks with aggregate deposits exceeding $3.2 billion had closed. Businesses either failed or managed to survive bankruptcy only by severely limiting their output. National unemployment rose from 3 percent to 25 percent, the highest figure in the country's history. During the worst of the Depression, more than 18 million Americans sought emergency relief; many were unable to secure any assistance. In Philadelphia, a city in which the Board of Pensions held a large number of real estate mortgages, more than 80 percent of the city's 280,000 unemployed received no relief assistance whatsoever.[1]

Religious institutions also felt the impact of the conditions. The Depression forced some congregations to share pastoral services and to dismiss associate and assistant pastors and Christian education directors.[2] Even with staff reductions, congregations could not pay all or part of their pension contributions, and many ministers became delinquent in their personal share of payments. In response, the board in 1932 established "The Temporary Emergency and Relief Fund" with an initial base of $25,000 derived from undesignated endowment funds. At its first meeting the committee selected to administer the Fund approved grants of $7,470 to fifty-one individuals.[3] Before economic conditions improved in the 1940s, the board estimated that its relief program had cost the board approximately $830,000 in cash outflow and reduced capital for investment.[4]

Despite these conditions, reports in the early 1930s were reassuring. While acknowledging a "slight increase" in delinquent payments, Secretary Henry B. Master expressed confidence that the board's conservative investment program, based on advice from informed staff and outside consultants, would handily ride out the Depression. In 1932 he told General Assembly commissioners, "It is difficult to conceive of any combination of circumstances which is likely to result in a net loss to the Board over a period of years. There is reason to confidently hope that the Board will go through this period of almost unparalleled crisis without impairment of resources."[5] Master reiterated the board's promise to provide a pension at sixty-five without requiring retirement, saying that the policy of the Presbyterian church was "to this extent more liberal than that of almost all other pension paying agencies of which your Board has any knowledge."[6]

While other boards were cutting back, the Board of Pensions wrote of expansion. In 1932 it created the Accumulations Department to enable participants to earn extra pension credits. Members could deposit funds over and above their 2½ percent contribution to build an account supplemental to their pensions. With savings institutions closed throughout the country, the board offered what it termed "a secure program" of investments, free from the fluctuating and uncertain banking world.[7] Nevertheless, the board found few Presbyterian ministers with money to invest. Citing burdensome operating expenses and lack of interest in the project, the board phased out the Accumulations Department in 1944.[8]

In 1934 the board announced the establishment of the Employees Pension Plan (EPP) for full-time church workers, clerical, support staff, and other lay employees not included in the Service Pension Plan (SPP), as a substitute for the new Social Security legislation then under discussion in Congress. Along with other major Protestant denominations, the PCUSA lobbied vigorously against the passage of legislation that would include lay and ordained employees, primarily on the grounds of the separation of church and state. In a poll taken by the Board of Pensions, 98 percent of Presbyterian clergymen and congregational treasurers opposed government intervention in the area of pensions for church employees.[9]

The EPP differed significantly from the SPP. It required retirement (men 65 and women 60) before any pension could be received. It also demanded ten years' employment by the church before the participant received any benefits. More importantly, it was a "money purchase" or accumulation annuity type of pension rather than the formula benefit provided by the SPP. Neither the amount nor the rate of benefits was fixed in advance, and there was no reserve fund except for the 3 percent portion paid by the employee. The employing organization (not the Board of Pensions) underwrote the balance of the pension payments (6 percent), but the board accumulated, invested, and distributed the dues, acting as the organization's agent. Like similar programs begun during this period, the EPP had provisions for limited disability payments and a small survivor benefit based upon accumulated credits.[10]

Although the board repeatedly stressed the denomination's moral responsibility to care for its employees who were not covered by the newly passed Social Security Act of 1935, the EPP received little response. In 1936 the board reported only 413 members in the EPP, most of whom were employed by the General Assembly or one of the national boards rather than by local congregations.[11] In 1947 only 671 workers were covered with 88 of that number employed by local churches. Referring to these figures, the board report concluded, "It is difficult to protest against the extension of Social Security Pensions to our secular lay employees, while the church fails to make proper provision for them."[12] Acknowledging the ineffectiveness of the EPP, the board closed the program in 1951 when lay church employees became eligible for Social Security, and then the board permitted full-time employees to become members of the SPP.[13]

The Board of Pensions seemed satisfied with its investment program. Commissioners elected Master moderator of the General Assembly in 1936, a recognition not previously accorded a Relief or Pension Board executive. Church papers praised his ability to preserve the SPP in the midst of the Depression. The editor of *The Presbyterian*, for one, wrote, "No one has brought forth better fruit from his labors."[14] When Master retired in 1937, he was elected a member of the board and saw his close friend, Reid Dickson, associate secretary since 1925, named as secretary.

In his initial report to the General Assembly, Dickson reaffirmed Master's optimism about the board's financial status. "We have every expectation of the Fund continuing in the future to operate within the projections and we have a balance in the Fund more than sufficient to cover the reserves... and a margin for future contingencies remains." He raised the Board's commitment to continue its policy of paying automatic pensions at sixty-five regardless of retirement and described it as a "sound experiment."[15] There was no reason for commissioners in 1938 to doubt that the SPP's advertised policy—"Economic security is the definite plan of the PCUSA"—was justified.[16]

The denomination was shocked one year later when the Board of Pensions announced two weeks before General Assembly that serious financial problems necessitated an immediate change in pension regulations. Unless the automatic pension at sixty-five was immediately discontinued, the announcement read, it would be necessary either to increase pension contributions or decrease pension benefits, poor alternatives during Depression conditions. By requiring actual retirement at sixty-five in order to receive a pension, the board estimated that it would save almost 30 percent in expenditures because most ministers would choose to continue to work and make contributions to the SPP.[17]

At the General Assembly meeting itself, incredulous commissioners received a financial report that described a $12 million dollar drop in the market value of board assets and contained a warning from actuary George Huggins that unless the proposed changes were approved the reserve fund would be short nearly $3 million and future pensions would be jeopardized. Stated Clerk William Barrow Pugh revised the assembly's agenda to permit extended discussion of the situation. Although many speakers preferred the automatic pension at age 65, commissioners reluctantly approved the board's recommendation to disband it. By an almost unanimous vote, the assembly for the first time amended the SPP.[18] Although the board consequently remained financially solvent, its reputation suffered. As one minister said, "The Church did not, in plain language, get a square deal from the Board. It should have been informed of the situation long before it became a crisis."[19]

Defending the board's action, Dickson argued that circumstances had changed so quickly that he could not have notified the assembly earlier. Moving to another area, however, he claimed that the automatic pension at sixty-five had created unemployment problems for younger ministers. Dickson related that during the Depression it was not uncommon for older ministers already receiving pensions to offer to serve congregations for less remuneration than younger men. Dickson said that the $12 million dollar drop in the market value of securities was strictly a "paper loss" which would be recovered when conditions improved. According to his statistics, the board had actually written off only $121,000 in bad investments since it had begun to issue pensions in 1927. "With all solemnity and sincerity," he assured his audience, "the Pension Plan is not in jeopardy."[20]

The board's financial problems stemmed from two premises on which the SPP had been based, both of which seemed attainable but which never materialized: that the board could earn approximately 5 percent on its total investment portfolio, and that it would have in hand $15 million through pledges and gifts to the Laymen's Fund by January 1931. Because the Depression occurred as many pledges were coming due, by 1931 only $12 million in cash were actually available to the board for investment purposes. Eight years later the total had risen only to $12,788,000. Even allowing for poor economic conditions, if the board had received the full $15 million in 1931 it would have earned approximately $2,200,000 more than it actually did and perhaps could have avoided or at least postponed the crisis of 1939.[21]

The board's investment philosophy proved to be the single most important factor in its financial crisis. The original charter specified that investments were to be limited to those sanctioned by the laws of Pennsylvania and that no loans were to be made to any member or officer of the board. After the acquisition of $600,000 from the Centenary Fund drive in 1889, the General Assembly appointed a lay committee to establish more specific investment policies. The committee recommended three categories, approved by the General Assembly: domestic securities in which trust funds could be legally invested; first mortgages on improved real estate in cities; first mortgages on railroad corporations paying dividends on their capital stock. The committee also suggested that investment funds be spread out in various parts of the country rather than being confined to Philadelphia and vicinity.[22]

The board evidently adhered to its policy to invest "at the highest rate of interest that can be obtained with absolute security."[23] It invested heavily in real estate mortgages (about 70 percent of its portfolio in 1927) and high grade government and railroad bonds. Its few preferred or common stocks came from gifts and bequests and usually were sold when conditions seemed favorable. During the years in which the board was investing large sums of money from the Laymen's Fund in the late 1920s, the value of all types of investments was highly inflated. With the 1929 crash and subsequent bank closings, bonds were forced on the market and declined greatly in value. Although the board had reduced its real estate mortgage holdings to about 34 percent of its total investments by the mid-1930s, it nevertheless owned many properties on which it had to foreclose and accept a lower profit margin than the 5½ percent it had previously received.[24]

During the Depression, annual investment earnings dipped below the 4 percent the board estimated it needed to cover the actuarial expenses of the SPP and to support operating expenses. Hoping to make higher returns even though it involved considerably more risk to the principal, yet not confiding in the General Assembly, the treasurer and several board members purchased lower quality bonds. They also acquired a substantial number of common stocks subject to fluctuation in a volatile market. They bought some bonds after they were in default, anticipating that they might pay off well when conditions improved. For a while it seemed as though the board's adventuresome investments would be successful. A sudden market slide in 1937–1938, however, exposed the board's risktaking and caused it to propose the elimination of the automatic pensions.[25]

The board's report to the General Assembly in 1939 triggered a year of confusion and antagonism between board officials and plan participants which one minister characterized as a "whispering campaign" filled with rumors, charges, and countercharges regarding the financial status of the SPP. Staff members were deluged with letters and telephone calls from members who complained bitterly about the sudden change in pension regulations without adequate forewarning. Some correspondents charged the board with moral culpability, and others warned that they were considering legal action if they did not receive satisfactory answers regarding board policies and procedures. One dissatisfied clergyman claimed that board members were inadequately prepared to explain financial matters. "They come before presbyteries and have been quizzed on the floor, and they have revealed abysmal ignorance. So the boys have come from presbytery and said, 'Hells bells, if they don't know any more than that there must be something wrong.'"[26]

Concurrent with external pressures, internal dissent among the staff threatened to disrupt the day-to-day operations of the organization. An investigation in 1939 concluded that the treasurer was arbitrary and unnecessarily harsh in dismissing certain employees, that he expressed "an unkind and un-Christian conduct" with other employees, and called for his resignation. Before the year ended, five other key staff members resigned, including one person who had served the board for twenty-nine years. Despite efforts to keep the board's troubles from the press, someone leaked stories to several Philadelphia newspapers. One member of the General Council summed up his estimation of the situation; "Things are in a mess at the Board."[27]

When the General Assembly convened in June 1940, the board's reputation was very poor. Behind the scenes, candidates for the office of moderator promised, if elected, "to clean up" the Board of Pensions and restore order. The assembly appointed a committee of ministers and laymen with instructions to hire legal counsel and to conduct a thorough investigation of all aspects of the board's work.[28] This marked the beginning of an extended period of supervision of board management and resulted in the resignations of board members, the dismissal of another treasurer, and the eventual demotion of General Secretary Dickson to a field representative position in southern California.[29]

Under the leadership of John Timothy Stone, the committee held extensive interviews with board members, staff, and plan participants to amass data relative to the investment policies and financial condition of the board. In addition to financial testimony, some witnesses alleged that a clique of staff and trustees were controlling board decisions outside the normal administrative channels. Others alleged that the board had become ingrown with a network of Princeton graduates and Philadelphia family connections. In describing the investment activities of the then incumbent treasurer, one ex-staff member said, "He was strong on speculation and sometimes he hit it. Lots of times he missed it."[30]

The committee presented its 170-page report to the General Assembly in 1941. It criticized the board for its speculative investments and charged it to restrict investments to high quality stocks and bonds. While acknowledging that the Depression had been a major factor in the board's financial crisis, the committee nevertheless instructed the board to preserve principal rather than seek a high rate of return. It mandated the board to diversify investment advice both within and outside the Philadelphia area. A final recommendation, that dues be raised 1 percent to compensate for losses, was deferred for a year.[31]

Events at the next General Assembly indicated that "the pension problem" would continue. Commissioners defeated the referred proposal to raise dues by 1 percent and required the Board of Pensions to give ninety days advance notice in writing of any proposed amendment to the SPP. They appointed a committee to work with the board in polling members regarding alternatives to the existing plan.[32] Because resulting suggestions necessitated raising large sums of money for a reserve fund, the existing program was reluctantly maintained and the 1 percent increase in dues was approved in 1943. Dissatisfied commissioners appointed yet another committee to investigate the board's financial activities and to recommend changes and improvements in operations.[33]

This committee consisted of five laymen with expertise in the fields of investments, insurance, and law, who had no previous association with the Board of Pensions. It made key staff changes and assembled a new group of board members, and in 1945 gave the board its first positive endorsement in a number of years. "The Board of Pensions is in the main well organized and well managed—its assets carefully handled. With assets of more than $40 million," it reported, "this is, indeed, a financial activity of major proportions."[34]

As a result of this study, the General Assembly lowered the interest assumption to 2½ percent so that the board would not have to make high risk investments to cover actuarial reserves and operating expenses. Although this would lower pensions, the safety of principal was to take precedence over a high rate of return. It called for periodic reviews of the board's investment activities and an increase in lay board members so that there would always be a preponderance of business and financial leaders in the decision-making process.[35] In 1948 the committee told the General Assembly that the board of Pensions was in excellent condition and that it was convinced that the board with its present leadership required no further supervision. For the first time in nearly a decade, the board was not under investigation.[36]

Thereafter, board members and staff tended to be conservative in espousing change either in plan features or investment policies. They adhered to the General Assembly's unqualified admonition: be conservative when dealing with the church's money. As a result, the board was more cautious in its interest assumptions than any of the large insurance companies. Rather than take any risks to accrue higher returns, the board relied on high grade investments that promised steady income over a long period of time. If improvements in the program were deemed necessary, the board's policy was to request permission to raise dues in order to absorb increased costs.[37]

Despite its conservatism, the board made one significant change regarding its leadership. Complaints about the long-established policy of having an ordained minister as its chief executive officer caused it to decide to hire a "competent business executive" with a new title, Executive Vice President, to head up operations. The board's search committee deferred selection of a new executive, however, until the end of World War II when more candidates would be available.[38]

When that time arrived, the committee selected Donald L. Hibbard, who had earned a Ph.D. in mathematics from M.I.T. A former captain in the U.S. Navy, he had worked for the Aetna Life Insurance Company and had served as president of Parsons College in Iowa. Although he intended to stay at the Board of Pensions only long enough to stabilize the program, he spent twenty-six years as the board's chief executive officer, retiring in 1972.[39]

Hibbard endeavored through improved communication to help the board regain its image as a reliable trustee of funds. Annual reports thus avoided technical language and used charts, graphs, and specific examples of how proposed changes would affect the individual. Hibbard also supervised a complete rewriting of SPP regulations, replacing legal terminology with more direct language. In addition, he periodically distributed free brochures such as "Federal Income Tax Information for Clergymen" and "How to Organize a Savings Plan" that evoked favorable responses from ministers.[40]

Hibbard believed that the board itself had a responsibility not simply to administer the SPP but also to initiate revisions, so he appointed a research committee to review policies. He led the board to have its work evaluated periodically by qualified independent research agencies to ascertain how its constituency felt about the administration of the SPP. Conducted by the University of Michigan Research Center in 1960, the first study indicated programmatic strengths and weaknesses that prompted proposed changes to the pension and welfare programs.[41]

Measured improvements to the SPP were in keeping with the General Assembly's mandate for the board to proceed cautiously. The board added group life insurance, increased disability benefits and widows' benefits, and in 1948 introduced educational grants for minor children attending college. Although it considered incorporating a major medical feature into the SPP, it did not do so primarily because the cost factor was difficult to estimate. As a temporary measure, the board in 1956 offered to aid member families whose medical expenses in any one year exceeded 10 percent of their total income with grants from the Welfare Fund, assisted when possible by the presbytery or employing organization.[42]

The introduction of a major medical plan came after the merger in 1958 with the United Presbyterian Church of North America strengthened the board's resources. Retirement pensions also increased in the united church with the UPNA's higher rate of calculating credits being adopted. To assure former UPNA ministers that they would receive larger benefits than promised, the board introduced a new special apportionment feature, the first of its kind among denominational pension plans. This provided that if operating margins developed in excess of the required actuarial reserves, the excess was to be distributed to members in fully funded benefits. The first such apportionment, 9 percent, became effective on January 1, 1964; a subsequent apportionment of 16.81 percent followed in 1971.[43]

The board's new major medical plan paid 80 percent of medical costs for a member and his/her family after the member had paid an amount equal to 5 percent of her/his annual salary. Included were hospitalization, x-rays, operating room costs, surgeons' fees, nursing costs, and drugs. The maximum lifetime benefit was set at $10,000 but later was extended.[44] Beginning September 1, 1962, the board established an arrangement with the Menninger Foundation in Topeka, Kansas, to provide diagnostic psychological examinations for members provided they pay transportation costs and $100 toward medical fees.[45]

Although the major medical plan met with general approval, the board received complaints that the deductible was too high and disability and death benefits too low. After requesting specific suggestions for improvement, the board proposed a major revamping of the SPP in 1968. Along with increased disability and educational benefits, the board proposed salary continuation benefits for widows or survivors for one year up to a maximum of $10,000 and extension of major medical coverage for one year after retirement.[46] Two years later it increased disability payments to 60 percent of salary with a $7,200 yearly maximum, lowered the medical deductible from 5 percent to 2 percent and paid for 100 percent of all hospital charges up to $1,000 and 80 percent thereafter. It also introduced increased death benefits to survivors formulated on a sliding scale based on age at time of death.[47]

Despite these improvements, many pensioners, especially those who had retired prior to participation in Social Security (1955) and whose salaries had been low, continued to receive inadequate pensions.[48] Ministers who retired in 1952 had an average pension of $799.55 and their widows only $331.86. Almost 1,900 ministers received less than $1,200 and nearly 3,000 widows collected less than $600 a year. The board estimated that about 25 percent of those individuals were wholly dependent on their pension incomes and needed special assistance from the denomination.[49] At the board's request, the General Assembly concluded that funds had to be diverted from other boards and agencies in order to increase pensions to an adequate level. Although funds never fully matched needs, supplements to low-income pensioners were first paid in 1956 from General Mission funds. By the mid-1960s, approximately

$1,000,000 per year was being divided among two to three thousand family units with inadequate pensions. The General Council proposed that pension dues be increased 2 percent and the additional income, about $2 million, be distributed among the lower-range pensioners. The board rejected this on the basis that such an action constituted an assessment tax for benevolence purposes and was therefore unconstitutional.[50]

Another suggestion for coping with inadequate pensions was that the board distribute equal pensions regardless of earned income. In a response to the General Assembly on the question of compensation and pensions, the board noted that ministerial salaries ranged from almost zero (national missionaries subsidized by the board) to approximately $30,000. If equality of pensions were to be immediately introduced, all widows would receive about $480 and all married couples about $960 annually, thus reducing every pensioner to a "needs basis." The board called attention to the fact that the Pension Plan already had equalization features—permanent disability was a flat amount and the salary continuation benefit had a limit of $7,500, later raised to $10,000, so that lower salaried widows might well receive a higher percentage of their husbands' annual salaries than widows of higher salaried ministers. The report concluded that the long-range solution was not equal pensions but an increase in denominational salaries.[51]

Along with the expansion of the SPP, the board developed guidelines for its welfare (or relief) program. In 1948, it created the Ministers' Emergency Relief Fund which granted aid on a dollar for dollar basis with matching funds from local churches and presbyteries. In 1952 the General Assembly provided additional welfare money and recommended that the Emergency Fund be used in cases of financial distress or when extended assistance was required. The board gave it a new title, Welfare Fund (later Assistance Fund), but the process remained essentially the same. The presbytery provided one dollar for each dollar from the Fund, and, if the local congregation was involved, the presbytery, congregation, and board each provided one-third of the assistance. In special situations, the entire amount could be drawn from the Fund. During the first year of its existence, with approximately 24,000 individuals eligible for aid, only forty-three persons requested funds, and a number of these attempted to pay back some of the money. By 1972 the total amount paid from the board's Assistance Fund was $252,610 with the average total grant of $1,157 to 427 families.[52]

Earlier in this volume, we described the development of the Homes Program, begun in the late nineteenth century with the opening of a ministerial retirement home in Perth Amboy, New Jersey. This program grew rapidly between 1955 and 1972, though earlier it had consisted only of four congregate homes, the largest of which had twenty residents in 1947, and the Ministers' Cottage for tuberculosis patients in Albuquerque, New Mexico. By the board's own admission, the congregate homes were inefficient in terms of operating costs and unattractive to potential residents, who tended to view them as poor houses.[53] A 1948 study recommended the creation of a responsible agency to supervise all homes, hospitals, and orphanages.[54] It also suggested that the homes program be diversified, offering alternatives to the congregate model, such as apartment rentals or ownable homes clustered around a main building containing medical and social assistance. Above all, it recommended that new homes should be located in residential or city-center locations so that residents could participate in social and cultural activities.

The General Assembly in 1949 established the Division of Welfare Agencies, linking it administratively to the Board of Pensions. The division's executive, John Park Lee, visited retirement homes throughout the country, attended conferences on social welfare, and kept Presbyterian institutions informed about new developments. He drew up uniform standards for Presbyterian-related homes and hospitals and organized the National Presbyterian Health and Welfare Association. The association assisted professionals and staffs in developing their skills and in relating more effectively to the denomination, and it promoted higher standards of operation and increased cooperation with other religious, secular, and governmental welfare agencies. The General Assembly transferred the division to the Office of Health and Welfare of the Board of National Missions in 1959.[55]

The Board of Pensions presented an outline of its new Homes Program in 1955 and had it in operation by the early 1960s. Surveys of Presbyterian ministers indicated that about 3 percent of clergy and widows preferred or needed a congregate-type home with separate living quarters but a central dining room. The board built three congregate homes: Plaza del Monte, Santa Fe (1961); the Mid-Continent Home, Kansas City (1967); and Prentiss House, Philadelphia (1971). As the new buildings became available, the older congregate homes were gradually closed: the L'Amoreaux Home in 1953, the Thornton Home in 1967, the Merriam and Haywood Homes in 1970, and finally Fynmere in 1974.[56]

Beginning with a cluster of modest homes (Morganwood, in Swarthmore, Pennsylvania, in 1957), the board built similar units for independent living in Lakeland, Florida; Santa Fe, New Mexico; Topeka, Kansas; Portland, Oregon; and Los Gatos, California. It also advertised its willingness to accept gifts of individual homes provided that the board retain the right to sell the home if it was unsuitable for its purposes. The first two donations came from Wichita, Kansas and Waverly, New York in 1961; by 1972, 135 houses or apartments located in ten different states had been accepted.[57]

Two experimental projects were discontinued because of inadequate response. In 1961 the board purchased and located ten trailers in St. Petersburg, Florida, within access to public transportation. Designed for ministerial and missionary couples during extended periods of convalescence, few people actually used them. They were sold in 1966 with proceeds going toward building six apartments in Lakeland, Florida.⁵⁸ The second experiment responded to concerns that minorities were not taking advantage of available housing opportunities. The board opened the United Presbyterian Apartments in Atlanta in 1973, hoping to attract black residents as well as others who might want to live in that locale. This facility never maintained capacity occupancy and was sold five years later.⁵⁹

As time passed, the board adapted its Homes Program to its constituency. In 1974 it took over management of Westminster Gardens in California, a retirement home for missionaries developed by the Commission on Ecumenical Mission and Relations (COEMAR). Other changes in recent years have included the sale of the Mid-Continent Home to the United Presbyterian Foundation of Kansas in 1975 and the closing of Philadelphia's Prentiss House in 1985. To meet the increased demands for independent living facilities, the board in 1977 purchased seventeen individual condominium units in the Imperial Southgate Villas Condominium Association in Lakeland, Florida, and has continued to expand its holdings of donated private homes.⁶⁰

The board also developed some nursing care services. In 1953 the board arranged with Desert Mission Inc., of Phoenix, Arizona, and St. Barnabas Hospital in New York City to care for chronically ill ministers and widows. At the Thornton Home in Newburg, Indiana, the board also established an infirmary consisting of a fully equipped facility for twelve patients. More recently, the board has arranged for priority use of nursing care beds in the Florida United Presbyterian Homes and the Philadelphia Presbytery Homes. Plaza del Monte in Santa Fe also has a contract for nursing with the Presbyterian Medical Services, Incorporated, in Santa Fe.⁶¹

Along with changes in its pension, assistance, and homes program the board also modified its investment policies. The board decided in 1963 to have a New York City bank handle all its investments, reserving the right of review by the board's Finance Committee.⁶² In 1972 it split total investments among three banks (about $100 million each) whose performance records were considered to be among the best in the country: Morgan Guaranty Trust Company of New York, the United States Trust Company of New York, and the National Bank of Detroit.⁶³

Perhaps the most significant shift in investment policies during the Hibbard administration was an increase in the anticipated rate of annual earnings and the inclusion of a larger percentage of common stocks in the portfolio. Because the interest rate of 2½ percent, set in 1954, was raised to 3 percent in 1966, the board was not required to hold as much money in reserve to pay pension benefits and could more readily issue special apportionments.[64] The board increased the amount of its assets invested in common stocks from about 10 percent in 1946 to almost 70 percent in 1970. Although the current yield of these investments was lower than that obtainable in fixed income investments such as government bonds, it had a potential growth in dividends and capital that could benefit plan participants.[65]

Another influence on investment policies during the 1960s was questions raised concerning the morality of supporting companies and corporations that practiced racial discrimination. The Commission on Religion and Race (CORAR), established in 1963, issued a "Desegregation Policy Statement" that urged affirmative action for desegregation by utilizing economic pressure in the purchase of goods and services, rental leases, and investments.[66] The Board of Pensions, as well as the United Presbyterian Foundation, resisted efforts of CORAR to engage them in such issues. The board wrote to the commission that while it was willing to take "constructive and positive action to implement policy statements," it was unwilling to do anything that could be interpreted as being financially irresponsible. Raising a number of practical problems, including the possibility of law suits, the board promised to be sensitive to racial justice issues but did not commit itself to any specific economic actions.[67]

In 1968 the assembly instructed its boards and agencies to invest 30 percent of their undesignated funds in minority owned and operated businesses in low income areas of the country. After securing legal counsel, the board agreed to provide $267,000 from its Assistance Fund rather than from monies specifically designated for the SPP. Although the board expressed concern that such an investment might limit its assistance, it endorsed in principle the purpose of the project and requested an annual report.[68]

One other development in the early 1970s had an impact on the board's relationship with the denomination. The first major reorganization of boards and agencies since 1923 occurred in 1972. Along with creating fourteen regional synods, the General Assembly approved a new General Assembly Mission Council (GAMC) responsible for coordinating the plans of basic mission objectives. In addition, the new structure included an Office of Equal Opportunity and Employment, a Council on Church and Race, a Council of Theological Seminaries, and three mission agencies: The Program Agency, the Vocation Agency, and the Support Agency. The Board of Pensions continued as a separate management body but was linked programmatically to the Vocation Agency. The president of the Board of Pensions functioned as the director of the Division of Personnel Assistance and Pensions of the Vocation Agency, thus relating the board more directly to the total vocational program. The board's annual report to the General Assembly henceforth would come through the Vocation Agency, which had the right to comment on the report but not to amend it.[69]

As the Hibbard era drew to a close, the Board of Pensions was receiving mixed reviews. A survey conducted by the Institute for Social Research at the University of Michigan in 1970 indicated a decrease of between 14 and 24 percent in the proportion of each sample group that thought the board was "doing a very good job" since the survey a decade earlier. Moreover, the proportion of those who thought the board was "not doing an adequate job" had about doubled. The most frequent comment called for better, more effective communication between the board and those whom it served. One woman commented, "I have not yet gotten over the shock of the letter I received adjusting my monthly pension starting the day before my husband died!"[70]

Of the plan itself, the general pattern was one of acceptance with little enthusiasm and dissatisfaction with little real discontent. The most widely endorsed change (82 percent of active and retired ministers) was that those with lower salaries should get pensions proportionately higher in relation to their incomes than those receiving higher incomes. A significant number (35 percent) wanted more coverage in the face of escalating medical costs. As the survey was being conducted, the board was actively working on both these problems although it anticipated no simple, effective solutions.[71]

Dissatisfaction with the board's performance surfaced at the General Assembly in 1972 when commissioners considered an overture from the Presbytery of Central Washington that charged that certain provisions of the SPP discriminated against female members by denying to their survivors benefits provided for male members.[72] After considerable debate, the assembly by a vote of 303-231 ordered an independent investigation of the board's basic philosophy, organization, and operating policies. On recommendation of the General Council, the assembly instructed the Vocation Agency to forward specific recommendations.[73]

After twenty-six years as chief executive of the Board of Pensions, Donald Hibbard retired in 1972. Board President Herbert B. Anderson praised Hibbard for protecting the financial integrity of the pension plan and designing it to provide flexibility. During his tenure, Hibbard raised retirement pensions, increased medical protection, and expanded its homes and assistance programs.[74] The board's carefully cultivated conservatism, however, although in part a response to pressures from General Assemblies in the 1940s and 1950s, raised questions in an age of rapid social change and rampant inflation. In the decade that followed, the discussion of these two issues would continue.

Chapter 11
A Decade
of Controversy and Change
1973-1983

Now don't give me the old malarkey about pension plans being tied to actuarial percentages. Don't tell me we cannot change our system. We made it; we can change it.
—*Monday Morning Magazine*, 1980

Both the United Presbyterian Church in the U.S.A. and the Presbyterian Church in the U.S. made significant adjustments between 1973 and 1983 as they attempted to adapt to social, economic, political, and theological change. General Assemblies were rarely routine as commissioners debated such issues as sexual equality, social responsibility through investment policies, peacemaking, poverty, and aging. Both denominations faced challenges from conservative coalitions that called for a spiritual renewal primarily through evangelistic outreach. Although this period cannot yet be definitively assessed, it undoubtedly set priorities for the reunited church—the Presbyterian Church (U.S.A.), which dates from 1983.

During this decade the Board of Pensions (UPCUSA) and the Board of Annuities and Relief (PCUS) on a number of occasions were questioned by the General Assemblies about their operational policies. Moreover, a variety of denominational interest groups wanted the elimination of what they considered inequities in the retirement plans. Leaders of the boards themselves initiated modifications of programs and policies. The resulting tensions, some of which are unresolved, provide the framework for discussing this decade of controversy and change.

Although the Board of Annuities and Relief retained its independent status in the PCUS reorganization, the Board of Pensions became a part of the Vocation Agency in the new UPCUSA structure. Immediately a Consulting Committee on Pensions was appointed to investigate concerns about the board expressed by various groups at the General Assembly in 1972. The committee specifically studied four overtures from 1973, relating to inadequate pensions, widows' benefits, medical coverage, and sexual discrimination. Representative in its composition, the Consulting Committee was chaired by Professor Dan M. McGill, chairman of the Department of Insurance, the Wharton School, the University of Pennsylvania. One of the foremost academicians in the field of pension research, McGill's *Fundamentals of Private Pensions* is considered the basic work in its field.[1]

After analyzing the existing program, the committee drafted certain principles to direct the board's overall work, some axiomatic to any pension plan but others reflecting areas of ongoing controversy. One principle specified that although differences in economic status established during a participant's active ministry should carry over into retirement, the plan should provide certain minimum benefits irrespective of previous salaries. Another stated that the assets of the plan must be segregated from other church funds to assure their exclusive use for meeting benefit commitments. The committee further maintained that the board's investment portfolio should be structured to provide maximum returns, although it acknowledged that management of such a portfolio should be sensitive to social, political, and moral judgments.[2]

When the Consulting Committee made its final report to the UPCUSA General Assembly in 1974, it affirmed that the basic structure of the Pension Plan was sound and that its benefits, on the whole, compared favorably with those provided by other denominations and comparable organizations. The committee recommended three improvements. First, it proposed that the General Assembly approve a minimum retirement benefit that would help people whose pension credits had accrued when salaries were extremely low. The annual benefit proposed was $80 multiplied by the number of years for which dues were paid. Introducing this minimum would increase the pension payments of approximately two-thirds of the participants. Benefits of these participants averaged only $1,317 a year at this time. Second, the committee proposed changing the "widow's benefit" to a "survivor's benefit," thus rectifying a disparity in the treatment of male and female members. The survivor's benefit was extended to include spouse, unmarried minor children, and dependent parents or siblings, when applicable. In addition, it permitted spouses to remarry after age sixty without loss of pension. Third, in response to complaints that the medical benefits had gaps that forced members to take out supplemental insurance, the committee agreed that the plan should pay 100 percent of reasonable and customary charges with a deductible of 2 percent of a participant's annual income. It proposed a provision for a supplement to Medicare at a minimal cost to pensioners and raised disability benefits. The General Assembly adopted all the recommendations.[3]

Concerns continued to be raised with both boards. For example, in the PCUS, the Committee on Women's Concerns petitioned the General Assembly in 1975 to seek both church and secular advice on alternate ways to provide equal benefits for men and women in the Employees' Annuity Fund. Because women tended to outlive men, their monthly pensions, based on the same dues at the same ages as men, were smaller in order to cover a longer anticipated life span. After considerable study, the Board of Annuities and Relief modified the EAF to equalize payments for male and female members. In 1978 all annuities paid to female members increased by 13 percent without any corresponding increase in contributions, and future accrued benefits were to be calculated without regard for the greater longevity of females as a group.[4]

A related issue was the provision of pension benefits for divorced spouses of the Board of Pension's plan members. In 1975 the Board of Pensions concluded that the type of aid required was within the scope of its Assistance and Homes Program and that no new program was required.[5] In 1976, the Board of Annuities and Relief dealt with a similar request by referring it to the Standing Committee on Church Order and Vocations. While noting that it was "sympathetic to the legal and economic situation of ex-spouses of PCUS members," the board did not deem it feasible to act. It promised, however, to monitor what other denominations were doing.[6] An overture from the National Capital Union Presbytery in 1978 asking that spouses of clergypersons be accorded "some pension equity commensurate with the careers they have shared with their clergy husband or wife" caused the boards to reconsider their previous actions.[7]

This question came before both boards, and each moved cautiously before responding. The Board of Pensions first suggested that a member could *elect* to convert a portion of her/his accrued benefits to the divorced spouse. The board's legal counsel advised against such action, because it would jeopardize the exemption from federal estate tax and state inheritance tax that plan beneficiaries presently held.[8]

After similar studies by the Board of Annuities and Relief, the PCUS General Assembly approved an amendment to the Ministers' Annuity Fund that permitted payments to eligible surviving divorced spouses under specified conditions. The board agreed in 1982 that it would honor any court-approved survivor divorce settlement that provided a benefit for a divorced spouse. As long as the plan member was alive, however, payments would be made directly to him/her, and it would be the member's obligation to fulfill the terms of the settlement. If the member died, the payment would be the normally accrued benefit at the time of the divorce, and any new spouse would have her/his payment reduced by that amount. Although some commissioners thought that the board should pay the divorced spouses directly, the board maintained that the legal problems involved were too complex: "Divorce proceedings are matters for civil authorities and the Board should not become involved therein."[9]

The most prolonged and certainly the most publicized controversy between the boards and their respective General Assemblies centered on the issue of social responsibility through investment policies. In the late 1960s, mainline Protestant denominations began to apply fiscal pressure on corporations whose policies or practices appeared incompatible with religious ethical standards. In 1966 the United Methodist Church withdrew $10 million from the First National City Bank of New York City to protest the bank's fiscal relationship with South Africa and apartheid, and the following year a variety of Protestant denominations, including the UPCUSA, supported shareholder resolutions criticizing Eastman-Kodak's minority hiring practices.[10]

In 1971 the UPCUSA General Assembly made an important strategy shift when it adopted Investment Policy Guidelines that transformed denominational investment functions from a largely passive social role into an active one and brought the church into direct institutional engagement with corporations. Some Presbyterians welcomed the concept as a sign of the church's willingness to order its own life by the same standards of accountability that it recommended to others. Some reacted negatively, including members of the business community. A survey conducted by the *Presbyterian Panel* in June 1981 indicated that up to 60 percent of all Presbyterians had become polarized on the issues of economics and social responsibility.[11]

The Investment Policy Guidelines established that church investments were an instrument of mission and included theological, social, and ethical considerations reflected in previous General Assembly actions and the *Confession of 1967*. Prominent in these considerations were concerns about peace, economic and social justice, and environmental protection. The PCUS General Assembly in 1976 approved similar guidelines proposed by the General Executive Board citing its historical position: "Our whole tradition, Biblical and Reformed, takes seriously both our *fiduciary responsibility* for funds entrusted to our care, and our *social responsibility* for Christian witness with said funds."[12]

Although both boards traditionally had prohibited investments in alcohol, tobacco, and gambling industries, these restrictions were noncontroversial and involved only a fraction of possible investment activity. Under the new strategies, General Assemblies, through delegated committees, began to raise questions about the ethical conduct of some of the country's largest and most profitable corporations. On various occasions they asked the boards to apply pressure on specific corporations by casting proxy votes, filing stockholder resolutions, or divesting themselves of all stocks in the targeted companies. Many board members believed such tactics might conflict with their primary fiduciary responsibility to plan participants and resisted taking any actions that they considered might be interpreted as fiscally imprudent.[13]

The UPCUSA General Assembly created a Committee on Mission Responsibility Through Investment (MRTI), a subcommittee of the GAMC, to identify and recommend to boards and agencies opportunities for responsible use of investments and to maintain a liaison with similar groups developing programs or researching investments. Represented were members of various General Assembly agencies and boards, including the Board of Pensions and the United Presbyterian Foundation. The MRTI depended heavily on the Interfaith Center on Corporate Responsibility (ICCR), a "sponsor-related movement" of the National Council of Churches supported by 17 denominations, more than 175 Roman Catholic Orders, and other religious groups. Although the ICCR itself owned no stock, filed no shareholder resolutions, and officially took no positions on specific issues, it provided an ecumenical arena for coordinating church strategies, giving individual denominations and organizations freedom to make autonomous decisions regarding their own investment policies.[14]

Initially the Board of Pensions indicated its willingness to comply with the Investment Policy Guidelines, promising to implement them "insofar as legally possible," language employed in the guidelines themselves. In a number of instances the board gave its proxy votes to the GAMC in support of shareholder resolutions initiated by the UPCUSA church, other denominations, or secular organizations concerned with business ethics. Though wary of possible precedents, board trustees thought that the board's compliance at this level did not infringe on any legal rights or responsibilities inherent in the board's charter and bylaws.[15]

Conflict with the GAMC occurred in 1976 when the Board of Pensions rejected a request from the MRTI that the board itself file a shareholder resolution with American Home Products protesting that company's alleged questionable practices in the marketing of infant formula products.[16] In defense of its action, the board issued a paper entitled "Clarification of the Pension Board's Role in Social Action," which essentially argued that taking the initiative in filing shareholder resolutions would consume considerable staff time, incur extensive legal expenses, and raise the possibility of suits either by targeted corporations or opposing plan members.[17] In reaching this conclusion, the board had been strongly influenced by the passage in 1974 of the Employee Retirement Income Security Act (ERISA) that changed the liabilities of trustees whose retirement plans were covered by law. It specified the importance of prudent behavior and created a previously ambiguous or nonexistent right of participants and their heirs to sue a pension plan and its trustees for breaches of these standards. Although ERISA did not apply to church programs such as the MAF and the Pension Plan, legal counsel advised the boards to adjust their policies to meet ERISA guidelines since they would likely be applied as precedent in any litigation between the boards and their constituents.[18]

The GAMC held an emergency meeting and voted to "instruct" the board to file the shareholder resolution with American Home Products. This precipitated an extended series of unproductive discussions between the two agencies. Subsequently both the board and the GAMC requested the General Assembly to appoint a special committee to listen to both sides and make a report to the assembly in 1978.[19]

Spokespersons for the board outlined to the committee its arguments against compliance with the GAMC's directive: loss of staff time, possible litigation, violation of the principle of prudent management of church funds. They maintained, however, that reluctance to file shareholder resolutions did not signify the board's insensitivity to social issues; indeed trustees took precautions to avoid unpopular investments.[20]

The GAMC countered with four propositions and in so doing raised the question of the relationship between the General Assembly and the board. It claimed that the General Assembly had clearly established policies and guidelines for church investment and that its authority vis à vis the board was unequivocally established by historical precedent; the assembly had instructed the Board of Pensions to implement these policies insofar as legally possible; no legal impediment existed to preclude the filing of shareholder resolutions; and the basic issues were not fundamentally legal or pragmatic but theological. GAMC leaders referred to a statement from the General Assembly in 1949 that indicated that boards were not self-perpetuating bodies and "must always function as servants of the church, in dependence upon the General Assembly" and noted that the board had never directly questioned the assembly's authority. They also argued that the so-called Prudent Man Rule binding trustees to administer funds with care, skill, and caution related specifically to the act of making investments, not the filing of shareholder resolutions. Concerning effort and expense, it suggested that if the board relied on the expertise of the ICCR and the MRTI as did other denominations and church organizations, the financial impact would be negligible. Finally, the GAMC volunteered to reimburse the board for any costs incurred resulting from legal actions or judgments. Moreover, they noted that the possibility of legal action being taken by a company against a church group was remote.[21]

GAMC representatives also queried the theological grounds on which the board declined. They concluded their presentation by saying, "We believe that God has called us to be responsible stewards toward all children and the whole of creation. When we think of the church's investment policies, the fundamental question before us is still, 'Do those who observe our activities and decisions regard what we do as showing forth the love and grace and peace of our Lord?'"[22]

Before the special committee had reached a decision on how to resolve the impasse, the board through its president, Arthur Brown, proposed a compromise that would enable both sides to achieve their objectives. The board recommended that the GAMC take responsibility for filing shareholder resolutions on the board's behalf, including expenses arising out of any legal actions, and that the GAMC purchase adequate liability insurance to reimburse the board for any financial damages it might sustain. With this protection, the board felt that it could authorize the GAMC to file in its name. The committee accepted the board's proposal and referred it to the General Assembly for approval.[23] Some commissioners still felt that even this action might endanger the security of the pension fund. On a motion from the floor, the General Assembly appointed yet another committee, which supported the actions of the previous committee. The GAMC subsequently took out a $10 million liability insurance policy from Lloyds of London and assumed responsibility for issuing shareholder resolutions on behalf of the board.[24]

This three-year controversy strained relations between the board and the GAMC and its MRTI committee. Leaders in both organizations hoped that future confrontations could be avoided, though in fact they did take place. In response to the 192nd General Assembly's call for peacemaking in 1980, the MRTI drafted "Provisional Guidelines on Military Investment" that directed denominational boards and agencies to refrain from investment in the nation's ten leading military contractors, any of the one hundred leading military contractors that were dependent on the military for more than 20 percent of their business, and companies that made key components for nuclear warheads. The guidelines permitted divestment decisions to be timed to avoid undue economic loss.[25]

When the guidelines were first released in 1981, the board again argued that such a directive could prevent it from maximizing the total return on its investments. Although initially the board took no vote on the guidelines, it reiterated its primary responsibility to Plan members and indicated that the board would "constructively propose alternative means of implementation" that would support GAMC policies without detriment to the United Presbyterian Pension and Benefits Plan or its members.[26] After further consideration, however, the board accepted the Provisional Guidelines, although six members requested that their negative vote be recorded in the minutes. The board's Social Responsibility Committee concurred, but with "grave reservations about the appropriateness and effectiveness of such divestment" and instructed President Arthur Ryan to express to the GAMC its concern.[27] It concluded that while the guidelines represented a sincere approach, "they are likewise an inappropriate and overly simplistic response to the issue, and divert attention from the real need for Peacemaking."[28]

Board minutes and personal testimony describe the tension between the MRTI and the board as each group defended its position. In attempting to reach accord, the MRTI made two changes in the wording of the guidelines. A reference to "investment securities" was changed to "common stocks" in order to make the type of investment more specific, and the operative verb "direct" was changed to "urge" so that the guidelines would not be perceived as an order that would abridge the board's authority for making investment decisions.[29] Nevertheless, at its October 1982 meeting, the Finance Committee of the board unanimously expressed its opinion that divestment was "not a practical communication vehicle either to the corporations involved, the church at large, or the members of the Pension and Benefits Plan." At the same meeting, a motion to withdraw the Board of Pensions from the denominational divestment program generated considerable support but was defeated on a divided vote.[30]

In March 1983 the board's Social Responsibility Committee conferred with MRTI representatives about their respective positions. Following the conversation, the board reaffirmed its desire to "struggle faithfully and responsibly to resolve the tension" and identified two acceptable strategies: shareholder resolutions and communication with congressional leaders, but it determined that no further dialogue was necessary other than participation of the board representatives at regular MRTI meetings.[31]

In its annual report to the General Assembly in 1983, the Board of Pensions indicated compliance with the military investment guidelines by excluding securities from twenty-one corporations whose military involvement met the guidelines' criteria. It noted, however, that such action was taken only because the board's investment advisors had concluded that the exclusions would not impair the productivity of the investment portfolio. Furthermore, the board unanimously reaffirmed its previously expressed concerns about disinvestment.[32]

The attitude of the Board of Annuities and Relief closely paralleled that of the Board of Pensions regarding the relationship between financial obligations and social responsibility. Because of its autonomy, Annuities and Relief was not subject to the investment guidelines approved by the PCUS General Assembly in 1976.[33] Although the board acknowledged its ethical concerns and standards in business transactions, it considered its funds unique from other programmatic accounts. In 1971, for example, when the PCUS General Assembly requested that its boards and agencies each contribute $10,000 to the Black Presbyterian Leadership Caucus for operating funds, the board declined to participate, citing its charter that restricted the administration of funds "solely for the separate purposes for which benefits are promised or contracted." The board emphasized that it was precluded from using such funds for social or charitable reasons, "it matters not how worthy that purpose."[34]

In another instance, in 1977 the PCUS General Assembly endorsed a "Message to the Churches on Southern Africa" in which it opposed apartheid and urged congregations and church agencies to commit themselves to a "serious re-examination of the manner in which our investments and other economic involvements in South Africa are perpetuating the system of racial injustice in South Africa."[35] Because the Board of Annuities and Relief did not initiate a response to the message, two commissioners to the 1978 Assembly, Glenn Dickson and Wayne D. Griffin, pastors in Suwannee Presbytery in Florida, filed a resolution asking that the board be instructed to take four actions: ascertain the extent of its investment in South Africa; seek to determine the manner in which these companies were doing business; plan a series of steps that would encourage companies in which it owned stock to act justly in their business dealings; and consider divesting itself of stocks in companies whose practices violated Christian standards of justice. The assembly referred the resolution to the board and asked for a response.[36]

A board-appointed committee that reported to the General Assembly in 1979 concurred that board members should be "aware of, sensitive to, and concerned about current social and moral implications of investments," but not at the expense of its fiduciary responsibility. The report contended that to raise questions of the "social usefulness" of an investment might be considered a violation of pension law and subject to governmental sanction.[37] The board declared that divestiture of stocks in companies whose practices "violated Christian standards of justice" would be neither legally prudent nor socially responsible. It further argued that to sell a company's securities to someone else would amount to an abandonment of social responsibility and would result in no basic impact on the essential problems. In fact, the board had voted unanimously not to divest itself of the securities it presently held in companies doing business in South Africa. The board promised to continue to monitor its portfolio and "to the extent that such investments are consistent with the trust imposed upon it," reiterated its commitment to the positive social and moral values contained in the investment guidelines adopted by the PCUS General Assembly.[38]

The board's response to the South African question was approved "as acceptable," but commissioners did not drop the matter entirely. They endorsed an overture asking that all church courts and agencies conform to the investment guidelines already adopted by the General Assembly or draw up some other "appropriate" guidelines.[39] In response the board again stated its interpretation of fiduciary responsibility and adopted what it considered to be appropriate guidelines for conducting its tasks. These guidelines contained four principles: fiduciary responsibility to participants; preservation of funds and best available returns with prudence and safety; adherence to General Assembly affirmations of social and moral values "to the extent that they are consistent with the trust responsibilities of the Board"; and consideration of the individual company's "recognition of human worth and dignity, employment practices and policies," and its general conformity with General Assembly guidelines. Beyond these internal constraints, the board refused to bind itself to specific courses of action.[40]

Another basic issue for both boards was how to deal with the inequality of retirement pensions among their members. Through its Joy Gift receipts and other sources, the Board of Annuities and Relief had by 1983 been able to raise its minimum income assistance formula to $8,100 for individuals and $11,600 for couples.[41] The UPCUSA assistance program, aided by the success of its similar Christmas Offering, had established a target income for retirees with twenty or more years of service of $11,000 for couples and $7,000 for individuals. Moreover, the Board of Pensions included two minimum benefits within the pension plan itself designed to offset low earning years. The first provided a minimum of $125 for each year of service prior to 1980, an equivalent of an effective average salary of $10,000 for forty years of service. The second was an alternative pension for each year of service *beginning* with 1980 based on the average of median salaries in the denomination for the five years preceding retirement. If an individual's actual accrued pension fell below the median, he/she was credited with the higher figure for those years.[42]

Many ministers still felt that the inflation of the 1970s was too hard on retirees on fixed incomes and that the denominations should begin to base retirement incomes on years of service rather than the traditional salary scales. Articles written by Presbyterian ministers in *Monday Morning Magazine* and other periodicals frequently raised the issue that ministers who served small congregations and missions, where salaries were low, received inadequate pensions. One clergyman expressed his frustration with the situation: "Now, don't give me the old malarkey about pension plans being tied to actuarial percentages. Don't tell me we cannot change our system. We made it; we can change it."[43]

In 1979, the Presbytery of San Diego (UPCUSA) presented an overture asking the Board of Pensions to revise its retirement plan so that everyone would be guaranteed a minimum pension of $8,000 for forty years of service with cost of living increments provided to keep pace with inflation. The assembly's Standing Committee on Pensions recommended "no action" because it deemed such a request "impracticable."[44] In 1980, however, a resolution to the PCUS General Assembly requesting "equalization of the retirement plan" prompted the assembly to instruct the GAMB to develop a

"Theology of Compensation" for pastors, with particular attention to current disparities in salaries and retirement benefits.[45]

The GAMB report in 1983 not only addressed a wide range of economic and theological considerations but devoted considerable attention to retirement-related issues. It featured a theological paper by Professor Walter Brueggemann that related Reformed theological principles to contemporary cultural contexts and demonstrated how the two interacted. Although the paper itself contained no directives, the committee presented six recommendations, one of which encouraged the Board of Annuities and Relief to develop a new pension plan by 1989 (if reunion failed to pass) that would pay a viable minimum pension income, provide larger pension incomes for lower paid ministers, and give greater weight to a formula based on length of service.[46]

Concurrently with the discussion of controversial issues, the boards experienced a variety of changes in their respective programs and personnel. Implementation of ERISA caused uncertainty for board officials because the new law defined "church" so narrowly (almost to the function of worship) that there was a question if employees of related church agencies could be included under the existing denominational programs. The Church Pensions Conference, an ecumenical organization to which both boards belonged, formed A Church Alliance for the Clarification of ERISA which produced a number of amendments to enable the various denominations to maintain their programs. Board executives Charles C. Cowsert and Arthur W. Brown testified before the United States Senate Joint Finance and Human Resources Committee and helped convince legislators to modify ERISA so that there was no need to prepare a second pension and benefit plan for church employees other than ordained parish ministers.[47]

During the decade from 1973–1983 both boards also experienced changes in leadership. After fourteen years, George Vick retired as executive secretary of the Board of Annuities and Relief in 1976. His successor, Charles C. Cowsert, a graduate of King College in Tennessee and Union Theological Seminary in Virginia, had experience as an army chaplain, a pastor, and a presbytery executive before becoming the denomination's Secretary of Stewardship and the Presbyterian Foundation's Associate Director and Treasurer. Under Cowsert the board altered its administrative procedures, increased its financial resources, and added a number of retirement and health features to the MAF and EAF. On January 1, 1983, J. Phillips Noble began a three-year term as executive secretary, continuing until the General Assembly approved the new benefits program in 1986. A graduate of King College and Columbia Seminary in Georgia, Noble had held a number of pastorates, including a ten-year relationship with the First (Scots) Presbyterian Church in Charleston, South Carolina, prior to assuming board leadership. Knowledgeable about denominational structures and their interaction with the board, Noble provided leadership that was a key link in the orderly integration of the two boards following church union.[48]

With the retirement of Donald L. Hibbard in 1972, the Board of Pensions selected Arthur W. Brown, Princeton University graduate, Presbyterian layman, and former manager of employee relations for Standard Oil of New Jersey, to become its new president. Brown had served on the 1972 reorganization committee that linked the Board of Pensions to the Vocation Agency, and his skills as a listener and communicator guided the board through this adjustment. During his eight years, he devised a means of supplementing retirement annuities for pensioners on the low end of the salary scale through the alternative pension program. Following Brown's retirement in 1980, the board elected layman Arthur M. Ryan, vice-president for administration in the Alma (Michigan) Plastics Company. Ryan, a Yale graduate with an M.B.A. from Harvard, had demonstrated skills in articulating ideas, managing office staffs, and directing financial institutions. Ryan has been an effective liaison with the Vocation Agency and the Church Pensions Conference in addition to his responsibilities with the board itself. His expertise in the areas of Social Security and income tax regulations has been helpful during a period in which a number of changes in these areas have affected the structuring of pension programs.[49]

The decade also saw changes in investment policies and procedures as board leaders continually reevaluated strategies in order to adapt to fluctuating economic conditions. Utilizing multiple investment advisors with specialized expertise in various areas, both boards increased their earnings. When interest rates were high in the late 1970s, the Board of Pensions deposited $50 million with Aetna and $25 million with Travelers and Connecticut General for extended periods at 15 to 16 percent interest.[50] The Board of Annuities and Relief retained the Trust Company of Georgia as its main fund manager but had separate fund managers working to provide a diversified portfolio. It also placed its securities in a street name (as did the Board of Pensions) to facilitate quicker and easier sales of stocks and bonds and initiated a lockbox checking account procedure to expedite the earning of daily interest on all of the board's funds.[51]

During the same time period, both boards adopted a less conservative stance regarding the relationship between fixed-income and equity (stocks) investments, moving to a 60 percent equity and 40 percent fixed-income ratio.[52] Because of such policies, the Board of Pensions could announce special apportionments of 10 percent in 1977 and 1982, 16 percent in 1980, and 5 percent in 1983. Between 1973 and 1983, the Board of Annuities and Relief distributed six good experience credits to MAF members totaling 53 percent and to EAF various increases totaling 41 percent.[53]

In terms of plan benefits, both boards enlarged and upgraded various aspects of their programs. Among other things, the Board of Annuities and Relief increased lifetime hospitalization limits to $2 million and improved disability coverage. Beginning 1 January 1983, the board instituted a voluntary dental plan with 292 organizations enrolling 576 employees and 246 dependent units.[54] It also provided for laypeople to transfer membership from the EAF to the MAF and changed the EAF from a "defined contribution" plan to a "defined benefits" plan, which made more funds available for good experience credits. Although the average pension of ministers in the MAF in 1983 was only $3,240 because of the number of older annuitants who had retired with extremely low incomes, another statistic provided a better indication of improvements. A minister who retired in 1963 with a pension of $300 a month would in 1983 receive $801.61 monthly, an increase of 167 percent.[55]

The Board of Pensions similarly improved its basic program in light of changing economic and social conditions. With increased medical and disability limits, including a supplement to Medicare, the board began to accept charges for the services of pastoral counselors and other qualified professionals. It also raised the lifetime family maximum for outpatient treatment of nervous and mental disorders to $15,000. Sharing with the Presbytery of West Florida, it employed a minister to counsel active and retired ministers regarding particular needs.[56] In terms of actual retirement pensions, the board reported that the average pension of a 1982 retiree was more than double that of her/his 1974 counterpart, showing an increase from $3,500 to $7,128.[57]

The board made a major change in 1982 when it deleted group contracts for lay employees and permitted coverage for nonordained professionals and staff on an individual basis. This came in response to recommendations made by a Task Force on Economic Security for Older Adults organized by the Advisory Council on Church and Society.[58] While the Pension Plan had always been open to various nonordained church workers, such coverage was not mandatory as it was with ordained clergy. As a result, many lay professionals were not enrolled in the Pension Plan by their employing organizations. Although the Task Force approved the board's action and its cooperation with the Vocation Agency in composing a section on compensation and benefits in "Guidelines for a Session Personnel Committee," it noted that "A burden continues to lie on presbyteries, congregations, and the Board of Pensions to witness to the covenant we have in Christ by meeting the retirement needs of lay employees."[59]

The Board of Pensions further expanded its benefits by adding retirement planning counseling. A 1983 consultation of people from the academic and business communities with experience in this area provided information with which the board planned pilot counseling programs that could be implemented by the reunited church.[60]

The Board of Pensions's relationship with the Vocation Agency, which linked it administratively more closely to a variety of church programs, resulted in expansion of its service to the denomination at an international level, as well. When Brown was president, he spent five weeks in 1978 in Pakistan, Thailand, and South Korea, advising churches in those countries on pension administration and development of new programs.[61] The board also trained four Korean American part-time ministry staff appointees under the auspices of the Program Agency to assist field representatives in pension matters among Korean American churches in the United States.[62]

Both boards underwent evaluations by independent agencies during the late 1970s and early 1980s. In 1979 the Hewitt Associates, an actuarial firm in the Chicago area, compared the boards' benefits with a dozen mainline Protestant denominations plus the YMCA and YWCA and a typical industrial pension plan. The UPCUSA plan tied for second place in the combined benefits ranking (retirement, disability, death, and medical), and the PCUS program compared favorably with the benefits of other denominations in size of pension, disability, and medical compensation, and was equal to or better than industrial plans except in the area of medical payments. From this study the boards implemented a number of changes prior to denominational reunion in 1983.[63]

Continuing its policy begun in the 1960s, the Board of Pensions authorized a ten-year evaluation by its constituents of the quality of its service. The 1981 survey conducted by the Research Division of the Support Agency revealed that the image of the board had improved considerably in a decade. Only 1 percent of the sample expressed dissatisfaction with the benefits provided by the plan, and between 61 and 75 percent reported being either very or quite satisfied. While there were some general complaints about the high major medical deductible (subsequently changed) and problems about communication in filing claims, the most general request from lay members, female clergy, and surviving spouses was that the board provide more accessible information about various features of the program itself. Through the survey, the board recognized that it should be more attentive to female clergy, clergy couples, and participants who had never been married or were married more than once.[64]

In a similar survey conducted by the Office of Review and Evaluation of the PCUS in 1982, the Board of Annuities and Relief received high ranking as an effective agent of the General Assembly. Of thirty-eight General Assembly functions, the Board of Annuities and Relief ranked first in terms of perceived effectiveness and second in terms of importance. Samplings of participants, board members, and middle court executives indicated that the board overall was viewed as "effective in assuming and carrying out its responsibilities." Annuitants awarded positive ratings to the board of 100 percent on promptness of checks, 98 percent on sensitivity to personal relationships, and 72 percent on simplicity of procedures. Primary concerns centered around whether benefits under personal health care were the best available for the cost and the lack of dental coverage, which was later added. A number of respondents expressed the need for fiscal advice with regard to retirement. Nevertheless, the report underscored expressed the church's overall confidence in the Board of Annuities and Relief.[65]

Perhaps the single most important change for the Board of Annuities and Relief and the Board of Pensions during the decade was the reunion of the UPCUSA and PCUS denominations formalized at the joint General Assembly meetings in Atlanta June 1–15, 1983. The formation of the new denomination, the Presbyterian Church (U.S.A.), was the end result of a series of reunion discussions that began in the nineteenth century following the creation of the Southern Presbyterian church in 1861.[66] For the two boards, this signaled a comprehensive reexamination of existing programs; accordingly they created the Unified Benefits Committee consisting of six members of each board, which held its first meeting in September, 1983. It studied the events of the previous decade, particularly the issues of divestment and of the relational definition of the board and the denomination. It also addressed the relationship of the board to its constituents as well as to the administrative structure of the church. In articulating its objectives at an early session, the committee described the complex nature of its assignment:

> We are faced with two incompatible but essential objectives: (1) the insulation of the Pension function from direct control by the Church, particularly in the area of investment and plan design and administration; (2) the inclusion of the Pension function as an organic and responsive participant in the organization and work of the Church.[67]

Epilogue

> The Benefits Plan with its orderly churchwide financing, its use of dues based on a percentage of salary and its benefits-leveling provisions is consistent with our theology and polity and is an expression of the community of the Church.
> —"How Plan Dues Are Established," *Board of Pensions Leaflet*, 1986

Working closely with the Board of Annuities and Relief and the Board of Pensions, the Unified Benefits Committee met eleven times between September 1983 and January 1986 as it followed the mandate of the General Assembly to formulate a new denominational retirement and benefits program. In order to focus on major areas of concern, the committee created four task forces: Benefits, Legal and Structure, Actuarial, and Assistance and Homes. By June 1985 the task forces and the full committee had developed a working draft of the new plan for use in a churchwide consultation process. In August 1985 the boards issued a progress report that outlined the major provisions of the plan and announced the times and locations of the consultations. More than 1,100 participants attended and submitted evaluations and responses to questionnaires. Based on this information, the Unified Benefits Committee reviewed the working draft and modified parts of the proposed plan. At their meetings on February 21, 1986, the respective boards unanimously approved a final document that was then submitted to the 198th General Assembly (1986) at its meeting in Minneapolis, Minnesota, in June. The new organization, the Board of Pensions of the Presbyterian Church (U.S.A.), presented its program entitled The Benefits Plan of the Presbyterian Church (U.S.A.). It recommended that J. Phillips Noble and Arthur M. Ryan serve as copresidents until December 31, 1988; at that time, Noble will retire and Ryan will continue as the sole chief executive. The General Assembly approved the new program and directed that it become effective January 1, 1987.[1]

The Benefits Plan incorporates concepts from both the PCUS and UPCUSA programs and introduces a number of options not available under either of the former plans. The framers of the new plan emphasized that it is a collective expression: "It is based on the principle that we should share each others burdens. This care and concern are supported by sound financing provided by the whole community of the church."[2] This is most evident in its use of percentages for major medical coverage and the establishment of a minimum pension. By calculating medical dues on a percentage of effective salary rather than using a flat rate premium, the plan reduces the dollar cost for smaller churches. At the same time, it reduces the dollar cost for lower-paid ministers by basing the deductible on a percentage of the effective salary. "This leveling of major medical costs reflects the sharing of each other's burdens in the community of the Church."[3]

The Benefits Plan also implements this collective dimension by supplementing retirement income for church workers whose career incomes were lower than many of their peers. In the past, in both the PCUS and UPCUSA plans, the accumulation of pension credits was based on 1¼ percent of annual effective salary, which meant that participants with low incomes received correspondingly low pensions. The new plan addresses this problem by including a "leveling-up feature" that permits pension credits to be accrued each year on *the higher* of either the member's effective salary or the median salary of all pastors serving churches.[4]

The plan also encourages a wider participation of lay employees, many of whom previously had no pension safety net. As an inducement to local congregations and other organizations, payment of dues toward retirement benefits for new lay employees can be waived for the first three years. Employers will be able to pay dues only on major medical coverage (8 percent) and disability and death benefits (1 percent). After three years when the full 20 percent dues would go into effect, the employee has immediate vesting rights in the pension credits that he/she will begin to earn. The plan also specifies that if an organization covers *any* professional or other lay employee, then it has to cover *all* such full-time employees on the payroll.[5]

The medical protection plan has a variety of levels of participation and introduces "cost containment" provisions that foster judicious use of services without impairing quality of care. The 8 percent medical payment has been subdivided into 4 percent for the member, 2 percent for the spouse, and 2 percent for children. In the event that a member does not have a spouse (or if the spouse was covered under another group medical plan), the 2 or possibly 4 percent may be applied to optional dental benefits, additional death benefits, or additional retirement savings. Cost containment features include payment to obtain second opinion on operations, reduction in payment for procurement of prior approval before nonemergency hospitalization, and complete reimbursement for out-patient surgery. These features and other options make the medical section of the Benefits Plan a much more efficient and flexible program than any of its predecessors.[6]

In its Assistance and Homes Program the new plan reaffirms its determination to offer financial aid and services to retirees whose salaries during active service were low in comparison with present economic conditions. The Assistance Program furnishes income supplements and offers nursing home assistance based on guidelines that ask applicants to use their own assets down to a stipulated level before requiring help from the board. The program also provides for shared grants with other participating organizations, such as local congregations or presbyteries where the board contributes one-half or one-third depending on the number of participants involved. An additional feature is the Diagnostic Psychiatric Program under contract with the Menninger Clinic in Topeka, Kansas, a program the board hopes to expand.[7]

Although need for ministerial retirement homes has declined in recent years due in part to the improving level of retirement income and the practice of giving ministers housing allowances instead of providing a manse, the Unified Benefits Committee opted to continue the Homes Program in its present general form without major expansion. While maintaining the program, the board also authorized an in-depth study similar to the one conducted in the 1950s that would supply information for future decisions. At present the Homes Program consists of eight clusters of independent living units, two congregate facilities, one nursing center, and approximately thirty individual homes in various parts of the country.[8]

Structurally the Board of Pensions will report directly to the General Assembly. It will, however, have overlapping membership at the elected level and staff cooperation on an adjunct basis with the Church Vocations Unit. Thus, the new board will be less closely related than the former Board of Pensions (UPCUSA), but more closely related than the former Board of Annuities and Relief (PCUS), to comparable program agencies.[9]

The board still faces resolution of some of the issues described in chapter 11. In 1983, 1984, and 1985, for example, the Board of Pensions in several instances deviated from the military-related investment guidelines because of what it considered to be valid fiduciary considerations and informed the General Assembly of its actions.[10] In 1985, the General Assembly approved a new set of guidelines for implementing a procedure of divestment in South Africa-related corporations. Both boards acknowledged their willingness to comply with the guidelines which called for selective divestment in a deliberately phased progression rather than immediate and total divestment. They noted, however, that their participation was voluntary rather than mandatory and that they continued to be guided by legal obligations specified in their charters and codified in the regulations of ERISA.

Conversations with GAMC and GAMB leaders indicate that relationships between their organizations and the boards have improved considerably since the controversies of the late 1970s, and they attribute this change in part to the cooperation of board trustees and staff, especially Ryan and Noble. That progress is being made can be seen by the response of the 1985 General Assembly Committee on Pensions and Annuities to an overture from the Presbytery of New Castle affirming the authority of the General Assembly to stipulate ethical and social policies under which investments could be made by the Board of Pensions and the Board of Annuities and Relief. After hearing from both boards and having sought counsel from the Advisory Council on Church and Society, the committee recommended nonconcurrence with the overture because it was satisfied that "insofar as legally possible," the boards were seeking to live within the guidelines of the General Assembly.[11]

The historical roots of the Board of Pensions (U.S.A.) suggest that programs and policies will continue to evolve as new generations respond to changing social and economic conditions. From the Widows' Fund of colonial times to the modern Board of Annuities and Relief and the Board of Pensions, the board and its predecessors have attempted to balance the interplay between legal and pragmatic considerations and ethical and theological principles, with varying measures of success. As the twenty-first century approaches, the board undoubtedly will pursue its examination of its program and its relationship to the denomination. Perhaps this survey will be useful to those who will make future decisions affecting board activities.

Notes

Chapter 1

1. David H. Fischer, *Growing Old in America* (New York: Oxford University Press, 1977), 42. For an excellent survey of attitudes toward old age in colonial America, see 26–27.
2. Lefferts A. Loetscher, *A Brief History of the Presbyterians*, 4th ed. (Philadelphia: Westminster Press, 1983), 56–58, and Leonard J. Trinterud, *The Forming of an American Tradition: A Reexamination of Colonial Presbyterianism* (Philadelphia: Westminster Press, 1949).
3. Loetscher, *Brief History*, 56–58, and Leonard J. Trinterud, *The Forming of an American Tradition*.
4. Trinterud, *The Forming of an American Tradition*, 60–61.
5. Guy S. Klett, *Presbyterians in Colonial Pennsylvania* (Philadelphia: Pennsylvania State University Press, 1937), 104–8.
6. "Minutes of the Corporation for the Relief of Poor and Distressed Presbyterian Ministers, and of the Poor and Distressed Widows and Children of Presbyterian Ministers," 3 March 1760. Hereafter referred to as "Corporation Minutes." Located in the Presbyterian Historical Society (hereafter referred to as PHS), Philadelphia, Pennsylvania, and the Presbyterian Ministers' Fund Insurance Company in Philadelphia.
7. Klett, *Presbyterians*, 109. In 1760 £1 sterling (London) was worth £1.58 Pennsylvania currency. See John J. McCusker, *Money and Exchange in Europe and America 1600–1775* (Chapel Hill, N.C.: University of North Carolina Press, 1978), 185.
8. Klett, *Presbyterians*, 110. See also Trinterud, *The Forming of an American Tradition*, 202–5.
9. Klett, *Presbyterians*, 111.
10. John Boyce, ed., *The Presbytery of Utica Centennial 1843–1943* (n.p., n.d.), 22–23.
11. Klett, *Presbyterians*, 182.
12. "Minutes of the Presbytery of Donegal," 5 October 1737.
13. "Minutes of the Presbytery of New Castle," 14 April 1731.
14. Guy S. Klett, ed., *Minutes of the Presbyterian Church in America 1706–1788* (Philadelphia: Presbyterian Historical Society, 1976), 31, 35–37. Hereafter referred to as *Church Minutes*.
15. Ibid., 40.

16. Ibid., 91.
17. Ibid., 61.
18. Ibid., 110, 175.
19. Ibid., 151, 159-60.
20. Ibid., 164.
21. Loetscher, *Brief History*, 58-59.
22. Ibid.
23. *Church Minutes*, 199.
24. Ibid., 304.
25. Ibid., 240-43. For the background of Alison, see Alexander Mackie, *Facile Princeps: The Story of the Beginning of Life Insurance in America* (Lancaster: Pennsylvania State University Press, 1956), 31-41.
26. A. Ian Dunlop, "Provision for Ministers' Widows in Scotland—Eighteenth Century," *Records of the Church History Society*, XVII (1967): 233.
27. J. B. Dow, "Early Actuarial Work in Eighteenth-Century Scotland," *Transactions of the Faculty of Actuaries*, vol. 33, part 3 (1975): 193-229. See also Henry G. Graham, *The Social Life of Scotland in the Eighteenth Century* (London: A. and C. Black Ltd., 1928), 226-65. The Scottish Fund continues today under the title of The Churches and Universities (Scotland) Widows' and Orphans' Fund.
28. "Corporation Minutes," 12 (n.d.).
29. "Corporation Minutes," 22 May 1761. See also Mackie, *Facile Princeps*, 1-6. The Fund also imposed a penalty of one year's premium on ministers who remarried because the second wives were usually younger than the first ones.
30. "Corporation Minutes," 21 July 1760. The Corporation did apply some pressure on young ministers by adding a rule that they had to become members within a year of their settlement in the synod or forfeit the right to take out a policy.
31. Cited in Trinterud, *The Forming of an American Tradition*, 48.
32. For a background of these men, see Mackie, *Facile Princeps*, 32-63. When William Humphreys succeeded Allen as treasurer in 1760, he refused any salary noting that he "desired that it might be entered in our Minutes, that he Freely bestowed his labour to promote ye good and charitable designs of the Corporation." "Corporation Minutes," 25 June 1760.
33. "Corporation Minutes," 20 December 1760, 18 May 1761.
34. Ibid.
35. *Church Minutes*, 254, and Guy S. Klett, *Journals of Charles Beatty 1762-1769* (University Park, Pennsylvania: Pennsylvania State University Press, 1962), 3-39.
36. *Church Minutes*, 245-46.
37. *Church Minutes*, 368, and "Corporation Minutes," 22 May 1761.
38. Mackie, *Facile Princeps*, 7-8.
39. Widows' Fund Membership Register, 1761-1875 (The Presbyterian Ministers' Fund Archives, Philadelphia, Pennsylvania).
40. Viviana A. Rotman Zelizer, *Morals and Markets: Life Insurance In The United States* (New York and London: Columbia University Press, 1979).
41. Margaret G. Myers, *A Financial History of the United States* (New York: Columbia University Press, 1970), 29.
42. Shepard B. Clough, *A Century of American Life Insurance* (Westport, Connecticut: Columbia University Press, 1946), 22-23; Marquis James, *The Metropolitan Life: A Study in Business Growth* (New York: The Viking Press, 1947), 13-14.
43. "Corporation Minutes," 17 November 1762, 8 July 1763.
44. Ibid., 19, 26 May 1763.

45. Ibid.
46. Klett, *Journals of Charles Beatty 1762–1769*, xxiii–xxiv.
47. "Corporation Minutes," 17 November 1762.
48. Ibid., 29 July 1766.
49. Ibid., 447–48, and "Corporation Minutes," 27 May 1767. The Corporation also made unilateral policy decisions that annoyed the synod. In 1768 the Corporation decided not to grant money to build meeting houses but to concentrate its efforts on assisting "poor and Vacant Congregations."
50. *Church Minutes*, 492–94 and "Corporation Minutes," 22 May 1771.
51. *Church Minutes*, 527.
52. "Corporation Minutes," 25 May 1774. After this settlement the Corporation divested itself of responsibilities for missionary activities. It continued to administer the residue of the old Fund for Pious Uses, however, until it was exhausted. A note in the "Waste Book" for 20 May 1782 says that £6 was paid to the widow of Francis Alison "being part of ye interest of the money belonging to ye old Synod of Philadelphia." See also Mackie, *Facile Princeps*, 99–100.
53. *Church Minutes*, 423.
54. Ibid., 433–44.
55. "Corporation Minutes," 26 May 1768. Earlier the Corporation had agreed to give the widow of a delinquent policyholder £30 "out of compassion for her situation." "Corporation Minutes," 21 May 1765.
56. Ibid., 23 May 1771.
57. Ibid., 12 October 1773. In 1772 a minister petitioned the Corporation to return his money "as he is poor, and unable to make yearly payments, and is about to leave the Province." Ruling that the request "must be hurtful to the design of the Fund," his request was denied. "Corporation Minutes," 28 May 1772.
58. "Corporation Minutes," 24 May 1779. See also Mackie, *Facile Princeps*, 149–50. Mackie devotes an entire chapter to early investment policies, 143–55.
59. "Corporation Minutes," 17 May 1781.
60. *Church Minutes*, 572.
61. *Church Minutes*, 579.
62. "Corporation Minutes," 22 May 1784.
63. Ibid., 28 May 1787.
64. *Church Minutes*, 594–95.
65. Trinterud, *The Forming of an American Tradition*, 291. See also *Archives of the State of New Jersey, First Series*, vol. XVIII (Trenton, N.J., 1893), 269–84 in which details of Witherspoon's petition are given.
66. *A Draught of a Plan of Government and Discipline for the Presbyterian Church in North-America* (Philadelphia, 1786), 24.
67. *Church Minutes*, 638. See also Trinterud, *The Forming of an American Tradition*, xx.
68. Clough, *A Century of American Life Insurance*, 23–24, and Mackie, *Facile Princeps*, 127–30. Identical charters were granted by Pennsylvania, New Jersey, and New York. The Congregationalists formed the Massachusetts Congregational Charitable Society in 1786 with provisions similar to that of the Widows' Fund and based on more accurate mortality tables supplied by the Reverend Richard Price. John Wesley set up a fund for "worn-out preachers" in 1763 and in 1774 the American Conference ordered an Easter collection for needy itinerants. In 1789 the conference approved a Fund for Superannuated Preachers and the Widows and

Orphans of Preachers. Each minister was expected to contribute two dollars at the annual conference meeting. The accumulated funds were dispensed to those ministers and dependents who needed assistance.

Chapter 2

1. Philip Schaff, *America: A Sketch of its Political, Social, and Religious Character* (Cambridge: Harvard University Press, 1961), 118.
2. Clough, *A Century of Life Insurance*, 24.
3. Ibid., 24-25.
4. "Corporation Minutes," 25 May 1791, and Mackie, *Facile Princeps*, 166-70.
5. Mackie, *Facile Princeps*, 191-92.
6. Ibid., 193.
7. Ibid., 194-96.
8. Widows' Fund Membership Register, 1761-1875.
9. Mackie, *Facile Princeps*, XX.
10. "Corporation Minutes," 18 May 1786, 17 May 1787.
11. "Corporation Minutes," 21 May 1793, and *Minutes of the General Assembly of the Presbyterian Church in the United States of America*, 1793, 68. Hereafter referred to as *GAUSA*. During the Old School-New School schism between 1837 and 1870, references to General Assembly minutes will be differentiated by (O.S.) and (N.S.).
12. "Corporation Minutes," 21 May 1793. On several occasions, however, the General Assembly endorsed the Widows' Fund and encouraged its members to participate. *GAUSA*, 1800, 197. It also directed the trustees of the assembly to pay "$400 of monies belonging to the Theological Seminary of N.J." to provide coverage for two professors. 1812, 512.
13. Mackie, *Facile Princeps*, 179-80.
14. "Corporation Minutes," 5 June 1804.
15. Ibid., 3 September 1805.
16. Ibid., 24 May 1797, and Mackie, *Facile Princeps*, 168-82.
17. "Corporation Minutes," 22 May 1799.
18. Ibid., 20 May 1800, and Mackie, *Facile Princeps*, 197-202.
19. James, *The Metropolitan Life*, 13-18.
20. An outstanding example of this new research is Zelizer, *Morals and Markets*.
21. *New York Times*, April 1853, 11.
22. *The United Presbyterian*, 22 August 1868, 5.
23. "Life Insurance," *The Presbyterian Magazine* (May 1857), 219.
24. "A Plea in Behalf of the Widows and Orphans of Deceased Ministers of the Presbyterian Church in the United States," *The Southern Presbyterian Review* (April 1869), 192.
25. Zelizer, *Morals and Markets*, 45-46.
26. *The Herald and Presbyter*, 11 February 1874, 8.
27. "Life Insurance," 320.
28. Ibid., 320-31.
29. Martha Stone Hubbell, *The Shady Side: or, Life in a Country Parsonage* (Boston, 1853), 324-25.
30. William B. Sprague, *Annals of the American Pulpit*, vol. 3 (New York, 1858), 186-92. See also Mackie, *Facile Princeps*, 102.

31. Zelizer, *Morals and Markets*, 82.
32. *The Presbyterian*, 14 June 1884, 8. See also *The Southwestern Presbyterian*, 17 April 1884, 6 for similar sentiments.
33. Zelizer, *Morals and Markets*, 68.
34. Ibid., 69.
35. "Life Insurance," 322-23.
36. Zelizer, *Morals and Markets*, 78-79.
37. Ibid., 78.
38. *The American Manual of Life Assurance Answering All Questions Necessary to a Full Understanding of the Whole Subject* (Newark, 1862), 74-78.
39. Mackie, *Facile Princeps*, 186-221, 207-21.
40. "Corporation Minutes," 27 May 1798.
41. Ibid., 28 May 1813.
42. "Corporation Minutes," 23 May 1820, and Mackie, *Facile Princeps*, 210.
43. Mackie, *Facile Princeps*, 210.
44. Fischer, *Growing Old in America*, 78-80, 92-93.
45. Ashbel Green, *Address to the Ministers and Congregations of the Presbyterian Church in the United States of America* (Philadelphia, 1824), 1-2.
46. Ibid., 5-6. Green also argued that the pension should not begin earlier than sixty-five because it would "reflect discredit on the ministry if many clergymen while enjoying firm health and a full salary, should be drawing an annuity."
47. Ibid., 8.
48. Mackie, *Facile Princeps*, 210-14.
49. "Corporation Minutes," 19 May 1837.

Chapter 3

1. For a background study, see George Marsden, *The Evangelical Mind and the New School Presbyterian Experience* (New Haven: Yale University Press, 1970).
2. Loetscher, *Brief History*, 76-78.
3. "Corporation Minutes," 17 May 1839.
4. Ibid., 16 May 1823, 25 May 1824.
5. In 1853, for example, when the company had a record enrollment of policyholders, all but two were from the Old School General Assembly.
6. "Corporation Minutes," 19 May 1837.
7. Ibid., 28 May 1841, 19 May 1845.
8. See, for example, *The Presbyterian*, 29 January 1848, 11 August 1848, 15 September 1849.
9. "Corporation Minutes," 19 May 1851.
10. Ibid., 22 May 1852.
11. Ibid., 22 May 1852, and Mackie, *Facile Princeps*, 262-68.
12. "Address of the Corporation for Relief of Poor and Distressed Presbyterians Ministers, etc.," (Philadelphia, 1852), 12-13. See also Mackie, *Facile Princeps*, 267-70.
13. "Corporation Minutes," 19 May and 22 December 1854.
14. Ibid., 22 May 1852.
15. Mackie, *Facile Princeps*, 270-71.
16. "The General Assembly and Ministerial Relief," *The Presbyterian Review* (July 1871), 5.
17. Zelizer, *Morals and Markets*, 6.

18. Joseph F. Hingeley, *The Retired Minister: His Claim, Inherent, Foremost, Supreme* (Chicago: Privately Printed), 153, 219–20. See also *The United Presbyterian*, 25 March 1897, 181 and 1 April 1897, 202 for a description of the United Presbyterian Association.
19. *GAM*, (N.S.) 1864, 297.
20. Widows' Fund Membership Register 1761–1875.
21. "Corporation Minutes," 17 May 1861.
22. Ibid., 10 September 1863, 19 May 1865.
23. *GAM* (O.S.), 1863, 59.
24. "Corporation Minutes," 10 September 1863.
25. *The Presbyterian*, 22 April 1871, 2; 1 July 1871, 2.
26. "Corporation Minutes," 3 April 1871.
27. Ibid., 20 April 1874.
28. *GAM*, 1876, 73.
29. "Corporation Minutes," 17 May 1875, and "Address of the Presbyterian Annuity and Life Insurance Company, 1875," 1–5. In 1876 the company agreed to "make insurance on the lives of human beings and grant annuities without regard to any sectarian or denominational connection whatsoever." "Corporation Minutes," 2 October 1876.
30. Ibid., 19 May 1880, 27 January 1881. See also *GAUSA*, 1881, 550.
31. "Corporation Minutes," 22 January 1894.
32. John Baird, *Horn of Plenty: The Story of the Presbyterian Ministers' Fund* (Wheaton, Illinois: Tyndale House Publishers, 1982), 184, 254.
33. Ibid., 165–282.
34. There may be exceptions to these generalizations, but we have not seen any material that indicates otherwise. We have relied on official publications and documents rather than personal letters and comments.
35. *An Historical Sketch of the Presbyterian Board of Ministerial Relief* (Philadelphia, 1888), 3.
36. For example, in *The Presbyterian Magazine* (June 1925), 312, Master wrote: "It is significant that the oldest Board in the Church—established in 1717—is the Board of Ministerial Relief."
37. Alexander Mackie to Sherman Skinner, 14 September 1951.

Chapter 4

1. *GAM* (PCUSA), 1794, 90. All references to General Assembly minutes in this chapter refer to the PCUSA unless otherwise noted.
2. *GAM*, 1975, 97.
3. *GAM*, 1799, 173–74.
4. *GAM*, 1800, 6–7. Board of Trustees of the General Assembly, Treasurer's Accounts, 1803–1830. We have examined these and other financial records from the period and cannot find any specific reference to funds given to ministers' dependents. Nevertheless, the *Presbyterian Digest* in tracing the history of ministerial relief work says, "To this Board of Trustees of the General Assembly was committed the cause of Ministerial Relief, and for fifty years the Assembly endeavored to secure sufficient funds to give a comfortable support to all our ministers' families that were found to be in need." *Presbyterian Digest*, II (Philadelphia: Office of the General Assembly, 1930), 731.
5. *The Presbyterian*, 6 June 1856, 86.

6. *The Presbyterian*, 25 July 1857, 116.
7. "Corporation Minutes," 22 May 1852.
8. *GAM* (O.S.), 1857, 218. A survey taken in 1857 confirms this generalization. At that time, most synods and presbyteries had no system for assessing and caring for the needs of retired ministers within their bounds.
9. In 1800 the General Assembly recommended to presbyteries "that when they settle ministers in their churches they endeavour to convince such ministers of the importance of their speedily becoming contributors to the Widows' Fund, whereby they may at once provide for the support of their families, and assist in supporting an institution so charitable and useful in the Church." *GAM*, 1800, 10.
10. Ibid., 1842, 217.
11. "Minutes of the Presbytery of St. Clairsville" (O.S.), 4 October 1842. In 1842 Scioto Presbytery (N.S.) created a fund for superannuated ministers within the bounds of presbytery. See the account of this effort in *The New York Evangelist*, 1 July 1886, 8.
12. "Minutes of the Presbytery of Transylvania" (O.S.), 28 April 1848, 16 April 1850.
13. *The Constitution of the Society for the Relief of Indigent and Superannuated Ministers of the Presbyterian Church and Their Families* (Charleston, South Carolina, 1857), 1–10.
14. *GAM* (O.S.), 1849, 254 and "Minutes of the Presbytery of Steubenville (O.S.), 10 April 1849.
15. Ibid., 266–67.
16. *GAM* (O.S.), 1852, 27.
17. *An Historical Sketch of the Presbyterian Board of Ministerial Relief* (Cincinnati, 1888), 9–10. Hereafter referred to as *Ministerial Relief Sketch*.
18. Ernest Trice Thompson, *Presbyterians in the South*, 2 vols. (Richmond: John Knox Press, 1963), I:524.
19. Ibid., 524–28.
20. *GAM* (O.S.), 1856, 531 and *The Presbyterian*, 31 May 1856, 80.
21. *The Presbyterian*, 31 May 1856, 80.
22. Ibid., 81.
23. *GAM* (O.S.), 1856, 85.
24. *The Central Presbyterian*, 31 May 1856, 85.
25. *The Presbyterian*, 31 May 1856, 85.
26. Ibid.
27. Ibid., 86.
28. *The Central Presbyterian*, 31 May 1856, 85.
29. *The Presbyterian*, 31 May 1856, 85.
30. Ibid., 85–86.
31. Ibid.
32. Ibid.
33. Ibid.
34. *GAM* (O.S.), 1857, 218.
35. *The Central Presbyterian*, 31 May 1856, 85–86.
36. *GAM* (O.S.), 1857, 218.
37. Ibid., 221.
38. *Ministerial Relief Sketch*, 12, and *The Presbyterian*, 12 June 1869, 5. The first contribution to the Permanent Fund was made by the Mentz Church, New York. The same year the Cumberland Church in New York gave $11 followed by the Port Byron, New York, congregation which gave $11 in 1852. *GAM*, 1899, 262.
39. *GAM* (O.S.), 1861, 397–98, and *Ministerial Relief Sketch*, 12–13.

Notes

40. *GAM* (N.S.), 1861, 473.
41. *GAM* (N.S.), 1864, 295–98.
42. *GAM* (N.S.), 1865, 339.
43. *Ministerial Relief Sketch*, 16–17, and *The American Presbyterian*, 17 May 1869, 164.
44. *GAM* (O.S.), 1863, 105.
45. *The Presbyterian*, 5 June 1869, 5.
46. *GAM* (O.S.), 1869, 916–17.

Chapter 5

1. Loetscher, *Brief History*, 85; Clifford Drury, *Presbyterian Panorama* (Philadelphia: Board of Christian Education, 1952), 167–68.
2. *An Historical Sketch of the Presbyterian Board of Relief for Disabled Ministers, and the Widows and Orphans of Deceased Ministers: With the Outlook for its Work*. (Philadelphia: Board of Relief, 1888), 17.
3. "The General Assembly and Ministerial Relief," *American Presbyterian Review* (July 1871), 5.
4. *GAM*, 1874, 68–69. All references to General Assembly minutes in this chapter refer to the PCUSA unless otherwise noted.
5. *GAM*, 1871, 557. The General Assembly approved a sustentation fund in 1871 intending to provide all Presbyterian pastors a salary of at least $1,000 annually, but that goal was never realized.
6. *GAM*, 1871, 665–66.
7. *GAM*, 1875, 620–21.
8. *The Presbyterian Banner*, 18 May 1873, 100.
9. *GAM*, 1874, 68. See also *The Presbyterian*, 6 June 1874, 3.
10. *GAM*, 1874, 45 and 1876, 513.
11. *An Historical Sketch*, 18–19.
12. "Minutes of the Board of Relief for Disabled Ministers and the Widows and Orphans of Deceased Ministers," 18 February 1879. Hereafter referred to as "Relief Minutes."
13. "Relief Minutes," 19 November 1891.
14. "Relief Minutes," 16 September 1879, 11 April 1901.
15. "Relief Minutes," 17 June 1879, 16 March 1880. "Clergymen's sons and daughters, whom God has blessed with wealth, or a moderate competence, will at once repudiate the thought of leaving an honored parent to be dependent on anything but themselves for a home and the necessities of life." *GAM*, 1880, 160.
16. "Relief Minutes," 21 June 1906.
17. "Relief Minutes," 15 October 1896.
18. "Relief Minutes," 21 June 1881.
19. "Relief Minutes," 21 November 1901.
20. "Relief Minutes," 19 March 1891.
21. "Relief Minutes," 16 September 1897.
22. "Relief Minutes," 19 March 1891.
23. "Relief Minutes," 21 March 1882, 16 September 1897.
24. *GAM*, 1880, 160, 1898, 273.
25. "Relief Minutes," 17 October 1912.
26. *GAM*, 1888, 251, 1889, 240.
27. *The Assembly Herald* (July 1904), 385–88.
28. "Public Meeting of Ruling Elders, Commissioners to the General Assembly, at

Cincinnati, Ohio, in behalf of the Board of Relief, 28 May 1885. See also *The Church at Home and Abroad* 16 (1894), 239–41. Hereafter referred to as *CHA*.

29. For a survey of Presbyterian women's organizations in the nineteenth century, see Lois A. Boyd and R. Douglas Brackenridge, *Presbyterian Women in America: Two Centuries of a Quest for Status* (Westport, Connecticut: Greenwood Press, 1983), 3–59.
30. *GAM*, 1876, 174.
31. *GAM*, 1883, 795.
32. In 1899 Agnew lamented that churchwomen seemed well disposed to send food and clothing to active missionaries but had failed to continue such benevolence when people retired. At his urging the General Assembly in 1899 passed a resolution asking churchwomen "to minister to those aged and needy members of our great church family by preparing and sending boxes of clothing and other such articles as will carry comfort to their homes and gladness to their hearts." *The Assembly Herald* (October 1899), 137.
33. "Report of the Synodical Committee of Philadelphia on Ministerial Relief," 22 October 1880, 13–17.
34. *The Presbyterian*, 22 April 1871, 3. Letters expressing similar sentiments were common in church newspapers and periodicals.
35. *GAM*, 1890, 258–59. This included ministers, missionaries, and stated supplies who had served the church for at least thirty years.
36. The first year saw nineteen apply, the second year fifty-eight. *GAM*, 1890, 259; *GAM*, 1891, 299. Until 1918 the Honor Roll was fixed at age seventy and a maximum of $400. In 1921 the board lowered the age requirement to sixty-five and raised the maximum payment to $600. The average payment in 1921 to Honor Roll recipients was only $424.01. Henry B. Master to John T. Stone, 23 February 1922.
37. *GAM*, 1891, 298.
38. *GAM*, 1901, 318, and *The Assembly Herald* (February 1900), 442–44. During the last thirty years of the nineteenth century the number of assisted families grew from 264 to 931. In 1903 there were 3,300 nonself-supporting churches and 1,600 ministers without pastoral charges. See *The Assembly Herald* (July 1903), 346–47.
39. *The Assembly Herald* (September 1902), 380 and *The Presbyterian Magazine* (June 1925), 313, (July 1925), 364.
40. *The Assembly Herald* (December 1912), 673.
41. Fischer, *Growing Old in America*, 150–51. The increase in retirement homes was due in part to impetus given by large corporations and industries that were pensioning older workers in order to make room for younger applicants. Retirement homes, however, never proved to be very popular in America. By 1910 only a small percentage of America's four million persons sixty-five and older (fewer than one in twenty) lived in so-called old age homes.
42. "The Ministers' House at Perth Amboy," *CHA* 5 (1889), 413–17.
43. Ibid., 416.
44. *GAM*, 1886, 211.
45. *GAM*, 1887, 225–26.
46. *GAM*, 1888, 254.
47. *GAM*, 1901, 34.
48. Over a twenty-year period the average number residing in Perth Amboy was twenty-one. From 1883–1901 only forty-eight ministers chose to live there, fifteen of that number with their wives. During that time, there were twenty-three widows, eleven orphans, and two female missionaries. In all, only eighty-four families were represented.

49. Relief Board, *Annual Report*, 1902, 10–11.
50. Ibid., 12.
51. Fischer, *Growing Old in America*, 152.
52. *Harper's Weekly*, 17 June 1872, 1. Carleton's opening stanza described the revulsion felt by the elderly parent at the prospect of moving to the local poor house. "Over the hill to the poor-house/I can't quite make it clear!/Over the hill to the poor-house/It seems so horrid queer!/Many a step I've taken a toilin' to and fro,/But this is a sort of a journey I never thought to go."
53. *GAM*, 1902, 10–11. Surveys conducted by labor unions indicated that residents of their homes missed the experience of a community—friends, neighbors, and familiar environs. "Brothers," wrote one railroad worker, "how many of us would leave our family and friends and homes of our childhood days and go to a Brotherhood Home, perhaps far distant, and end our days in a strange place with strangers?" William Graebner, *A History of Retirement: The Meanings and Function of an American Institution* (New Haven: Yale University Press, 1980), 143–44.
54. "Relief Board Minutes," 17 November 1904.
55. Relief Board, *Annual Report*, 1896, 5. See also *CHA* 22 (1897), 33–35.
56. "Relief Board Minutes," 15 November 1900.
57. *The Assembly Herald* (May 1901), 190.
58. *The Assembly Herald* (November 1905), 617.
59. To its credit, the board continued to maintain a retirement home program because it felt that it met a need that otherwise might have gone unfulfilled. For an excellent summary of the history of these homes, see "The First Hundred Years: Centennial of the Homes Program for the Board of Pensions," published by the Board of Pensions in 1983.
60. "Relief Board Minutes," 19 January 1888.
61. Ibid., 17 December 1896.
62. Ibid., 18 March 1920.
63. *The Assembly Herald* (January 1899), 33.
64. "Relief Board Minutes," 21 November 1918.
65. "Relief Board Minutes," 18 September 1890. This would not have been considered unreasonable, however, given nineteenth-century definitions of sibling roles.
66. "Relief Board Minutes," 21 April 1898.
67. "Relief Board Minutes," 16 September 1897.
68. "Relief Board Minutes," 10 November 1895.
69. "Relief Board Minutes," 21 June 1923, 16 December 1920.
70. "Relief Board Minutes," 1 May 1913.
71. "Relief Board Minutes," 20 December 1917.
72. "Relief Board Minutes," 18 March 1920.
73. "Relief Board Minutes," 15 November 1923.
74. "Relief Board Minutes," 21 April 1982.
75. "Relief Board Minutes," 17 November 1927.
76. "Relief Board Minutes," 18 March 1926.
77. Relief Board, *Annual Report*, 1914, iv; 1915, 20.
78. *The New Era Magazine* (August 1916), 462–63.
79. *The New Era Magazine* (November 1919), 632.
80. *GAM*, 1923, I:76–77. In 1930 the Board of Pensions noted that the General Assembly had assigned it this responsibility in 1923 but gave the board neither authority nor money. The board expressed its willingness to assist in giving the denomination accurate information about homes and hospitals but said that

nothing substantial could be done "until a practical solution is worked out." "Board of Pension Minutes," 15 May 1930.

Chapter 6

1. Winthrop Hudson, *Religion in America* 3d ed. (New York: Scribner's, 1981), 293–326, and *GAM*, 1898, 78.
2. *The Assembly Herald* (February 1900), 442–44.
3. Graebner, *A History of Retirement*, 11–13.
4. Ibid., 108. See also George Swetnam, *Andrew Carnegie* (Boston: Twayne Publishers, 1980), 151–52.
5. Hingeley, *The Retired Minister*, 241–44.
6. "Minutes of the Presbytery of Iowa," 11 September 1901.
7. *GAM*, 1902, 170.
8. *GAM*, 1905, 134.
9. *GAM*, 1906, 109–14. It also had a benefit for widows and orphans. Women (missionaries and deaconesses) could join but had no survivor benefits.
10. *GAM*, 1906, 116–17. Huggins described his role in the early history of the Sustentation Fund in a letter to Reid Dickson, 7 July 1942 (PHS).
11. *The Assembly Herald* (June 1916), 338, (June 1917), 295.
12. *Sustentation Fund Report*, 1911, 3.
13. *The Assembly Herald* (February 1911), 200.
14. B. J. Agnew to the Executive Commission, 5 March 1903.
15. B. J. Agnew to the Executive Commission, 30 November 1906. Agnew later opposed merger in his report to the General Assembly in 1910. See *Annual Report*, 1910, 14–16.
16. *GAM*, 1908, 115; *GAM*, 1910, 66. Sustentation field representatives worked on an incentive plan. For cash and subscriptions totaling more than $15,000 a month, they received an additional twenty-five dollars in salary. "Sustentation Fund Minutes," 17 January 1911.
17. "Relief Board Minutes," 7 December 1911.
18. John R. Sutherland to the Executive Commission, 21 March 1911. According to Sutherland, the chief obstacle his fund faced was opposition from members of the Relief Board. "They openly stated that the plan would prove a failure, and when they began to fear that their prediction would not be fulfilled, their opposition became more open and pronounced. They evidently believed that the success of the Sustentation Plan would militate against the interests of said Board, and that it would lessen its annual income." See also *The Assembly Herald* (August 1911), 394.
19. *The Assembly Herald* (September 1911), 417–19.
20. *The Presbyterian*, 18 May 1911, 32.
21. *The Assembly Herald* (September 1911), 418.
22. *The Presbyterian Banner*, 25 May 1911, 7.
23. *GAM*, 1911, 207.
24. Ibid., 1912, 230.
25. *Relief Board Report*, 1912, 20–21, and *The Assembly Herald* (July 1911), 195.
26. John R. Sutherland to the Executive Commission, 21 July 1910.
27. *GAM*, 1912, 233, and *The Assembly Herald* (July 1912), 402.
28. *The Assembly Herald* (December 1912), 672.
29. *The Assembly Herald* (December 1918), 616–17.
30. "Relief and Sustentation Minutes," 21 February 1918.

Notes 163

31. *GAM*, 1918, 133, and *The Assembly Herald* (December 1918), 616–17.
32. *The Assembly Herald* (November 1919), 634.
33. *The Presbyterian Magazine* (July 1922), 423.
34. *GAM*, 1922, I:89–90, and *The Presbyterian Magazine* (June 1922), 369, (July 1922), 461.
35. *GAM*, 1923, I:55–56, and *The Presbyterian Magazine* (March 1924), 13, (February 1927), 82–83.
36. For a critical analysis of the Sustentation Fund, see Charles L. Burrall, Jr., "Church Pensions—Past, Present and Future," 1 December 1977 (PHS).
37. *The Presbyterian Magazine* (February 1927), 81–82.
38. George A. Huggins to Reid Dickson, 7 July 1942, and Hingeley, *The Retired Minister*, 150–206.
39. George A. Huggins, "The Church Pensions Conference," 10 October 1956. Present at the first meeting were J. F. Hingeley (Methodist), George C. Lenington (Reformed Church in America), Henry H. Sweets (Presbyterian Church, U.S.), Everett T. Tomlinson (American Baptist), and William A. Rice (Congregationalist). Hingeley's book, *The Retired Minister*, utilized information he gained from these interdenominational contacts.
40. Correspondence in PHS indicates that the controversy between Relief and Sustentation continued unabated even after federation of the two groups. Several lay members of the Relief Board carried on a sustained campaign against Sustentation and, according to Foulkes, had an "obsession about destroying Sustentation." William H. Foulkes to Stanley White, 16 April 1917.
41. *GAM*, 1923, I:59–188.
42. Special Committee on Reorganization and Consolidation of the Boards and Agencies, 1922–1923, *Correspondence, Minutes, and Reports*, PHS.
43. Ibid.
44. *GAM*, 1922, I:158–59. The other three boards were also instructed to add three women to their list of trustees. This marked the first time in denominational history that women were so recognized. The first three women elected to Relief and Sustentation were Mrs. George Grant Snowden of Rosemont, Pennsylvania, Mrs. Oliver R. Williamson of Chicago, Illinois, and Mrs. William Jennings of Harrisburg, Pennsylvania.
45. "Relief and Sustentation Minutes," 19 October 1922, and *GAM*, 1923, I:77.
46. Will H. Hays, *Memoirs of Will H. Hays* (New York: Doubleday, 1954), 560.
47. *The Presbyterian Magazine* (June 1927), 337.
48. *GAM*, 1924, I:108–9, and *The Presbyterian Magazine* (April 1925), 198
49. *The Presbyterian Magazine* (January 1925), 18–19.
50. *The Presbyterian Magazine* (June 1925), 312–13.
51. *The Presbyterian Magazine* (February 1925), 79. The Plan also contained a clause that permitted a contributor to withdraw one's 2 ½ percent at 4 percent interest should one resign his or her position and be ineligible to receive a pension.
52. *The Presbyterian Magazine* (September 1925), 464.
53. *The Presbyterian Magazine* (July 1924), 348.
54. *The Presbyterian Magazine* (June 1925), 312–13, (April 1924), 182.
55. *The Assembly Herald* (September 1911), 420.
56. *The Presbyterian Magazine* (July 1925), 365.
57. Ibid.
58. "Relief and Sustentation Minutes," 21 October 1926, and Hays, *Memoirs*, 561–62.
59. Hays, *Memoirs*, 564–65.

60. *The Presbyterian*, 2 June 1927, 17, and Hays, *Memoirs*, 566.
61. *The Presbyterian Magazine* (July 1927), 383–84.
62. Ibid. In his "History of the Board of Pensions," 1972, 25, Donald L. Hibbard, secretary of the Board of Pensions from 1946–1972, states that the Laymen's Committee initially asked the Prudential Life Insurance Company to run the pension program rather than entrust it to the Board of Relief and Sustentation. According to Hibbard, Edward D. Duffield, president of Prudential, rejected the offer, arguing that the church needed to have a vital interest in the program and without a total involvement the program would fail. We have found no direct confirmation of this story in any of our primary sources but there is no reason to doubt Hibbard's recollections which he obviously picked up from personal contact with older board members and staff. The issue apparently was discussed in the 1920s as indicated by an article written by George A. Huggins, "Church Pensions or Commercial Insurance?" *The Presbyterian Magazine* (March 1927), 166–67. Huggins made a strong case for church management of the pension program based on theological and pragmatic grounds.
63. *The Presbyterian Magazine* (March 1928), 134, (July 1928), 383–84.
64. *The Presbyterian Magazine* (June 1925), 312.

Chapter 7

1. Ben M. Barrus, Milton L. Baughn, Thomas H. Campbell, *A People Called Cumberland Presbyterians* (Memphis: Frontier Press, 1972), 32–44 and R. Douglas Brackenridge, *Voice in the Wilderness: A History of the Cumberland Presbyterian Church in Texas* (San Antonio: Trinity University Press, 1969), 1–11.
2. Wallace N. Jamieson, *The United Presbyterian Story* (Pittsburgh: Geneva Press, 1958), 11–60.
3. B. W. McDonnold, *History of the Cumberland Presbyterian Church*, 2d ed. (Nashville, 1888), 250.
4. Barrus et al., *A People Called Cumberland Presbyterians*, 205–6.
5. "Minutes of the Little River Presbytery" (CP), 9 December 1857.
6. *St. Louis Observer*, 5 June 1888, 4.
7. *Minutes of the General Assembly of the Cumberland Presbyterian Church*, 1833, 12. Hereafter referred to as *GACP*.
8. Barrus et al., *A People Called Cumberland Presbyterians*, 211.
9. *GACP*, 1873; 1874, 34–35.
10. *GACP*, 1880, 36–37.
11. *GACP*, 1881, 35–36.
12. Ibid.
13. *GACP*, 1882, 84. See also the *St. Louis Presbyterian*, 29 September 1881, 4.
14. *GACP*, 1890, 86.
15. *GACP*, 1906, Appendix:92.
16. *GACP*, 1890, 87.
17. *GACP*, 1886, 120.
18. *GACP*, 1892, 107.
19. *GACP*, 1890, 100; 1901, Appendix:70a–71a.
20. *GACP*, 1887, 106–7.
21. *GACP*, 1896, 97.
22. *GACP*, 1891, 100.

23. *The St. Louis Observer*, 11 December 1890, 12.
24. *GACP*, 1894, 124–25.
25. *GACP*, 1890, 88.
26. GACP, 1906, Appendix 2:6a–10a.
27. *The United Presbyterian*, 5 December 1868, 2.
28. *The United Presbyterian*, 11 April 1868, 2.
29. *Minutes of the General Assembly of the United Presbyterian Church of North America*, 1862, I:71. Hereafter referred to as *GAUPNA*.
30. *GAUPNA*, 1864, II:14.
31. Ibid.
32. *GAUPNA*, 1969, II:34.
33. *GAUPNA*, 1870, III:150.
34. *GAUPNA*, 1877, IV:477; 1879, V:72; 1883, V:719; 1901, X:328–29.
35. *GAUPNA*, 1873, III:545.
36. *GAUPNA*, 1895, IX:781.
37. *GAUPNA*, 1875, IV:163.
38. *GAUPNA*, 1885, VI:286.
39. "Minutes of the Board of Ministerial Relief" (UPNA), 2 January 1877.
40. "Minutes of the Board of Ministerial Relief" (UPNA), 4 January 1910.
41. "Minutes of the Board of Ministerial Relief" (UPNA), 8 September 1892.
42. "Minutes of the Board of Ministerial Relief" (UPNA), 23 June 1884.
43. *GAUPNA*, 1882, V:578.
44. *Woman's Missionary Magazine* (January 1894), 93–94; (November 1899), 88–89; (July 1899), 329–30.
45. Jamieson, *The United Presbyterian Story*, 106–7.
46. *GAUPNA*, 1898, IX:598.
47. For a historical overview of these programs, see *The United Presbyterian*, 15 June 1922, 1–14; 17 April 1930, 9–12; 2 May 1949, 10–11.
48. *GAUPNA*, 1909, XII:316, and *The United Presbyterian*, 2 May 1949, 10.
49. *GAUPNA*, 1916, XIV:23.
50. *GAUPNA*, 1917, XIV:290–91.
51. *GAUPNA*, 1928, XVII:148.
52. *GAUPNA*, 1928, XVII:150.
53. Board of Ministerial Pensions and Relief, *Annual Report*, 1958, 2–4.

Chapter 8

1. Loetscher, *Brief History*, 104–6, and Thompson, *Presbyterians in the South*, I:551–71.
2. Cited in Thompson, *Presbyterians in the South*, II:36.
3. "Minutes of the Synod of Georgia," 1862, 18. See also Thompson, *Presbyterians in the South*, II:36–62.
4. *The Southern Presbyterian*, 25 January 1866, 1.
5. Thompson, *Presbyterians in the South*, II:18–19.
6. *GAM*, 1900, 690. All references to General Assembly minutes in this chapter are from the Presbyterian Church in the United States (PCUS).
7. *The Central Presbyterian*, 31 May 1866, 2.
8. John N. Craig to F. R. Beattie, 28 December 1899.
9. *GAM*, 1863, 129–30; 1864, 274.

10. *GAM*, 1867, 148; 1868, 274.
11. *GAM*, 1869, 404, and *The Christian Observer*, 9 June 1869, 2.
12. *GAM*, 1873, 351.
13. Ibid. Most of the sustentation reports in the 1860s and 1870s contained similar accounts of ministerial destitution.
14. *GAM*, 1890, 78–79.
15. *The Christian Observer*, 29 May 1901, 2.
16. *GAM*, 1882, 562.
17. *GAM*, 1883, 39, 73.
18. *GAM*, 1884, 234.
19. *GAM*, 1894, 237.
20. *The Christian Observer*, 19 May 1895, 7.
21. *GAM*, 1895, 396.
22. John N. Craig to F. R. Beattie, 28 December 1899.
23. *GAM*, 1900, 690.
24. For a description of the Free Church program, see *GAM*, 1900, 686. For a background of Wilson, see Henry A. White, *Southern Presbyterian Leaders* (New York, 1911), 394–408.
25. *The Christian Observer*, 9 June 1869, 1.
26. *GAM*, 1869, 396.
27. *The Christian Observer*, 17 August 1870, 1.
28. *The Southwestern Presbyterian*, 3 June 1869, 2.
29. *The Christian Observer*, 5 October 1870, 1.
30. *The Central Presbyterian*, 12 April 1871, 1.
31. *The Central Presbyterian*, 28 April 1869, 1.
32. *The Central Presbyterian*, 21 April 1869, 1.
33. *The Southwestern Presbyterian*, 8 June 1871, 1.
34. *GAM*, 1870, 524–26.
35. *GAM*, 1873, 542.
36. *GAM*, 1876, 208. See also *The Christian Observer*, 24 May 1876, 2.
37. *GAM*, 1900, 691.
38. *The Christian Observer*, 3 June 1885, 5.
39. Ibid.
40. *GAM*, 1885, 421.
41. *GAM*, 1899, 418.
42. *The Southwestern Presbyterian*, 30 July 1896, 4.
43. *The Christian Observer*, 23 May 1900, 1.
44. *GAM*, 1900, 653, and *The Southwestern Presbyterian*, 14 July 1901, 3.
45. *The Christian Observer*, 30 May 1900, 3.
46. *GAM*, 1900, 684–93.
47. Ibid., 691–93.
48. *GAM*, 1901, 111–13.
49. *The Christian Observer*, 13 February 1901, 2. The original records refer to the committee as "The Executive Committee *on* Ministerial Relief (italics added). For consistency's sake, we have used "of" in such instances.
50. *GAM*, 1902, 310–11.
51. *The Presbyterian Standard*, 4 January 1902, 6.
52. *The Presbyterian Standard*, 12 February 1902, 4, and *The Southwestern Presbyterian*, 29 May 1902, 2.
53. *The Southwestern Presbyterian*, 29 June 1902, 12.

54. *GAM*, 1904, 81.
55. Ibid., 13, and *The Southwestern Presbyterian*, 1 June 1904, 4.
56. *The Southwestern Presbyterian*, 4 June 1904, 4, and *The Christian Observer*, 1 June 1904, 12.
57. *GAM*, 1904, 44, and *The Christian Observer*, 1 June 1904, 26-27. See also *The Presbyterian Standard*, 31 August 1904, 14.
58. *GAM*, 1910, 20-21, and *The Christian Observer*, 27 July 1904, 2.
59. For a brief summary of Sweets' work in education, see *The Presbyterian Outlook*, 16 February 1948, 10-11. Sweets' personal papers (1890-1952) and most of his publications and addresses are in the archives of the Historical Foundation of the Presbyterian and Reformed Churches, Inc., Montreat, North Carolina. The papers were unprocessed at the time of publication of this book.
60. *GAM*, 1935, 17.
61. "Minutes of the Executive Committee on Ministerial Education and Relief," 12 January 1905. Hereafter referred to as "Executive Committee Minutes."
62. *Annual Report of the Executive Committee on Ministerial Education and Relief*, 1906, 3. Hereafter referred to as *Annual Report*.
63. "Executive Committee Minutes," 9 February 1917.
64. "Executive Committee Minutes," 14 January 1925.
65. "Executive Committee Minutes," 21 April 1918.
66. *GAM*, 1914, Appendix:112-13. See also *The Christian Observer*, 31 May 1893, 9 and 5 July, 5.
67. *GAM*, 1914, Appendix:113.
68. Ibid., and "Executive Committee Minutes," 7 February 1911.
69. *Annual Report*, 1911, 21-23, and "Executive Committee Minutes," 8 March 1912.
70. *GAM*, 1911, Appendix:122.
71. "Executive Committee Minutes," 16 April 1914.
72. *GAM*, 1921, 57.
73. *Handbook on Christian Education and Ministerial Relief* (Louisville, 1925), 16-17. For the first ten years the Graham Building averaged a net yield of $55,605.19, but its eventual deterioration, along with the financial problems of the Depression, caused the church to offer it for sale.
74. *GAM*, 1912, 23. For a background of the Woman's Auxiliary, see Hallie Paxon Winsborough, *The Woman's Auxiliary of the Presbyterian Church in the United States* (Richmond: Presbyterian Committee of Publication, 1927), 36-41.
75. Thompson, *Presbyterians in the South*, III:387.
76. *GAM*, 1912, 23.
77. Patricia Houck Sprinkle, *The Birthday Book: The First Fifty Years* (Atlanta: PCUS Board of Women's Work, 1972), 216-17.
78. *GAM*, 1899, 430.
79. *The Presbyterian Survey* (1933), 596; (November 1933), 692-94.
80. *GAM*, 1983, 644. See also Ralph Bugg, "From Pious Fund to Joy Gift," *The Presbyterian Survey* (October 1982), 34-35 and Cecil W. Hannaford, "A Very Important Gift" (November 1981), 26.
81. *GAM*, 1923, 68-70.
82. *Annual Report*, 1924, 2.
83. "Executive Committee Minutes," 4 April 1950, 15 February 1957. See also *The Christian Observer*, 26 December 1956, 15.
84. In addition to his participation in the Church Pensions Conference, Sweets also worked with the Council of the Reformed Churches and is committed to encourage

contributory pensions among Presbyterian denominations. See *Annual Report,* 1916, 16–17.
85. *GAM*, 1909, 10.
86. *GAM*, 1911, 53.
87. *GAM*, 1918, 34.
88. *Annual Report*, 1919, 11–12.
89. *Annual Report*, 1923, 46.
90. *Annual Report*, 1922, 13–26.
91. *Annual Report*, 1924, 17–19, and *GAM*, 1924, 40. The Ministers' Annuity Fund in its final form can be found in *GAM*, 1930, 140–45.
92. *GAM*, 1924, 40; 1925, 46; 1927, 36.
93. *Annual Report*, 1935, 27.

Chapter 9

1. *Annual Report*, 1935, 27.
2. "Executive Committee Minutes," 21 January 1938.
3. *Annual Report*, 1940, 92.
4. *The Presbyterian of the South*, 27 July 1932, 1.
5. Henry H. Sweets to B. Pollard Cardozo, 12 February 1938.
6. Henry H. Sweets to B. Pollard Cardozo, 12 February 1938.
7. Henry H. Sweets to Wade H. Boggs, 16 March 1938.
8. Henry H. Sweets to Wade H. Boggs, 25 January 1938.
9. Henry H. Sweets to Wade H. Boggs, 27 March 1940.
10. "Executive Committee Minutes," 20 June 1940, and Henry H. Sweets to Wade H. Boggs, 8 February 1940.
11. Henry H. Sweets Papers, Historical Foundation, Montreat, North Carolina.
12. Ibid.
13. *GAM*, 1942, 72–75.
14. *GAM*, 1977, 139–46; 1981, 338.
15. Alice Eastwood, "In Memoriam of Henry H. Sweets, 1872–1952" (Atlanta, 1952), 4.
16. *The Southern Presbyterian Journal* (October 1943), 4.
17. *Annual Report*, 1948, 61.
18. *Annual Report*, 1949, 50.
19. R. Douglas Brackenridge and Francisco O. Garcia-Treto, *Iglesia Presbiteriana: A History of Presbyterians and Mexican Americans in the Southwest* (San Antonio: Trinity University Press, 1974), 109–10.
20. *GAM*, 1946, 77.
21. *Annual Report*, 1949, 54–56.
22. *GAM*, 1958, 66. See also *GAM*, 1964, 101–6; 1978, 123–24.
23. C. Darby Fulton to Henry H. Sweets, 20 October 1940.
24. Henry H. Sweets Papers.
25. Ibid., 2 November 1943, and "Executive Committee Minutes," 7 November 1944.
26. *World Missions Annual Report*, 1963, 165; and 1966, 131. In 1979 the Board of Annuities and Relief assumed pension responsibility for eighty missionaries who had retired prior to 1966 under agreements with the former Board of World Missions. *GAM*, 1980, I:434.
27. *GAM*, 1949, Appendix:131.
28. Ibid., 131–32.
29. *GAM*, 1949, Appendix:148–49.

Notes 169

30. Charles Currie to Miriam Schmidt, 28 April 1955. See also the *San Antonio Express-News*, 11 March 1958, 10.
31. *GAM*, 1949; Appendix:150.
32. "Board Minutes," 10 July 1951, and *GAM*, 1952, 56.
33. *Annual Report*, 1953, 25–26.
34. *Annual Report*, 1960, 24–25.
35. *Annual Report*, 1968, 22–23.
36. *Annual Report*, 1973, 7–8.
37. *Annual Report*, 1922, 13, and "Executive Committee Minutes," 17 March 1922.
38. "Board Minutes," 21 April 1949.
39. "Board Minutes," 16 March 1954. At the same meeting the board turned down a suggestion that a memorial to Henry Sweets be in the form of a retirement home for ministers.
40. "Executive Committee Minutes," 7 November 1944.
41. *GAM*, 1973, Appendix:223.
42. *Atlanta Constitution*, 23 March 1967, 12.
43. *Annual Report*, 1973, 225.
44. "Board Minutes," 27 February 1962.
45. *GAM*, 1979, 379, and George H. Vick, interview with R. Douglas Brackenridge (RDB). Lewisburg, West Virginia, 1985.
46. *GAM*, 1972, I:118.
47. Ibid., 118–19.
48. "Board Minutes," 24 February 1970.
49. *The Presbyterian Outlook*, 5 July 1972, 8, and *The Presbyterian Survey* (July 1972), 4–5.
50. *The Presbyterian Survey* (August 1972), 17–21. See also (December 1972), 9; (April 1973), 64.
51. *The Presbyterian Survey* (May 1973), 33.
52. *GAM*, 1973, I:222.
53. *The Presbyterian Outlook*, 25 June 1973, 6.

Chapter 10

1. Andrew Achenbaum, *Shades of Gray: Old Age, American Values, and Federal Policies Since 1920* (Boston and Toronto: Little, Brown, Publishers, 1983), 29–30. For a background of this period, see Robert T. Handy, "The American Religious Depression, 1925–35," *Church History*, 29 (1960), 2–16.
2. *Ninth Annual Report of the Board of Christian Education*, 1933, 19–20. By 1933 there was widespread concern in the denomination regarding the status of unemployed Presbyterian ministers. The Department of Vacancy and Supply reported that "a greatly increased number of thoroughly capable and highly desirable ministers were out of employment."
3. "Minutes of the Board of Pensions," 21 January 1932, and 19 May 1933. Hereafter referred to as "BOP Minutes."
4. *Annual Report of the Board of Pensions*, 1943, 14. Hereafter referred to as *BOP Report*. Some members wanted to change the board's name to the Board of Pensions and Relief. This was successfully resisted by Master who argued that the word "relief" connoted charity and would have an adverse effect on the work. "General Council Minutes," 19 March 1931.
5. *BOP Report*, 1932, 20.

6. Ibid., 8.
7. Ibid., 10–12.
8. *BOP Report*, 1944, 37.
9. *BOP Report*, 1935, 6–8; 1939, 5.
10. *BOP Report*, 1935, 10–11; 1947, 21.
11. *BOP Report*, 1936, 19.
12. *BOP Report*, 1947, 21.
13. *GAM*, 1951, I:133.
14. *The Presbyterian*, 4 June 1936, 4, and *BOP Report*, 1937, 19–20.
15. *BOP Report*, 1938, 9–10.
16. *The Presbyterian*, 18 May 1938, back cover.
17. *BOP Report*, 1939, 14–15.
18. *The Presbyterian*, 1 June 1939, 9, and *GAM*, 1939, 81.
19. "Minutes of the Special Committee on the Board of Pensions 1940–41," dated 14 October 1940, 57 (PHS).
20. Reid Dickson, "Report on Service Pension Plan," September 1939, 1–11. Record Group 21, (PHS).
21. *Factual Information From the Board of Pensions* (Philadelphia, 1940), 41–49.
22. *Report on the Centenary Fund* (Cincinnati, 1889), 20–21.
23. "Relief Board Minutes," 19 December 1890.
24. *Factual Information From the Board of Pensions*, 40–41.
25. "Minutes of the Special Committee on the Board of Pensions, 1940–41," 14 October 1940, 57–85, and Donald L. Hibbard, "History of the Board of Pensions," 27–28.
26. "Minutes of the Special Committee on the Board of Pensions, 1940–41," 12–13 November 1940.
27. "General Council Minutes," 24 October 1939, 7–9; 6 March 1940, 7.
28. *GAM* 1940, 120–23.
29. *The Presbyterian*, 30 May 1940, 11.
30. "Minutes of the Special Committee on the Board of Pensions 1940–41," 15 October 1940, 57.
31. *GAM*, 1941, 83–107; 263–334.
32. *GAM*, 1942, 110.
33. *GAM*, 1943, 227–33.
34. *GAM*, 1945, I:129.
35. Ibid., 130–40.
36. *GAM*, 1948, I:148.
37. Hibbard, "History of the Board of Pensions," 29.
38. *BOP Report*, 1944, 39.
39. Donald L. Hibbard, interview with RDB and Lois A. Boyd (LAB), Longmont, Colorado, 15–16 June 1984. At the time of writing this book, the tapes have not been transcribed. They will be deposited with the Presbyterian Historical Society in Philadelphia as part of its oral history collection.
40. *BOP Report*, 1948, 20; 1949, 32–42.
41. *BOP Report*, 1960, 19–25.
42. *BOP Report*, 1956, 1.
43. Hibbard, "History of the Board of Pensions," 40–41, and *BOP Report*, 1962, 4; 1971, 3.
44. *BOP Report*, 1957, 11.
45. *BOP Report*, 1962, 5.

46. *BOP Report*, 1967, 5-30.
47. *BOP Report*, 1969, 5-48.
48. Attitudes toward participation in Social Security had dramatically changed since the 1930s when the program was first introduced. The General Assembly in 1952 expressed its desire that Social Security laws be changed to allow ministers to participate on a voluntary basis. They entered the program as "self-employed" individuals to avoid potential church-state conflicts. Only a small percentage of Presbyterian ministers chose not to enter the program and by 1970 the board reported that 97 percent of Presbyterian ministers were participating in Social Security. See *BOP Report*, 1951, 9-10; 1953, 7-9; and Hibbard, "History of the Board of Pensions," 33-34.
49. *BOP Report*, 1952, 3.
50. *BOP Report*, 1966, 29-61, and Hibbard, "History of the Board of Pensions," 32-33. In 1972 the General Assembly designated the 1973 Christmas Offering to be utilized for inadequate pensions. Contributions totaled nearly one and a half million dollars. Subsequently, portions of the Christmas Offering have gone for this purpose. *BOP Report*, 1972, 16-17.
51. *BOP Report*, 1963, 17-18.
52. *BOP Report*, 1952, 30-31; 1972, 11.
53. Hibbard, "History of the Board of Pensions," 14-15.
54. *BOP Report*, 1948, 24-33; 1949, 25-30.
55. *BOP Report*, 1951, 38-53; 1955, 44; 1958, 43. The annual reports of this Division are valuable sources of information about the network of Presbyterian institutions engaged in care for the elderly.
56. *BOP Report*, 1953, 26-27; Hibbard, "History of the Board of Pensions," 14-18; Moreland, "The First Hundred Years: Centennial of the Homes Program for the Board of Pensions," 5. Linn Fenimore Cooper had donated to the board his family home, "Fynmere," in Cooperstown, New York, together with twenty-eight acres of land in memory of his parents, James Fenimore Cooper and Susan Linn Cooper.
57. Moreland, "The First Hundred Years," 4-5, and *BOP Report*, 1972, 8-9.
58. *BOP Report*, 1965, 26.
59. Moreland, "The First Hundred Years," 5, and "BOP Minutes," 14 February 1979.
60. Moreland, "The First Hundred Years," 6, and *GAM*, 1983, I:506.
61. *BOP Report*, 1952, 25-26; Moreland, "The First Hundred Years," 5-6; Arthur M. Ryan, interview with LAB and RDB, Philadelphia, Pennsylvania, 12 May 1987.
62. *BOP Report*, 1963, 4, and Hibbard, "History of the Board of Pensions," 43-45.
63. *BOP Report*, 1972, 13.
64. *BOP Report*, 1966, 10.
65. *BOP Report*, 1969, 59.
66. *GAM*, 1966, I:415-16.
67. "BOP Minutes," 20 February 1964.
68. "BOP Minutes," 21 November 1968.
69. *GAM*, 1972, I:730-38, and *Presbyterian Life* (July 1972), 33-35.
70. "Perspectives: The Board of Pensions in Relation to its Members," Institute for Social Research, The University of Michigan, Ann Arbor, Michigan, 1971, 152-58.
71. Ibid., 62, 114.
72. *GAM*, 1972, I:100, 198, 377.
73. Ibid., 371, 1054.
74. *A.D. Magazine* (July 1973), 43.

Chapter 11

1. Dan M. McGill, *Fundamentals of Private Pensions*, 5th ed. (Homewood, Illinois: Pension Research Council, 1984).
2. *BOP Report*, 1973, 6–8.
3. Ibid., 24–39, and *A.D. Magazine* (July 1974), 45–46. The complete report of the committee with appendixes containing a summary of the suggestions received as a result of questionnaires, was printed and distributed separately. See *Report of the Vocation Agency's Consulting Committee on Pensions* (February 1974).
4. *GAM* (PCUS), 1975, I:110; 1977, I:389–93; 1980, I:432.
5. *GAM* (UPCUSA), 1975, I:183, and *BOP Report*, 1975, 21–22.
6. "Minutes of the Board of Annuities and Relief," 28 October 1977.
7. *GAM* (UPCUSA), 1978, I:421, and *GAM* (PCUS), 1978, I:129. Since this was a union presbytery, the request was directed to both the UPCUSA and PCUS assemblies. See also *A.D. Magazine* (June–July 1978), 45.
8. *GAM* (UPCUSA), 1979, I:77, 481.
9. *GAM* (PCUS), 1982, I:324; 1983, I:645–46.
10. For a background of these movements, see Robert Ruoss, "Churches vs. Corporations: The Coming Struggle for Power," *A.D. Magazine* (February 1973), 38–46; Otto S. Folin, "Church Investments and American Corporations," *Church and Society* (March–April 1972), 5–13; *A.D. Magazine* (February 1975), 15–26.
11. "The Church and Transnational Corporations," *Church and Society* (March–April 1984), 9, 27–28. This issue includes and expands upon material presented to the General Assembly in 1983 by the Task Force on Transnational Corporations. See *GAM* (U.S.A.), 1983, I:208–39.
12. *GAM* (UPCUSA), 1971, I:596–603; 1972 I:39; *GAM* (PCUS), 1976, Appendix:514.
13. Arthur W. Brown, interview with RDB, Philadelphia, Pennsylvania, 18 June 1985. The Board of Annuities and Relief traditionally avoided investment in tobacco companies. When it approved participation in the Sun Belt Investment Fund which included two tobacco firms, it did so only on the basis of eliminating those two companies. "Minutes of the Board of Annuities and Relief," 30 October 1981. On the other hand, the Board of Pensions, while noting that it had excluded from its portfolio companies whose principal business involved liquor, gambling, and tobacco, recognized that such was inconsistent with its opposition to divestment in general. "We would not be willing to initiate such a prohibition and there is considerable sentiment in favor of abolishing it." "The Board of Pensions' Comments on MRTI's Draft Paper Entitled 'Some Reflections on the Context for Considering Divestment as a Strategy in the Management of the Church's Resources in a Socially Responsible Way,'" 11 November 1983, 2–3. This particular paper sets forth the board's major objections to divestment and amplifies its understanding of fiduciary responsibility.
14. "The Church and Transnational Corporations," 28–29. *GAM* (UPCUSA), 1972, I:39; 1975, I:442–44. At the same time, the assembly also established the Advisory Council on Church and Society "to maintain and strengthen the prophetic voice of the church," 1972, I:713. For an overview of this group's work, see *GAM* (U.S.A.), 1983, I:333–35.
15. *BOP Report*, 1972, 15 and Arthur W. Brown, interview with RDB, Philadelphia, Pennsylvania, 18 June 1985.
16. *BOP Report*, 1976, 29, and "BOP Minutes," 20 December 1976.
17. "BOP Minutes," 19 February 1977. Later in the same year the board drafted new

investment policies that directed the Finance Committee to be "sensitive to the social and ethical teachings of the General Assembly and the *Confession of 1967* as they focus on Peace, Racial Justice, Economic and Social Justice, and Protection of the Environment." "BOP Minutes," 15 June 1977.
18. For a background of ERISA, see McGill, *Fundamentals of Private Pensions*, 29-38. *BOP Report*, 1975, 10, and *GAM* (PCUS), 1979, I:414-16.
19. *BOP Report*, 1976, 29.
20. Gordon Manser to G. Daniel Little, 3 January 1977. Manser was chairman of the Board of Trustees and Little was chief executive officer of the GAMC.
21. "The Views of the Committee on Mission Responsibility Through Investment," presented to the Special Committee on Shareholder Resolutions, 31 October 1977, 1-19.
22. Ibid., 20-21.
23. "BOP Minutes," 22 November 1977, and *Annual Report*, 1977, 29.
24. *GAM* (UPCUSA), 1979, I:129-30.
25. *GAM* (UPCUSA), 1982, I:261. The Board of Pensions was asked to implement these guidelines "insofar as legally possible within the fiduciary obligations for which their respective Trustees are personally responsible." Attached to the guidelines was a background paper by Dana W. Wilbanks, "Theological and Ethical Reflections on Proposed Mission Responsibility Through Investment Criteria," 261-63.
26. "BOP Minutes," 18 February 1981. The new title for the UPCUSA "Service Pension Plan" was adopted in 1977 to reflect changes in the nature of the program since its creation in 1927. See *GAM* (UPCUSA), 1977, I:705.
27. "BOP Minutes," 14 October 1981.
28. "BOP Minutes."
29. "BOP Minutes," 15 April 1982, and Arthur W. Brown, interview with RDB, Philadelphia, Pennsylvania, 18 June 1985.
30. "BOP Minutes," 20 October 1982.
31. "BOP Minutes," 3 March 1983.
32. *GAM* (UPCUSA), 1983, I:508-9. On the advice of investment counselors, the board later added some of the excluded corporations to its investment portfolio. *GAM*, 1984, I:555.
33. *GAM* (PCUS), 1977, I:468. In 1973 the General Assembly affirmed that all monies designated for the MAF, EAF, and relief funds "should be kept inviolate and should be separated in fact and in management from non-fiduciary program operations within the Church." *GAM* (PCUS), 1973, I:75.
34. "Board of Annuities and Relief Minutes," 29 October 1971.
35. *GAM* (PCUS), 1977, I:177-80.
36. *GAM* (PCUS), 1978, I:97, 130.
37. *GAM* (PCUS), 1979, I:414-16.
38. Ibid., 417-19.
39. *GAM* (PCUS), 1979, I:95, 190.
40. "Board of Annuities and Relief Minutes," 29 February 1980. Although the board was not under MRTI guidelines, it adjusted its investment portfolio after the 1983 reunion to exclude most military-related corporations. "Board of Annuities and Relief Minutes," 22 February 1985.
41. *GAM* (U.S.A.), 1983, I:644.
42. Ibid., 692. The title of the UPCUSA Service Pension Plan had been changed in 1977 to the U.P. Pension and Benefits Plan to reflect changes in the nature of the program since its creation in 1927. See *GAM* (UPCUSA), 1977, I:705.

43. *Monday Morning Magazine*, 17 March 1980, 6. For other examples, see 7 March 1972, 12; 5 November 1979, 10–11; 17 March 1980, 4–6; 12 May 1980, 6.
44. *GAM* (UPCUSA), 1979, I:77, 530.
45. *GAM* (PCUS), 1980, I:94. In 1981 the General Assembly approved an overture from Middle Tennessee Presbytery asking the board to study "how much restructure of the payment plan of retirement benefits... contributed by the Church as employer, together with the earnings on this portion could be computed on the basis of time of service rather than on salary earned." *GAM* (PCUS), 1981, I:58–59.
46. *GAM* (PCUS), 1981, I:693–94.
47. *GAM* (UPCUSA), 1977, I:381; (PCUS), 1979, I:420; "Board of Annuities and Relief Minutes," 21 June 1978, 16 October 1980.
48. *GAM* (PCUS), 1982, I:319. W. Terry Young, "Recognition of Service of Dr. Charles C. Cowsert," (n.d.), and "Biographical Information, James Phillips Noble," September 1983.
49. *Monday Morning Magazine* (August 1972), 18; Arthur W. Brown, interview with RDB, Philadelphia, Pennsylvania, 18 June 1985; Donald Smith, interview with RDB, New York, New York, 15 July 1985.
50. "BOP Minutes," 29 November 1976. For a description of the operation of an Index Fund designed to eliminate most of the investment transaction costs, see *BOP Report*, 1979, 12–14.
51. "Board of Annuities and Relief Minutes," 29 October 1982.
52. "BOP Minutes," 16 June 1982, and "Board of Annuities and Relief Minutes," 30 October 1981.
53. *BOP Report*, 1975, 7; 1978, 39; 1979, 9, and *GAM* (U.S.A.), 1983, I:643–44.
54. *BOP Report*, 1975, 7; 1978, 39; 1979, 9, and *GAM* (U.S.A.), 1983, I:643–44.
55. "At Your Service," Board of Annuities and Relief (Atlanta: April 1985), 1; *GAM* (U.S.A.), 1983, I:643.
56. "BOP Minutes," 18 June and 14 October 1981, and *BOP Report*, 1981, 21.
57. "BOP Minutes," 18 June and 14 October 1981, and *BOP Report*, 1981, 21.
58. *GAM* (UPCUSA), 1981, I:190–94.
59. *GAM* (U.S.A.), 1983, I:347–48.
60. *GAM* (UPCUSA), 1982, I:466–71, and *GAM* (U.S.A.), 1983, I:505–6.
61. "BOP Minutes," 21 June 1978.
62. "BOP Minutes," 18 June 1981.
63. *GAM* (UPCUSA), 1979, I:310, and *GAM* (U.S.A.), 1983, I:645.
64. "BOP Minutes," 2 March 1983, and *GAM* (U.S.A.), 1983, I:505.
65. *GAM* (PCUS), 1982, I:229–30.
66. John M. Mulder, "Road Signs on the Way to Reunion," *A.D. Magazine* (June 1983), 15–17.
67. "Minutes of United Benefits Committee," 12–13 November 1984.

Epilogue

1. *GAM* (U.S.A.), 1986, I:698–99.
2. "Your Benefits Plan. How Plan Dues Are Established," Board of Pensions Leaflet, 1986.
3. Ibid.
4. Ibid.
5. "Your Benefits Plan and The Local Church," Board of Pensions Leaflet, 1986.
6. "Your Benefits Plan: How and Why To Use Medical Benefits Effectively," Board of Pensions Leaflet, 1986.

7. "The Benefits Plan and The Assistance and Homes Program," Board of Pension Leaflet, 1986. See also *GAM* (U.S.A.), I:708–21.
8. *GAM* (U.S.A.), 1986, I:704–5. At its meeting on 24 October 1987, the Board of Pensions voted to amend its Homes Program from one based on the management of board-owned housing to one based on housing assistance supplements. Over a period of time the board proposed to dispose of its individual and congregate homes (with the exception of Westminster Gardens). The 1988 General Assembly, however, instructed the board to keep, in addition to Westminster Gardens, Morganwood (in Swarthmore, PA.) and Sombroso Oaks (in Los Gatos, Calif.), and to sell no more housing clusters without General Assembly approval. The Assembly also charged the Board to evaluate the Homes Program and report to the Assembly in 1991. *Presbyterian Survey* (July–August, 1988): 30.
9. *GAM* (U.S.A.), 1986, I:374, 389.
10. *GAM* (U.S.A.), 1984, I:555–56, and *GAM* (U.S.A.), 1985, I:629.
11. *GAM* (U.S.A.), 1985, I:30, 679.

Bibliography

Primary and secondary materials utilized in the research and writing of this book are for the most part located in five places: Presbyterian Study Center (Montreat), North Carolina; The Presbyterian Historical Association, Philadelphia, Pennsylvania; the Office of the Board of Pensions, Philadelphia; the Office of the Board of Annuities and Relief, Atlanta, Georgia; the Presbyterian Ministers' Fund Office, Philadelphia. One or both of the authors have visited these locations and have had access to all relevant materials. We have also interviewed both current and retired board officials and staff. During the course of our research, we have accumulated a considerable quantity of materials, all of which will be deposited in the Presbyterian archives.

Much of the material at the board offices in Philadelphia and Atlanta consists of financial records, assorted pamphlets, brochures and newsletters, and correspondence between the board and the program participants. Because of the personal nature of the latter correspondence, files of current plan members are restricted from public examination. Executive correspondence and official records were, however, available. The Board of Annuities and Relief has Board Minutes (1904–present) along with Relief Records (1910–1964) and other miscellaneous financial notebooks and registers. The Board of Pensions has sent most of its noncurrent archival materials to the Presbyterian Historical Association and keeps only recent Board Minutes in its files. Thanks to a recent project supervised by Research Historian Gerald Gillette and sponsored by the Board of Pensions, virtually all of the official records relating to the Board of Pensions and its predecessor organizations are available on microfilm at the Presbyterian Historical Association.

Taped interviews conducted by the authors will be deposited with the Presbyterian Historical Association. Although they have not been transcribed, they will be available to scholars within the restrictions placed on them by the interviewees, interviewers, and the general policies of the society.

Unless otherwise indicated in the bibliography, materials relating specifically to the Presbyterian Church in the U.S. are at The Historical Foundation and those relating to the United Presbyterian Church in the U.S.A. and its uniting denominations (Cumberland Presbyterian Church and the United Presbyterian Church of North America) are at the Presbyterian Historical Association.

Record Groups

There are a number of Record Groups at the Presbyterian Historical Association that contain information relative to the history of the Board of Pensions and its predecessors. Relevant materials are in the following Record Groups:

RG 122,	Records of former Stated Clerk William B. Pugh
RG 125,	Records of former Stated Clerk Lewis S. Mudge
RG 121,	Records of former Stated Clerk Eugene Carson Blake
RG 81,	Records of Foreign Missions and COEMAR
RG 60,	Papers of Alexander Mackie
Unprocessed,	Miscellaneous records of the Board of Pensions, primarily secretary and treasurer correspondence and notes.

Reports and Minutes

Presbyterian Church in the United States of America (PCUSA)
  Minutes of the Presbyterian Church in America 1706–1788. Edited by Guy Klett. Philadelphia: Presbyterian Historical Society, 1976.
  Minutes of the General Assembly 1789–1958 (includes Old School and New School Minutes 1837–1869).
  Annual Report and Minutes of the Board of Ministerial Relief, 1876–1918.
  Annual Report and Minutes of the Board of Relief and Sustentation, 1918–1929.
  Annual Report and Minutes of the Sustentation Fund, 1909–1918.
  Annual Report and Minutes of the Board of Pensions, 1927–1958.

The United Presbyterian Church in the United States of America (UPCUSA)
  Minutes of the General Assembly, 1958–1983. Annual Report and Minutes of the Board of Pensions, 1958–1983.

Presbyterian Church in the United States (PCUS)
  Annual Report and Minutes of the Executive Committee of Home Missions 1879–1902.
  Annual Report and Minutes of the Executive Committee of Ministerial Relief 1901–1904.
  Annual Report of the Executive Committee of Ministerial Education and Relief 1905–1910.
  Annual Report of the Executive Committee of Christian Education and Ministerial Relief, 1911–1949.
  Annual Report and Minutes of the Board of Annuities and Relief, 1950–1983.
  Minutes of the General Assembly, 1861–1983.

The Cumberland Presbyterian Church (CP)
  Minutes of the General Assembly, 1830–1906.

United Presbyterian Church of North America (UPNA)
  Minutes of the General Assembly, 1858–1958.
  Annual Report and Minutes of the Board of Ministerial Relief, 1873–1928.

Annual Report and Minutes of the Board of Ministerial Pensions and Relief, 1928–1958.

The Presbyterian Church (U.S.A.)
Minutes of the General Assembly, 1983–1986.
Annual Report and Minutes of the Board of Pensions, 1983–1986.
Annual Report and Minutes of the Board of Annuities and Relief, 1983–1986.
Minutes of the Unified Benefits Committee, 1983–1986.

Books and Articles

Achenbaum, W. Andrew. *Shades of Gray: Old Age, American Values, and Federal Policies Since 1920*. Boston and Toronto: Little, Brown Publishers, 1983.

Armstrong, Maurice W., Lefferts A. Loetscher, and Charles A. Anderson. *The Presbyterian Enterprise: Sources of American Presbyterian History*. Philadelphia: Westminster Press, 1956.

Baird, John. *Horn of Plenty: The Story of the Presbyterian Ministers' Fund*. Wheaton, Illinois: Tyndale House Publishers, 1982.

Barrus, Ben M., Milton L. Baughn, and Thomas H. Campbell. *A People Called Cumberland Presbyterians*. Memphis: Frontier Press, 1972.

Clough, Shepard B. *A Century of American Life Insurance*. Westport, Connecticut: Columbia University Press, 1946.

Fischer, David H. *Growing Old in America*. New York: Oxford University Press, 1977.

Graebner, William. *A History of Retirement: The Meanings and Function of an American Institution, 1885–1978*. New Haven: Yale University Press, 1980.

Hays, Will H. *Memoirs of Will H. Hays*. New York: Doubleday, 1954.

Hudson, Winthrop. *Religion in America*. 3rd ed. New York: Scribner's, 1981.

James, Marquis. *The Metropolitan Life: A Study in Business Growth*. New York: The Viking Press, 1947.

Jamieson, Wallace N. *The United Presbyterian Story*. Pittsburgh: Geneva Press, 1958.

Klett, Guy S. *Presbyterians in Colonial America*. Philadelphia: Pennsylvania State University Press, 1937.

Loetscher, Lefferts A. *A Brief History of the Presbyterians*. 4th ed. Philadelphia: Westminster Press, 1983.

———. *The Broadening Church*. Philadelphia: Westminster Press, 1954.

Mackie, Alexander. *Facile Princeps: The Story of the Beginning of Life Insurance in America*. Lancaster, Pennsylvania: Presbyterian Minister's Fund, 1956.

Marsden, George. *The Evangelical Mind and the New School Presbyterian Experience*. New Haven: Yale University Press, 1970.

McGill, Dan M. *Fundamentals of Private Pensions*. 5th ed. Homewood, Illinois: Pension Research Council, 1984.

Myers, Margaret G. *A Financial History of the United States*. New York: Columbia University Press, 1970.

Thompson, Ernest Trice. *Presbyterians in the South*. 3 vols. Richmond, Virginia: John Knox Press, 1963, 1963, and 1973.

Trinterud, Leonard J. *The Forming of an American Tradition: A Reexamination of Colonial Presbyterianism.* Philadelphia: Westminster Press, 1949.

Zelizer, Viviana A. Rotman. *Morals and Markets: Life Insurance in the United States.* New York and London: Columbia University Press, 1979.

Unpublished Materials

Burrall, Charles L., Jr. "Church Pensions—Past, Present and Future," 1 December 1977.

Hibbard, Donald L. "History of the Board of Pensions," Philadelphia, 1972.

"Minutes of the Corporation for the Relief of Poor and Distressed Presbyterian Ministers, and of the Poor and Distressed Widows and Children of Presbyterian Ministers," 1760–1856.

"Minutes of the Presbyterian Annuity Company," 1856–1875.

"Minutes of the Presbyterian Annuity and Life Insurance Company," 1875–1887.

"Minutes of the Presbyterian Ministers' Fund," 1888–1900.

"Widows' Fund Membership Register," 1761–1875.

Periodicals

A.D. Magazine, 1972–1980
The Assembly Herald, 1894–1918
The Central Presbyterian, 1856–1908
The Christian Observer, 1840–1875
The Continent, 1870–1926
The Christian Union Herald, 1880–1955
The Cumberland Presbyterian, 1880–1906
The Herald and Presbyter, 1869–1925
Monday Morning Magazine, 1936–1986
The New Era Magazine, 1919–1921
The Presbyterian, 1831–1948
The Presbyterian Advance, 1910–1934
The Presbyterian Banner, 1952–1937
The Presbyterian Journal, 1875–1904
Presbyterian Life Magazine, 1948–1972
The Presbyterian Magazine, 1921–1933
The Presbyterian of the South, 1909–1944
Presbyterian Outlook, 1944–1986
The Presbyterian Quarterly, 1887–1904
The Presbyterian Review, 1880–1889
The Presbyterian Standard, 1858–1931
The Presbyterian Survey, 1911–1986
The St. Louis Observer, 1880–1900
The St. Louis Presbyterian, 1874–1889
The Southern Presbyterian Review, 1847–1885

The Southwestern Presbyterian, 1869–1908
The United Presbyterian, 1858–1958

Interviews

Brown, Arthur W. Interview with R. Douglas Brackenridge (RDB). Philadelphia, Pennsylvania, 18 June 1985.
Cowsert, Charles C. Interview with RDB. Winchester, Virginia, 25 June 1985.
Griffin, Bailly. Interview with RDB. Atlanta, Georgia, 17 May 1985.
Guerrant, Horace. Interview with RDB. Atlanta, Georgia, 17 May 1985.
Hibbard, Donald L. Interview with RDB and Lois A. Boyd (LAB). Longmont, Colorado, 15 and 16 June 1984.
McGill, Dan M. Interview with RDB. Philadelphia, Pennsylvania, 17 July 1985.
Noble, J. Phillips. Interview with RDB. Atlanta, Georgia, 16 May 1985.
Ryan, Arthur M. Interview with RDB and LAB. Philadelphia, Pennsylvania, 17 July 1985.
Smith, Donald. Interview with RDB. New York, New York, 15 July 1985.
Vick, George H. Interview with RDB. Lewisburg, West Virginia, 14 June 1985.

Index

Accumulations Department (PCUSA), 120
Ad Interim Committee on Restructuring Boards and Agencies (PCUS), 115–16
Aetna Life Insurance Company, 126, 144
Aged and Infirm Ministers' Fund (UPNA), 82
Agnew, Benjamin L., 54, 59, 60, 63, 66, 67, 68
Albuquerque, N. M., 61
Alexander, Archibald, 28, 29, 31, 32
Alexander, John, 83
Allen, Perry S., 36
American Home Products, 137
Anderson, Herbert B., 132
Andrews, Jedidiah, 9
Annuities and Relief (PCUS), Board of, 112–18, 133, 134, 135, 140–43, 146–48, 151. *See also* Executive Committee of Christian Education and Ministerial Relief
Apartheid, 136
Assistance Fund (PCUSA), 126, 135, 149
Atlanta, Ga., 114, 130
Austin Presbyterian Theological Seminary, 110

Baird, John, 37
Baptists, 70
Barnes, Albert, 29

Barr, W. W., 83
Beattie, Francis R., 96
Beatty, Charles, 13
Beecher, Henry Ward, 26
Benefits Plan, 148–50
Birthday Offering (PCUS), 102, 103
Black Presbyterian Leadership Caucus, 140–41
Boggs, Wade H., 110, 113
Boyd, Adam, 16
Brainard, David, 14
Breckenridge, John, 29
Brown, Arthur W., 143, 144, 146
Brown, Charles, 51
Brown, James, 83
Bruen, Alexander M., 56
Bryan, William Jennings, 66, 67
Burnside, Robert W., 84

Carleton, Will, 58
Carmichael, John, 22
Carnegie, Andrew, 64, 97
Cattell, William C., 54, 55, 57
Cecil, Russell, 96, 97
Centenary Fund, 54–55
Christian Education and Ministerial Relief, Executive Committee of, 98–113
Christmas, observance of, 103
Church and Race (UPCUSA), Council on, 131

182

Church and Society (UPCUSA), Advisory Council on, 145, 151
Church Pension Fund (Episcopal), 70
Church Pensions Conference, 70, 99, 104, 143
Civil War, 34, 51
Clergy's Friendly Society of Baltimore, 94
Clergymen's Mutual Insurance League, 33
Confession of 1967, 136
Congregationalists, 70
Connecticut General Life Insurance Company, 144
Consulting Committee on Pensions (UPCUSA), 134-35
Converse, A.D., 92
Corporation for Relief of Poor and Distressed Presbyterian Ministers and of the Poor and Distressed Widows and Children of Presbyterian Ministers. *See* Widows' Fund
Corporation for the Relief of the Widows and Children of the Clergymen in the Communion of the Church of England in America, 18
Cowsert, Charles C., 143
Craig, John N., 89, 91, 94, 95
Cross, Robert, 11
Cumberland Presbyterian Church, 77-82
Currie, Charles, 113, 114

Dabney, Robert L., 88
Dales, J. B., 83
Darby, William J., 79, 80
Davies, Samuel, 10
Depression (Great, of 1930s), 102-103, 107, 119-20, 122, 125
Desert Mission Inc., 130
Dickenson, Jonathan, 10
Dickson, Reid, 121, 122
Disabled Ministers (o.s.), Fund for, 34, 38, 40-49

Division of Welfare Agencies (PCUSA), 129
Divorced spouses, 135-36
Downer Home, 58
Duffield, Edward D., 72
Duffield, George, 14, 25
Dulles, Avery, 36
Dulles, John Foster, 36
Dulles, John Welsh, 36

Eastman-Kodak, 136
Eastwood, Alice, 103, 104
Education (PCUS), Executive Committee of, 98
Edwards, Jonathan, 10
Emergency and Relief Fund (PCUSA), 120
Employee Retirement Income Security Act (ERISA), 137-38, 143, 150
Employees Pension Plan (PCUSA), 120-21
Employees' Annuity Fund (PCUS), 110, 112, 115, 144, 145
Engle, Cornelia, 103
Equal Opportunity and Employment, Office of (UPUSA), 131
Equitable Life Assurance Society of New York, The, 32
Ewing, Finis, 77
Ewing, John, 22-23
Executive Committee of Christian Education and Ministerial Relief (PCUS), 98-113
Executive Committee of Education (PCUS), 98
Executive Committee of Foreign Missions (PCUS), 111
Executive Committee of Home Missions (PCUS), 89, 91
Executive Committee of Ministerial Relief (PCUS), 96-98
Executive Committee of Publication (PCUS), 98
Executive Committee of Sustentation (PCUS), 89, 93

Index

Fidelity Mutual Life Insurance Company of Philadelphia, The, 65
Fine, John, 46
First National City Bank of New York City, 136
Florida United Presbyterian Homes, 130
Fogleman, William, 115
Foreign Missions (UPNA), Board of, 84
Foreign Missions (PCUS), Executive Committee of, 111
Foulkes, William H., 68
Franklin, William, 57
Fredericksburg Collegiate Institute, 100–101
Free Church of Scotland, 91
French Revolution, 19
Fulton, C. Darby, 111
Fulton, James M., 84
Fulton, John A., 116
Fulton, Mrs. J. Gault, 104
Fund for Disabled Ministers, 34, 38, 40–49
Fund for Pious Uses, 7, 9–11, 13, 37–38, 41
Fund for Superannuated and Disabled Ministers in Need, and for the Destitute Widows and Orphans of Deceased Ministers, The, 82
Fynmere Home, 129

General Assembly Mission Board (PCUS), 115–16, 137, 143, 150
General Assembly Mission Council (UPCUSA), 131, 138, 139, 150
Getty, William, 83
Graham, C. E., 102
Great Awakening, 10
Green, Ashbel, 28, 29
Greene, George F., 72

Hale, George, 48, 51
Hanna, J. P., 83
Harpe, Gene T., 117
Harrison, Henry, 83
Hawes, Samuel H., 96

Hays, George P., 54
Hays, Will H., 72, 75, 76
Haywood Home, 59, 61, 129
Heard National Bank Building (Jacksonville, FL) 102
Hebreton, W. W., 68
Hibbard, Donald, 114, 126, 130, 132, 144
Hodge, Charles, 26, 29
Home Life Insurance Company of New York, 113
Homes, retirement, 56–62, 101, 128–30, 149–50
Home Missions (PCUS), Executive Committee of, 89, 91
Hubbell, Martha Stone, 25
Hudson, Irene Hope, 103
Huggins, George A., 65, 70, 122
Hunter, Robert, 61, 69
Hussey, Charles L., 84

Imperial Southgate Villas Condominium Association, 130
Income Assistance Formula (PCUS), 114–15
Insurance Company of North America, 20
Interdenominational Secretaries Conference, 70. *See also* Church Pensions Conference
Interfaith Center on Corporate Responsibility, 137, 138, 139
Invalid Ministers' Fund (PCUS), 90–91
Investment policies, 130–31, 136, 137–42

Janeway, Jacob J., 28, 43
Jones, Joseph H., 43, 47
Jopling, Robert W., 108
Joy Gift (PCUS), 103, 111, 113, 115, 142

Kane, John J., 32
King, Samuel, 77

L'Amoreaux Home, 59, 129
Lakeland, FL 129, 130

Lamont, Robert J., 36
Lane, Margaret, 103
Laymen's Committee (PCUSA), 72–76, 122
Leavitt, H. H., 46, 47
Lee, John Park, 129
Life insurance, 11, 52, 93. *See also* Presbyterian Annuity Company, Presbyterian Ministers' Fund, *and* Widows' Fund
Loomis, Nelson H., 69
Los Gatos, Cal., 129
Louisville, Ky., 98, 99, 114
Louisville Theological Seminary, 96
McAdow, Samuel, 77, 78
Macalester, Charles, 35
McCandless, James, 83
McElroy, Isaac, 97, 98, 99
McGill, Dan. M., 134
Mackemie, Francis, 8
Mackie, Alexander, 36, 38
McKinley, William B., 72
Mallard, Robert Q., 95
Marts, Arnaud C., 75
Master, Henry B., 37, 69, 71, 72, 74, 75, 76, 120, 121
Matthews, Mark, 66, 74
Medicare, 113
Mellon, Andrew W., 75
Mellon, Richard, 75
Menninger Foundation, 127, 150
Mercer Home, 58
Merriam Home, 58–59, 129
Merrill Home, 59
Methodist Episcopal Church, 70
Mexican American pastors, 110–11
Michigan, University of, Research Center, 126
Mid-Continent Home, 82, 129, 130
Ministerial Annuity Fund (UPNA), 85
Ministerial Pensions and Relief (UPNA), Board of, 86
Ministerial Relief and Sustentation (PCUSA), Board of, 63–76
Ministerial Relief Fund, 47–49
Ministerial Relief Plan (UPNA), 84–85

Ministerial Relief (c.f.), Board of, 79–82
Ministerial Relief (PCUSA), Board of, 53–68
Ministerial Relief (UPNA), Board of, 83–86
Ministerial Relief (U.S.A.), Board of, 51–62, 66, 67, 68
Ministers' Annuity Fund (PCUS), 105, 107–18, 142, 145
Ministers' Emergency Relief Fund, 128
Ministers' Memorial Cottage, 61, 129
Minton, Henry C., 66
Mission Responsibility Through Investment, Committee on, 137–40
Morgan Guaranty Trust Company of New York, 130
Morganwood, 129
Munce, John, 95
Murray, William W., 94

National Bank of Detroit, 130
National Missions (PCUSA), Board of, 129
National Presbyterian Health and Welfare Association, 129
Native Americans, 14–15, 41
Neel, Samuel M., 98
New Jersey Society for the Better Support of the Widows and the Education of the Destitute Orphans of Presbyterian Ministers, 17
New Jersey, College of, 19
New School Presbyterians, 30–31, 34–35, 47–49, 51
New York and Philadelphia, Synod of, 12–18, 20
New York, Synod of, 10
Nicholson, John, 22, 23
Noble, J. Phillips, 143, 148, 150

Old School Presbyterians, 30–31, 34–35, 38, 42–47, 51, 87

Patterson, Epenetus, 45
Patterson, Robert, 21, 22, 23, 27
Patterson, Robert M., 27

Index   185

Patterson, Robert M., 27
Patterson, Robert II, 27, 32, 33
Pegram, Madeline, 104
Pennsylvania Company for Insurance on Lives and Granting Annuities, 20
Pensions (PCUSA/UPCUSA), Board of, 37–39, 76, 119–47. *See also* Ministerial Relief and Board of Ministerial Relief and Sustentation
Perth Amboy Home, 56–58, 60
Pew, John O., 64
Phelps Cottage, 61
Philadelphia Presbytery Homes, 130
Philadelphia, Presbytery of, 8
Philadelphia, Synod of, 8, 9, 10, 11
Plan of 1792, 20–21
Plan of 1824, 28–29
Plan of 1852, 32–33
Plaza del Monte, 129
Pollock, J. T., 90
Portland, Oregon, 129
Prentiss House, 129, 130
Presbyterian Annuity and Life Insurance Company, 36
Presbyterian Annuity Company, 30–36, 44, 45, 52. *See also* Presbyterian Ministers' Fund; Widows' Fund
Presbyterian Center in Atlanta, 114
Presbyterian Church in the United States. *See* Annuities and Relief (PCUS), Board of; Executive Committee of Christian Education and Ministerial Relief (PCUS)
Presbyterian Ministers' Fund, 11, 36–39, 94, 105. *See also* Widows' Fund; Presbyterian Annuity Company
Price, James, 84
Price, Richard, 20
Program Agency, 131
Protestant Episcopal Church, 70
Publication (PCUS), Executive Committee of, 98
Prudential Life Insurance Company of Newark, 72
Pugh, William B., 122

Redman, John, 20
Reed, Villory D., 53
Reformed Church of America, 34
Relief Fund for Disabled Ministers and the Widows and Orphans of Deceased Ministers (PCUSA), 51–52
Relief Fund for the Widows and Orphans of Ministers at Their Decease (PCUS), 91–94
Religion and Race (UPCUSA), Commission on, 131
Retirement homes, 56–62, 101, 128–30, 149–50
Review and Evaluation (PCUS), Office of, 146
Rhoades, Jacqueline, 118
Robinson, Stewart, 90
Rockefeller, John D., 97
Rogers, Ebenezer P., 43–44
Rogers, Will, 75
Ryan, Arthur M., 140, 144, 148, 150
St. Barnabas Hospital, 130
St. Petersburg, Fla., 130
Santa Fe, N. M., 129
Saunders, Alexander P., 100
Schaff, Philip, 19
Schmidt, Miriam, 112
Scotland, Church of, 11, 13, 15
Service Pension Plan (PCUSA), 73–76, 119–32
Smith, Robert, 12
Smith, William, 18
Snowden, J. Ross, 35
Social Security, 109, 120, 121, 127
Society for Promoting Life Insurance Among Clergymen, 52
South Africa, 136, 141–42, 150
Southwestern Presbyterian Sanatorium, 61, 113
Speer, Robert E., 75
Spring, Gardiner, 87
Spurgeon, Charles H., 26
Stinson, Thomas, 83
Stockholder resolutions, 137
Stone, John Timothy, 71, 124
Support Agency, 131, 146

Sustentation Fund (PCUSA), 64–70, 104
Sustentation (PCUS), Executive Committee of, 89, 93
Sutherland, John R., 64, 65, 66, 68
Swarthmore, Pa., 129
Sweets, Henry H., 98–110, 113

Teacher's Insurance and Annuity Association of America, 64
Tennent, Gilbert, 10, 20
Theological Seminaries (UPCUSA), Council on, 131
Thornton Home, 59, 61, 81–82, 129
Thornton, Emeline, 81
Thornwell, James H., 45
Topeka, Kans., 129, 150
Travelers Life Insurance Co., 144
Trust Company of Georgia, 114, 144

United Benefits Committee, 147, 148
United Presbyterian Church in the United States of America, 78, 133–44
United Presbyterian Church of North America, 34, 77–78, 82–86
United Presbyterian Foundation, 131
United States Trust Company of New York, 130

Van Gelder, George, 43
Vick, George H., 115, 116, 143

Vocation Agency, 131, 131, 132, 134, 144, 145, 146

Wallace, Robert, 11
Watts, George W., 101
Webster, Alexander, 11
Welfare Fund (PCUSA), 126. See also Assistance Fund
Westminster House, 58. See also Perth Amboy Home
Weyerhauser, Fred G., 72
Whitefield, George, 10
Widows' Fund, 11–29, 30, 31, 32, 37, 38, 39, 40, 41, 42, 151. See also Life insurance; Presbyterian Annuity Company; Presbyterian Ministers' Fund
Wigglesworth, Edward, 20
Wilkinsburg Home (UPNA), 84
Wilson, J. Leighton, 90, 91, 92, 93
Winsborough, Hallie Paxton, 102
Witherspoon, John, 17, 19
Women's Concerns (PCUS), Committee on, 135
Women's General Missionary Society, 83–84
Women, 55, 68, 80, 83–84, 102–4, 112–13, 117–18, 132
World Missions (PCUS), Board of, 112

www.ingramcontent.com/pod-product-compliance
Lightning Source LLC
Chambersburg PA
CBHW031245290426
44109CB00012B/443